CHRISTIAN ETHICS
AND SECULAR SOCIETY

By the same author
ASKING THE RIGHT QUESTIONS: Church and Ministry

CHRISTIAN ETHICS
AND
SECULAR SOCIETY

by

F. R. BARRY

HODDER AND STOUGHTON

Printed in Great Britain for Hodder and Stoughton Limited,
St. Paul's House, Warwick Lane, London, E.C.4, by
Billing & Sons Limited, Guildford and London

PREFACE

THIS is a book that I have long wanted to write – it might be better to say, this is a subject about which I have long wanted to write a book – but have not hitherto found opportunity. The occasion was given by a course of lectures delivered in St Michael's Church, Cornhill, in the spring and autumn of 1965. What is offered here is the substance of what was said then, now written out in a greatly expanded form. The lectures involved laborious preparation and a vast amount of reading – perhaps too much – from which I collected far more material than could possibly be used in the actual lectures. When it came to the point I could not bear to scrap it. The result is that what was first intended as a paperback has grown into a long book. Even so, I am painfully aware how much is left out that ought to have been included in any adequate treatment of the subject. The book is intended for the general reader and does not trespass in academic quadrangles; I have hoped, however, that it might be some use, as background reading, to students in the colleges.

Since the MS was completed nine months ago several important volumes have been published which – for that reason – I was not able to use. It is too late now to put in anything more; and a man of my age cannot wait indefinitely. Such as it is, the book must go on its way.

I wish to thank the Trustees for my appointment, so kindly extended from one year to three; the Rector, the Revd Norman Motley, for his co-operation and end encouragement; and my publishers, Messers Hodder and Stoughton, for accepting the book before they had even seen it and the interest that they have taken in it.

Westminster   F. R. B.

June 1966

CONTENTS

page

PART ONE

PART TWO

ACKNOWLEDGEMENTS

I have to thank the Oxford University Press for permission to use the quotation from Cochrane's *Christianity and Classical Culture*, and from R. M. Hare's *The Language of Morals*; Messrs. Nisbet for the quotation from Reinhold Niebuhr, *The Nature and Destiny of Man*; the S.C.M. Press for the use of the same author's *An Interpretation of Christian Ethics*; and the Harvard University Press for the extract from Lovejoy, *The Great Chain of Being*. The use of U.N. documents on crime prevention I owe to the good offices of Bishop Craske. If I have unwittingly infringed any copyright I hereby offer apologies.

PART ONE

Chapter One

THE MORAL VACUUM

I

OUT of what remains of the Christian legacy north-western Europe and the United States have built a form of society in which, though it still professes to be Christian, every man's religion is his own affair. Are his morals too? It is no academic question. No society known to us has existed without an acknowledged public morality, that tradition of accepted social *mores*, normally embodied in a legal system, out of which conscious morality has been born. It is hard to imagine that any society can function as an organic social order, or indeed continue to exist at all – except as 'a war of everyman against everyman' – on a basis of pure moral individualism.[1] But if that is agreed, where is the foundation for a public morality in the world today? This is no merely local or western problem. The external forms of Western civilisation will soon be established over the whole earth in standardised, global uniformity. Every man today is a citizen of the world. Through technical and economic pressures and the virtual abolition of distance the human race is completely interdependent – no man's thoughts are really his private affair any more than his material activity – and yet it is lethally at cross-purposes. Man's future and even his physical survival may be said to be bound up with the development of a body of recognised international law built on a commonly recognised morality. (See p. 274.) But on what foundations can that be laid down? Can Christianity still be the moral guide of our own fast-changing Western society, in its moral confusion and spiritual bankruptcy? What, more precisely, *is* Christian morality and how

[1] For some corrective to this, see Chapter Six. Of course I am assuming the modern, 'open-ended' society, not a monochrome, 'sacral' polity. Meanwhile, in fairness, I quote the following: 'It should be surprising to many of our moralists that the modern world works, in spite of the fact that it does not correspond to their ideal of a world with a common morality, harmony of interests, and co-operative or compromise solution of conflicts. The unity of mankind is tougher than is implied in the denunciations of some of our prophets.' Munby, *God and the Rich Society*, Oxford University Press, 1961, p. 132.

far is it valid apart from Christian belief? What has it to offer to twentieth-century man? Or is there any viable alternative – any 'objective', self-commending morality which can command the allegiance of man as man, whatever religion he may or may not profess – what is sometimes called 'the religion of all good men'? If there is, what has Christianity to say about it, and what makes its own ethic specifically Christian?

Ethics is sometimes called the cement of society. But a fluid society does not need cement, which must either constrict it or be cracked. What it needs is a permanent centre of moral reference, not so much a map as a true compass-bearing, as mankind moves out over uncharted seas to a still unpredictable destination. Can it find that in the Christian moral law? Christians believe that through all historical changes their Lord remains unchallengeable and un-challenged, yesterday and today the same and for ever. Believing that he is the Way, the Truth and the Life, it follows for them that the Christian moral law is not simply a private code for Christians, like the rules of a club or the charter of a college, but the declaration of God's will for all men at all times and at all stages of their development. For if Christianity is true at all, it is not merely the truth about 'religion', it is the truth about life itself and the moral constitution of the universe. This, as St. John said, is 'the real thing', this is 'true God and eternal life' – what life is *for*, what life really means. Christianity holds, of course, that in Jesus Christ something new came into the world – a newness of life, a creative redirection which was to change the whole course of history, which is still dated Before Christ or after. But there is, all the same, a real sense, and it is implicit in the Logos doctrine, in which it can rightly be said that what Christ reveals has always been operative in the Creation. What men's eyes had seen and their hands had handled was 'That which was from the beginning' (I John i: 1). 'By him all things were made.' As St. Augustine was to write later, 'What is now called the Christian religion existed among the ancients and has never failed from the beginning of the human race, until Christ came in the flesh; since when true religion, which was al-ready in existence, began to be called Christianity'.[1] So, accord-

---

[1] *Retractations*, I, 13, quoted by Inge, *Christian Ethics and Modern Pro-blems*, 7th edition, 1932, p. 17. For discussion, see Micklem, *A Religion for Agnostics*, S.C.M., 1965, pp. 60, 61.

ingly, it would be said that Christian morality just *is* morality, permanently valid and authoritative through all the fogs and tempests of revolution. 'The rain descended and the floods came and the winds blew and beat upon that house; and it fell not; for it was founded upon the rock' (Matthew vii: 25). Can that tremendous claim be substantiated?

People call this glibly the post-Christian era. It is not, I think, by any means so clear as it seemed to be even ten years ago that this is a true historical diagnosis. There are signs that reflective minds are beginning to see through the great 'modern' myth; the tide of opinion may be turning again, if not yet to Christian belief – that will probably take two generations – at least away from an unexamined positivism. Yet it is still widely and generally assumed that Christianity is so bound up with a cosmology and a social order which have now been overrun by events as to be no longer either credible or relevant to the human situation. In a course of lectures given last year, and now published as *Questioning Faith* (S.C.M.), I tried to meet some of the obvious objections (to which I am as sensitive as the next man), to deal with some of the many genuine difficulties which stand between modern minds and Christianity, and to show how in its central affirmations it interprets and 'makes sense of' human life more adequately than any of its rivals. But of course the real test of its relevance will be in what it has to say about ethics.

The business of Christianity is not only to explain the world but to change it and transform it, and to help hard-pressed men and women in the tragic dilemmas of our time to live with integrity and to find fulfilment – in Christian language, to enter into salvation. It is in the sphere of morals that religious questions present themselves most acutely to men today, just as all the sharpest moral questions are at bottom theological and religious. And it is here that the churches and what they stand for are felt by many sincere minds to be failing them. Some are afraid that an authoritarian ethic based, as it claims to be, on a revelation, can offer them only *a priori* dogmas – stock reactions and stereotyped formulas – with no understanding of the personal issues. They consult anyone rather than a clergyman and if they come to us they begin by saying, 'I don't suppose you will understand my difficulty'. Others think that the Christian moral principles belong to another age, not to our own. While others, as we must recognise with humility, honestly think they are positively harmful. No mere 'recall to Christian moral standards' in the pulpit manner will meet this situation. There is too much misunderstanding to be cleared up before any appeal of that kind will be listened to. We need a penetrating exploration of what Christian ethics really are – and are Christians themselves quite sure that they know? That entails not only a study of the Bible and other sources of Christian moral teaching but also a constant relation to theology and the light it throws on the Christian understanding of the nature and destiny of man. Conversely, and at the same time, it involves a fuller and more empirical observation of the actual constitution of human nature and the springs of human motivation than moral theology has always brought to it[1] – for what man *ought* to be and to do can obviously not be in contradiction to the way in which, in fact, he is made.

It has been too much assumed that what *must* be, in the sense of being logically necessary, is in fact the case; but the fact may defy the logic. The scholastics, for example, took for granted that the heavenly bodies, being 'perfect', must and could only move in perfect circles – till it was observed that they move elliptically.[2] Moreover, to understand the Christian ethic we must study it all the time in its history, watching Christian thought and life in action in various cultural and historical settings. We shall then be in the position to ask the question, What has an essentially religious ethic – for that, we shall see, is what in itself it is – to contribute to the actual situation in that pluralist and secular society in which now and in future Christians have to live? The Christian ethic is not a code of rules to be looked up in the index to a textbook in the vicar's study, or in the New Testament. It is a response to concrete situations. And furthermore, it is always deve-

---

[1] 'A generation which has been so largely stripped of its late illusions and all too hasty confidence in humanity may naturally be expected to turn to self-examination to seek an answer to the most searching and pressing of all contemporary questions, What is man and what is the matter with him?' Lovejoy, *Reflections on Human Nature*, Johns Hopkins Press, Baltimore, 1964, p. 10.

[2] Basil Willey, *The English Moralists*, Chatto and Windus, 1964, p. 132. (But see note on p. 129.) Mediaeval thought tended to turn logic straight into ontology. But 'We must not be bogged down in a thought-world tenanted by universals rather than by things . . . The primary object of the metaphysician, as it is the primary object of thought in general, is the real in the sense of the existent singular.' Canon Hawkins in *Prospect for Metaphysics*, ed. by Ian Ramsey, Allen and Unwin, 1961, p. 119.

loping. We must never identify Christian morality with the pre-
scriptions of earlier Christian periods, whether primitive, mediaeval or Victorian.

II

Christian ethics depend on Christian theology. If the fundamental doctrine is untrue, the case for Christian morality falls to the
ground.[1] Most of the great Victorian agnostics – themselves men
of the highest moral integrity – took for granted that Christian
morality would survive the abandonment of Christian faith. The
Victorians went in for religious doubts; about ethics they had 'no
manner of doubt whatever'; they were sure that they knew the
moral answers. That was partly because they were Victorians, with
their self-assurance and built-in sense of duty – limited though that
may have been and declining at times into 'respectability'. But
it was also because they had grown up in that all-pervading evange-
lical atmosphere which was the characteristic of the period. They
were not agnostic about ethics, for Christian morality was in their
blood-stream, but about the reasons for accepting that when one
no longer believes in Christianity. As Cockshut points out in his
study, *The Unbelievers*,[2] 'they were not trying to discover how they
ought to behave, for their consciences formed by generations of
Christianity told them that clearly enough. They were trying to
establish *why*, now that the religious motive was removed, they
ought to behave as their consciences told them.' But once the religious motive *was* removed, how long would men's consciences tell
them the same thing? These men, Cockshut goes on, 'were left
defenceless on the arrival of a new generation whose consciences
worked differently. They provided their successors with no answer
to Nietzsche and all those later prophets who actively hated Christian ethics.'

Some understanding of that situation is, it may be suggested,
a necessary background for any discussion of Christian morality in
our own similar yet so different setting as it has developed 100
years later.

First, we must understand why they were agnostics. Christianity
in the mid-nineteenth century was faced by a major intellectual

---

[1] See note at the end of the chapter.
[2] Cockshut, *The Unbelievers*, Collins, 1964, pp. 157, 158.

B

crisis, of which neither Tractarians nor Evangelicals seem to have had any real appreciation, and the Church in England was not equipped to meet it. Orthodoxy appeared to be committed to a literalist interpretation of Scripture, a pre-critical approach to miracles and a generally obscurantist attitude towards the new knowledge brought by the natural sciences. It seemed too, on the whole, to have little concern with the moral and religious implications of what at that time was called 'the social problem'. Christianity, therefore, as then taught, seemed to many to be incompatible with freedom of thought or acceptance of new truth. Confronted as they were by a choice with which they ought never to have been faced, between Christian belief and intellectual honesty, too many people of independent mind found themselves forced into some form of heterodoxy. Orthodox Christianity seemed to stand at once for intellectual obscurantism and for a reactionary social outlook. (For the situation in the universities see p. 146.) The Church, as it seemed to them, was against the future – and that is a cautionary tale for us. They therefore rejected official Christian doctrine. But as most of them were deeply imbued with it, they had to look both for a religious substitute and for some other justification of the ethic which they had learnt from the Christian tradition. Some sought both in a 'modernist' theology.

One of the most important and interesting of these men and women was Thomas Hill Green, the Professor Grey of *Robert Elsmere*, who dominated the Oxford of his time and exercised a far-reaching influence, which can still be felt, on Christian social ethics as well as on Liberal social legislation. (Asquith had been his pupil at Balliol.) Green does not appear in Cockshut's gallery, and indeed he can hardly be called an unbeliever – he told his wife on his deathbed that he believed in God and the future life. But in what sense did he believe in Christianity? Certainly not in its dogmatic formulas. Strongly affected by German thinking and Hegel's philosophical idealism, Green proposed to strip Christianity of all its historical and dogmatic elements – he was indeed one of the first 'demythologisers'. Its essence is in the life and the 'idea'. 'Everything significant in traditional Christianity can', he said, 'be put better by Idealism'. God is conceived as the 'higher' or 'possible' self, realised by devotion and self-sacrifice in a morally purposive and progressive universe. Self-sacrifice for the 'common good' or, in different words, 'simple Christian citizenship' thus becomes the dynamic of Christian ethics. On the one hand, there-fore, Green supplied professed agnostics like Sidgwick and Leslie Stephen with 'an untheological humanism based on ethics'; on the other he fired Christian believers like Henry Scott Holland and Charles Gore, with new visions of a 'social Gospel'. He was indeed very largely responsible, directly or indirectly through his pupils, both for the London Ethical Society and for the publication of *Lux Mundi* and the founding of the Christian Social Union.[1]

Marx 'stood Hegelianism on its head'. So, it has been remarked, Hegelianism seemed able to stand Christianity on its head, till God, Freedom and Immortality seem to mean something like their opposites – Man, dialectical determinism and social progress.[2] Is it quite certain that 'radical' theology, of course without being consciously aware of it, is not prone to be doing the same thing to-day? Beatrice Webb is recorded to have said that it was during the middle decades of the nineteenth century that the impulse of self-subordinating service was transferred, consciously and overtly, from God to man.[3]

Much of Green's teaching, like any effective teaching, was con-ditioned by its own time and place. Perhaps his most enduring contribution was to have established moral values in the founda-tions of political theory – 'Will, not force is the basis of the state' – and by will he meant the self-revealing Spirit. For many he saved their Christian beliefs – but by a theology which now seems un-tenable. He gave his generation 'a reason for doing what their con-sciences told them they ought to do' – but how far could we now confidently appeal to it? The distinguished line of Christian sociology which ran from Scott Holland and Gore to William Temple may be said to have started from Green's lecture room. But Green's idealistic metaphysics, which seemed at the time to bring so much support to Christian 'idealism' (in the other sense) have not survived the new philosophical criticism. His optimism about human nature, and the social order that sustained it have been shattered by the world wars and their sequels, and the whole

[1] This paragraph leans heavily on Richter, *The Politics of Conscience*, Weidenfeld and Nicholson, 1964. This is a captivating study of Green and his work against the religious, social and intellectual background of his time and in the setting of Jowett's Balliol. See also the sketch in Bryce's *Studies in Contemporary Biography*, Macmillan, 1903.

[2] Richter, p. 116, but this not an exact quotation.

[3] Richter, pp. 131, 132.

structure of moral presuppositions in which our fathers and grand-fathers lived seems to many in this bewildered generation as though it had been built on a bottomless pit.

The Victorians lived in a stable society – and these thinkers seem never to have heard of Karl Marx – in which all the pressures of tradition supported (a very protestant) Christianity. We live in a fluid, transitional society in which what is traditional is suspect, and the pressures are all in the opposite direction. The moral situation at any time is part of the wider cultural situation. Moral standards are undergirded by tradition and transmitted in the social inheritance. When society is relatively stable they are handed down through the social institutions, among which the family normally counts for most, from one generation to another. When there is any violent interruption of social continuity and tradition, the ancient certainties seem to be less certain and parents are less sure what to teach their children. We cannot assess the changes in moral outlook in isolation from all the other factors which enter into the social situation. These may include demographic factors. One would, for example, like to know more to what extent the moral and religious changes of the late fourteenth and fifteenth century were due to the rupture of social continuity inflicted on Europe by the Black Death. In any rapidly changing society, when traditional patterns are being broken up and the social fabric appears to be giving way, moral standards are bound to be in con-fusion. It is one of the commonplaces of history. The two world wars are within our own experience.

The classic case is Greece in the fourth century where, as the ancient regimes dissolved, the Sophists preached a complete moral scepticism. Morality was 'nothing but' a convention, a code im-posed by 'them' for their own advantage; Justice is but 'the in-terest of the stronger'. (Thrasymachus in Plato's *Republic* is the dramatisation of that doctrine.) It happened in England in the seventeenth century, with the shifting of economic and class balances, and Hobbes's 'state of nature' reflects that. Hobbes's natural man, says Christopher Hill, is 'bourgeois man with the policeman removed'.[1] It is happening on a world-scale today as the scientific and technical revolution is hammering society into new shapes, breaking down the old community patterns to create the 'urban situation' in which people have no roots in a common life,

[1] *Puritanism and Revolution*, Secker and Warburg, 1958, p. 279.

and are thus deprived of the support of the social customs and expectations (standards that decent people must live up to) which
had hitherto sustained the traditional ethic. At the same time and
increasingly all the time, secular ways of thinking about life are
supplanting the religious tradition by which the Christian ethic
had been nurtured. It is no longer possible to assume what the
Victorians could take for granted. A general moral confusion is
inevitable.

What is commonly called the Christian ethic has a pre-Christian
ancestry behind it. The Christian Church did not invent morality,
as some Christians so oddly seem to think. The law and the prophets are part of the Christian legacy. Moreover, as we shall see
(Chapters Two, Four) the Church has drawn right from the beginning on the great tradition of Greek moral philosophy. Not its
least contribution to history was that it preserved through the
Dark Ages and handed down to the new Germanic kingdoms what
was best in the Graeco-Roman legacy (Chapter Five). (One of the
weaknesses of the Reformation was its tendency to jettison all that,
as being bound up with the Pope and 'legalism', and, in its rightful desire to return to Scripture, to lay an almost exclusive emphasis on the Biblical and Hebraic elements.) Thus the ethics of the
Christianised West, derived as they are partly from classical
sources, deepened and enriched by Christianity, as well as from the
Bible and Church tradition, are not exclusively Christian in origin.
But for a thousand years or so in England they have been sustained
and upheld by the Christian faith which has given them both their
authority and their motive. Now that the majority of the population doubt or repudiate the Christian faith they are finding themselves left in a moral vacuum – and that is an exceedingly dangerous place to be. What happened when the house was left empty?[1]

---

[1] This chapter and most of the others had been written before the publication of Lord Devlin's important book, *The Enforcement of Morals*,
O.U.P., 1965. I have however been able to use it in Chapters Nine and
Ten. On p. 92 he speaks of the vacuum that is caused when a society no
longer acknowledges a supreme spiritual authority. See the valuable discussion of the predicament of a Christianised but no longer Christian
West, pp. 92, 93. On p. 25 he says: 'No society has yet solved the problem
of how to teach morality without religion. So the law must base itself on
Christian morals and to the best of its ability enforce them, not simply because they are the morals of most of us, nor simply because they are the
morals taught by the established Church – on these points the law recognises the right to dissent – but for the compelling reason that without
the help of Christian teaching the law will fail.'

III

It looks as though before we can even begin to revindicate Christian ethics, we shall first have to re-establish ethics – some acknowledged basis of moral obligation, some objective standard of moral reference. And that is not likely to be at all easy. The whole trend of contemporary thinking, both at the higher academic levels and in popular opinion, is against it. Moral philosophy in the universities disclaims the right and the capacity of expounding to people what they ought to do.[1]

Indeed it is doubted whether ethical statements are statements about anything at all beyond the attitude of the man who makes them. Are moral statements merely 'emotive' – that is, are they merely expressions of 'pro-attitudes' or, as Braithwaite would say, 'declarations of policy' – or how far can we claim for them an objective truth which has some status in reality? For that, after all, is the fundamental question.[2] If there is a moral law, on what does it rest? The current repudiation of metaphysics gives the question intense practical urgency. Is there anything that can fill the moral vacuum? Why *ought* anybody to do anything, and where can he find a valid standard of reference to guide him in knowing what he ought to do? If people reject the Christian answer, where can they find another to put in its place? For that is at the moment notoriously lacking. Science has come adrift from moral goals, and planners do not know what they are planning for; and the man

[1] See, for example, the Foreword by Ayer to Nowell Smith's *Ethics*, Pelican, 1954. 'There is a distinction which is not always sufficiently marked, between the activity of a moralist who sets out to elaborate a moral code or to encourage its observance, and that of the moral philosopher, whose concern is not primarily to make moral judgements but to analyse their nature.' In other words his concern is with logic and language. Nowell Smith himself remarks: 'The question, what shall I do and what moral principles shall I adopt? must be answered by each man for himself' (p. 320).

[2] Logical positivism tended to rule out all ethical and theological statements as strictly meaningless, because incapable of empirical, scientific, verification. Under pressure of sheer common sense and concern for the uses of language this has largely given way to logical and linguistic analysis; compare the title of Hare's book *The Language of Morals*. (For critical analysis of logical positivism in its ethical bearings, see W. D. Ross, *Foundations of Ethics*, Oxford, 1939, pp. 30, 38. On the whole matter see Chapter Two.)

in the street is constantly exposed to the insinuations of mass media for which moral distinctions are virtually obliterated – they are not so much 'immoral' as a-moral.[1]

Moreover, any idea of an objective standard runs counter to popular opinion. As Darwin's theory of natural selection was torn out of its biological context and given (quite wrongly) an ethical connotation – to support some very unethical moral theories; so today Einstein's theory of relativity is widely taken, equally illegitimately, to imply that moral standards are merely 'relative'. The claim that any standards are absolute is apt to be branded as 'undemocratic', intolerant or even 'un-Christian'. (For 'Christian' conduct means being kind to the cat and not to stop it from clawing up the carpet.)

Thus moral confusion meets the naked eye. Perhaps the first reaction of Christians to it ought to be to thank God that so many men and women, despite all the confusion and moral anarchy, do manage to hold on to high moral principles and to live upright and charitable lives. How far Christians are justified in talking, as preachers do, about general 'moral collapse', is a question about which we had best not dogmatise. *Is* this generation more wicked than its predecessors? In the nature of things it is almost impossible to obtain reliable evidence for an answer. But in some ways, surely, it is a great deal better. There is a far more sensitive social conscience and a much stronger abomination of cruelty than in the earlier 'Christian' society, and that should be thankfully and humbly recognised. On the other hand there is much that is alarming – the continuing increase in crimes of violence, not least by teenagers and even children, drug-addiction, the slaughter on the roads, the sacrifice of personal values to mammon, and that inordinate sexuality, ruthlessly exploited for the money in it, which threatens to pollute the atmosphere. But by common consent many of these evils ought to be regarded as chargeable rather to defects in the structure of society than to breakdown in personal morality. And they cannot be dealt with merely moralistically. Moral exhortation and talk about 'Christian ideals' are among the least rewarding of human activities. Under twentieth century conditions the Christian ethic cannot be put into practice without long-range social and political action. As a former Lord Chancellor has ob-

[1] See *Discrimination and Popular Culture*, Pelican, 1965.

served, 'It is no good dreaming dreams of utopia if one cannot draft the appropriate legislation'.[1]

The probability is that moral advance moves in a spiral rather than a straight line, and no generation, involved in its own present, can be sure whether the curve is rising or falling. Perhaps it is arrogant in us that we should wish to be. It is God, not man, who pronounces the last judgement. The Church is not here to condemn the world but to save the world, and it will not be saved by censorious attitudes. Christians may find some emotional release in denouncing the vices of the age; but they will do nothing more constructive that way. What we ought to be asking is not How wicked are people? but How can we best serve and help them in a time of unprecedented moral difficulty?

'What is desperately needed today is an understanding and sympathy on the part of those who represent the Church towards the often intolerable burdens which unnatural circumstances, economic and otherwise, place on the shoulders of those who are trying to keep the Commandments and who therefore, if they fail, need encouragement and sympathy rather than censure and who, if they succeed, must often be regarded as having achieved heroic sanctity.'[2]

The world over, the technical revolution is creating a social and moral situation of which hitherto neither the Church itself nor mankind as a whole has had any experience. It cannot be met by cut and dried ethical formulas. Every new technical invention brings its own new moral problems with it – nuclear energy is the obvious instance – and civilisation cannot find the answer to the ethical problems raised by its own achievements. Human sin will spoil all God's gifts and turn what is good to evil uses. But it ought to be emphasised, all the same, that some of the most pressing moral problems of our time have been set by man's achievements – that is, in the end, by God's creative work in man; and what we must always be looking for is the growing-point and the positive indication of God's purpose. Some of these are discussed in more detail later (Chapter Ten). Christians do not cherish any illusion that they can be solved apart from the grace of God.

But why do Christians make such a fuss when Humanists talk

[1] Lord Kilmuir, *Political Adventure*, Weidenfeld and Nicolson, 1964, p. 7.
[2] The late Gerald Vann, O.P., in *Moral Dilemmas*, Collins, 1965, p. 80.

about morals without religion? It would not have shocked St. Paul or St. Augustine. Nobody surely doubts that there can be good men who are not or do not call themselves believers; of course there are and all of us know scores of them. (It does not follow that God is not at work in them.) The great tradition of Christian moral theology which runs through St. Augustine to St. Thomas, has always affirmed that there is a moral law bearing its own evidence and authority, and that man can apprehend moral values apart from any specific relation to God. It does not need Christianity to tell us that it is better to be kind than cruel or that a man is more than his appetites. That belongs to the moral inheritance of mankind. And it is important for Christians to maintain this; partly because it provides an effective buttress against relativism and subjectivism, partly because the acceptance of revelation presupposes an independent moral judgement. For if we do not know what Goodness is, how can we recognise God when he is revealed to us? If we do not know what Goodness is, then even to say that God is good is meaningless. If we do not know what we mean by moral duty then we cannot say with any meaning that it is a duty to obey the law of God. Moreover, the 'image' of God may be corrupted if it has 'escaped the control of an unsurrendered, independent moral judgement'. From this point of view, it is highly important for Christians to insist that morals do not depend on religion and to safeguard the 'autonomy' of the moral will.[1]

That, however, cannot be the last word. It is one thing, and an important thing, to say that morals are in that sense 'autonomous' even (if you like) 'natural to man'. But it is quite another thing to say that religion and ethics are unrelated (that *could* lead to religion without morals). We have still to ask whether *in the long run* man's moral experience can be interpreted or vindicated apart from belief in God and whether it does not point beyond itself to a transcendent and self-revealing Goodness.

When Humanists talk about morals without religion they are claiming that morality can be validated simply from within man himself and without any transcendental reference. The question is whether that claim can be justified and how far it can stand up to the test of life. I do not believe that ultimately it can. Moral standards are not self-sustaining; they are vitalised and sustained by

[1] W. G. Maclagan, *The Theological Frontier of Ethics*, George Allen and Unwin, 1961, p. 187.

convictions that reach out beyond themselves, as the tree draws strength from the soil that nurtures it. How far is it possible to believe in man if we do not believe in something more than man? If he does not stand in some real sense 'outside' nature, if spirit has no status in reality, what claim or authority have his moral values? I do not think, as I try to work out later (Chapter Three) that human life and human moral experience can be understood or even described adequately except in relation to that which transcends them, or that in the long run moral obligation can be vindicated on any ground short of at least some form of theism.[1]

Christians maintain that Christian theology is the secure and valid basis of Humanism, because man realises his humanity – that which is distinctively human in him – only in his relationship with God. That is, of course, what Humanists cannot accept. Yet at a time when all human values are in danger of being over-whelmed it is tragic waste if Christians and Humanists, instead of being allies and collaborators shout at one another from entrenched positions. They should be engaged in mutual conversations. But on what common ground can they communicate? What Humanism has stood for in the past has been man standing out apart from nature in his human prerogative and dignity, while rejecting the Christian interpretation of that. In its great representatives like Sir Julian Huxley it has found room and welcome for religious values – even though it has been 'religion without God'. Today, however, it seems to mean something different. 'The middle ground of a truly "humanistic" interpretation of man which used to be pre-sented as an alternative to religious ethics has been largely cap-tured from two sides, by the naturalists and the supernaturalists, mainly by the former. As a consequence, the word "Humanism", which used to imply the essential discontinuity between man and nature, nowadays has only the negative meaning of "non-theism". Intellectuals who call themselves humanists are more often than not actually naturalists; in one way or another they "homogenise" man with the physical or social contexts to which undoubtedly in large measure he belongs.'[2]

Undeniably this makes conversation difficult. Possibly we can

---

[1] For this paragraph see the recent book by Owen, *The Moral Argument for Christian Theism*, Longmans, 1965, and for further discussion of 'natural' morality see Chapter Two.

[2] Paul Ramsey, *Basic Christian Ethics*, S.C.M., 1953, p. 266.

find common ground in the Stoic-Christian theory of natural law to which I have already alluded and attempt to explore more deeply in the next chapter. Or even in some empirical observation of how man is actually constituted. But conversation and dialogue there must be. The physical and social sciences can tell us many things about human nature which traditional Christian theology did not know, and could not have known, for it had no means of knowing them. Christianity knows things about human nature which science *qua* science, does not know and cannot know.

Our aim, surely, must be to find our way to an understanding of man in the modern world which shall do full justice to both.[1] And Christians must recognise that any attempt to 'place' human life and find a meaning for it is in itself essentially religious, even though it may seem to give anti-religious answers. All along the line we must reach new understandings of what Christian morality means *now*, in a setting so radically different from anything foreseen by our Christian ancestors.

IV

The New World which the West began to enter in the sixteenth century was at once 'a place and an idolum' – new countries of geographical discovery and at the same time a new country of the mind. It meant both the Atlantic and *The New Atlantis*. It was a migration of the human spirit from its own inner life to the external world. Bacon, as Mumford says in a lively passage, turned mediaeval values upside down.[2] 'One of the chief marks of the ideological new world of science was to be the progressive abandonment of the inner and subjective in every form . . . Thomas Aquinas's world presented man as shut up in himself – surrounded by self-conditioned ideas or divine revelations. Science opened up the external world and bade it welcome, but it shut out the self; it enlarged the horizon but contracted the centre; here lay the beginning of a deeper split in the Western personality . . . The most important problem of all was left out of the new world-picture of science: who is to control the controller of nature?' Religion is life experienced in depth. In this new world the dimension of depth

[1] Cp. Gregor Smith, *The New Man*, S.C.M., p. 390.
[2] Chapter Seven on The New Hemisphere in *The Condition of Man*, Secker and Warburg, 1944.

was lost. The whole weight of emphasis fell, and falls still, on what was external, quantitative and mechanical – on getting things done rather than on being people. The sciences which the new world has created are 'masterly symbolic fabrications: unfortunately the symbols of science were treated as if they represented a higher order of reality, when they actually represented only a higher order of abstraction . . . in other words, the physical sciences tended to identify the quantitative with the real, the qualitative with the unreal'. This is the mental climate that we inherit, and to it have added a vast new technical mastery. The result has been that during the whole period the inward man has been decaying while the outward man is renewed from day to day. A real danger of modern civilisation is that it should mould a new kind of human being, who is, so to speak, all outside but no inside, immensely competent in the external order, but with no 'soul', no interior life of his own. What is commonly called the Renaissance has gone one way and the Reformation another; they have never yet succeeded in getting married. There is a radical rift in the modern mind. The deep unconscious hungers of the psyche are starved or suppressed and find no satisfaction in a rational, intellectualised culture – this is what men mean when they talk about 'alienation' from the life of twentieth-century society. The result can be seen in the mounting incidence of mental illness and psychoneurotic 'breakdown', in the growing recourse to addictive drugs and sedatives – and perhaps through obscure compensation-mechanism it lies behind many of the crimes of violence. It could yet lead to a social 'loss of nerve' and the breakdown of Western civilisation.

Now, as we shall see (Chapter Seven) Christianity itself was one of the forces that made for the dissolution of the smaller and cosier world of the Middle Ages and for leading man out to a new stage in his history – and ongoing history is the work of God even though it may seem to us 'his strange work'. But at this critical moment, Christianity, instead of coming out to meet the New World and pointing men to the real presence of God in it, forgot its own doctrine of creation and allowed them to think that they had to choose between the excitement and enterprise of the new era and the traditional religious world-view which had, apparently, not very much to say to it; and men had no doubt which they were going to choose.

In result, since the end of the fifteenth century there has been an increasingly secularised and less God-centred attitude to experience. Confined at first to the educated élite, it has now, with the spread of general education and the apparatus of publicity, captured the masses of the population. For all practical purposes God had ceased to matter. And indeed such misleading associations have now gathered round the very name, that the mention of God no longer rings any bell.

The result of all this is that the West has been gradually coming adrift from its classical and its Christian inheritance; and this process has now come to a climax in the widespread abandonment of belief in God and, as many Christians at least maintain, the moral collapse which has been its consequence. At this point Christians have got to be very careful. The call for a return to Christianity in order to re-establish moral standards – assuming that moral standards *have* collapsed – is one to be made with the utmost compunction. We cannot *use* the Lord God as social vitamin. Moreover, as we have already insisted (p. 25) mankind can discern moral values without any specifically religious reference. There can be 'morality without religion'. Nevertheless, Western civilisation and the Christian morality which has sustained it have been so deeply rooted in faith in God and the Christian belief about Jesus Christ, that if the fundamental faith is abandoned, the structure could only too easily disintegrate. Can any society live without a faith? The fall of the Roman Empire may be a warning that without interior spiritual cohesion, no strengthening of external organisation can protect a society from dissolution. When we examine the prevalent moral standards, it looks as though the Victorians' expectations may be falsified by long-term events. Once faith in God is abandoned, we may be, morally speaking, on an inclined plane on which there may be no stopping just where we want to stop. The 'modern' age may be heading for the abyss. There are prophets today, and by no means only Christians, who believe that this is in fact what is happening – and here the Old Testament prophets are terrifying. A faithless and stubborn generation which in its arrogance has forsaken God and defied his law, by which men and nations live, will find itself under God's righteous judgement and Western civilisation will destroy itself. That sombre prediction *may* yet prove to be true. But if it does that will be the consequence not of any historical determinism but of causes that lie in the minds and hearts of men.

For the new society need not have been godless. To whatever extent it has been so, the Church cannot escape some of the blame for that. The Church cannot play providence to history but it ought to be able to see God in history. Christians do not worship a cultic deity but the Lord Almighty, Creator of heaven and earth (*rerum Deus tenax vigor* – a phrase which no one has yet been able to English). If it sees the movements of history as though they were mere revolts against itself, it will never be able to redeem history.

v

In this country and nearly everywhere else in the world Christians have now to live in a secular, not a monochrome, uni-credal society and must make up their minds how they stand towards it. It is futile to hanker after the kind of 'Christendom' which has now left the stage of history. But there is no necessity in the nature of things why a secular society should be secularist. That indeed is the central, unanswered question of mid-twentieth century civilisation (see pp. 138-139). But the Church was partly to blame for what happened before and must learn the lesson of those mistakes today. One fatal result of its clericalisation was that at heart it had little real concern for the life of the layman in the world at all. It was prone to identify the Christian life too narrowly with the purely churchly aspects; and it wrongly attempted to bring the new knowledge and the new economic and technical developments under *direct* theological control. But the moral sovereignty of Christ is one thing, religious imperialism quite another. Because it had not at that time understood the value of secular life in itself as an element in God's creative work, it adopted one of two mistaken attitudes, which were equally disastrous in effect. Either it tried to 'Christianise' the secular by bringing it under religious regulation, or it took refuge in a cocoon of pietism, leaving the secular world to go its own way. If religion was not thrown out, it stayed out, and became a man's own private affair, with diminishing relevance to the life around it. Both those mistakes must be avoided.

Christ is Lord of all life and nothing less, and Christianity cannot be departmentalised: the Church cannot withdraw from that position. But that does not mean and must never be allowed to mean any claim to ecclesiastical dictation; nor does it mean that our faith alone will tell us how to deal, let us say, with juvenile delinquency or how to solve the problems of immigration. Thus while, on the one hand, there is nothing human to which Christian morality is irrelevant, there are yet many problems which cannot be solved, immediately and directly, by any purely 'religious' methods. There are technical factors involved in moral choices and if we are trying to find out what is God's will and verify our Christian obedience we must have recourse, on such matters, to the experts, whether or not they believe in Christianity. On the other side, Christians bring to these dilemmas the insights derived from their own faith and loyalties. We have something to receive from the world, for God is operating in the world, as well as a Gospel to offer to the world – though that Gospel will make little impact if the ethical teaching of the Church seems to be confined to matters of personal piety. The teaching Church may yet have much to learn; and we shall do well to recall the Lord's reminder 'he that is not against us is for us' (Luke ix: 50).

To speak with authority need not mean to dogmatise. As we must not try to impose Christian ethics on the statute book of a pluralist society,[1] so we must not be 'laying down the law' too glibly. We must never claim to know all the answers. We can do much harm by giving the impression that there is some ready-made 'Christian answer'. All of us, Christians and Humanists alike, are in the same predicament together. We are all alike being carried along by forces which nobody yet fully understands, and none of the questions arising can be answered simply by quoting texts from the Bible or looking up the rules in the book of words. Christian faith in the Lordship of Christ does not imply that we know 'the Christian answer' to the complex ethical issues of our time. There is no ready-made Christian ethic which can just be 'applied' – as though it were paint or wall-paper. Moral decisions which are already laid on are not really moral decisions at all. Indeed, it has been well said that the essence of Christian obedience is responsible freedom.[2] Moral decisions have always to be made inside an actual, concrete situation – all ethics are 'situational' in that sense – and no authority, human or divine, could say just what Christians ought to do in circumstances that had not yet arisen.

[1] See, however, pp. 228 ff.
[2] See Stephen Bayne, *Christian Living*, Seabury Press, Chapters I and II.

To say that, as we shall see later (Chapter Five) does not imply that there are no absolute Christian moral principles which no changing circumstances can alter. Of course there are – 'heaven and earth shall pass away but my words shall not pass away' (Matthew xiii: 30). But the word 'ought' always involves *doing* something, and what action those principles require of us must differ from one situation to another. All moral *systems*, if they are to be applicable to the circumstances in which they are constructed, are bound to be to some extent limited and relative to their own time and place. Aristotle's *Ethics*, with all their penetration, reflect the outlook of upper-class Athenians. St. Thomas's moral theology reflects the social conditions of the thirteenth century and could, in fact, only have been written then (see p. 133). We must not try to 'absolutise the relative'. If we do, the result may be merely formalistic. The basic Christian facts do not change; but Christian theological formulations have changed and are now changing rapidly in response to social and economic changes. So the Christian moral principles do not change, but new social and economic facts intervene to change the situation and thus require fresh interpretations of them. New social techniques become available; society comes to be organised in new patterns; new medical or psychological knowledge may affect the Christian judgement on various points. Even during the last twenty years Christian moral judgements have been strikingly modified with respect to birth-control, for example, or homosexuality or suicide (for fuller treatment, see Chapter Ten). Christian moral principles do not change; there is no relativity in the law of Christ. But what it implies is inevitably alterable. When new facts change the moral context they will change the actual content of obedience.

The traditional Christian ethic was tailored to a far less complicated society, with few of the vast organised power-structures with which Christian action has now to come to terms. At all times and in all circumstances we are to love our neighbour as ourselves. That command is of absolute obligation. But under modern conditions it may require political, social, economic and even strategic measures to implement it. What ought we to *do* if our neighbour is a murderer – or a joint-stock company – or an invading army? Frankly, so far from knowing the Christian answer to the complex ethical questions of our time, that is just what we have got to try to find out. To most of the current problems in social ethics there are widely divergent Christian answers. Possibly no one answer *is* 'the Christian answer'.

Thus any relevant study of Christian ethics will be more like a voyage of discovery than simply acquiring text-book information.

NOTE: ETHICS AND THEOLOGY

'Christian ethics depend on Christian theology.' Till recently that remark would have been regarded as a truism if not a platitude. Many questions, however, are now being raised, in Christian circles as well as outside them, about this traditional relationship (see pp. 25, 237). Professor Maclagan's book is one example. He writes from a standpoint friendly to Christianity. The book is not an attack on Christian morals; it is a very searching examination of opinions held by many Christian moralists about the relation of morals to theology. But he writes as a professional philosopher and accordingly any discussion of his argument which was anything but blatantly superficial would have to be on a level of technicality which would be quite out of place in a book of this kind, even if I were qualified to offer it. His enquiry, moreover, moves within strict limits. It concerns what might be called the conceptual frontier between what morality is and what religion is. But morality is a pretty abstract term, and his question is, as he says himself (p. 23) quite a different question from that of the positive *content* of morality. No system of ethics happens *in vacuo*. The moral ideals which people hold are moulded by and largely derived from their social and cultural tradition, in which religion plays a large part. Indeed, in spite of the noble agnostics (p. 17) most people's ethical standards and ideals are probably derived mainly from their religion. (This is not the same as Dr. Maclagan's question about their ultimate moral *authority*.) And self-evidently, distinctively Christian ethics do derive from the Christian religion; otherwise the phrase has no meaning. Some approve of them and some reject them, but that is what Christian ethics are. That is really all I have been saying.

But the question is sometimes asked in a wider reference. May not the dependence of ethics on theology tend to cramp the style of Christian ethics? Ought not Christian ethical appraisements of

C

any actual moral situations to be made on more strictly ethical grounds alone, with less dependence on theological 'principles'? If we invoke too much theology may we not get stuck in cut and dried formulas which do little to solve the concrete problem? As to that, I should certainly agree that we cannot rely too much on moral syllogisms. We cannot expect to find the moral answer by a process of logical deduction from abstract, *a priori* concepts, as scholasticism was too prone to do and perhaps moral theology is prone to do. What gets left out are men and women. There is such a thing as Christian common sense. I think that any relevant Christian ethic needs a strong admixture of empiricism – a good deal of this book is indeed a plea for that. But any ethic, even the most empirical, depends on a theology of some kind, some attitude to life or world-view, and its distinctive quality derives from that. There is a recognisably Christian ethic, as there is a Buddhist or a secularist. The Christian derives from the Christian world-view, from those beliefs about God and man which constitute the Christian religion; and, if the ultimate Christian beliefs are false – or to put it bluntly, if Jesus Christ was wrong – then clearly the whole case for Christian ethics – I do not say for 'morality' – falls to the ground. In this sense surely it is hardly disputable that Christian ethics depends on Christian theology.[1]

[1] 'There is no such thing as an ethic which has been developed by pure reason without presuppositions . . . The difference between the Christian ethic and secular moral philosophy is not that the former has presuppositions and that the latter is free from them, it is that they derive their presuppositions from different sources.' G. F. Thomas, *Christian Ethics and Moral Philosophy*, Scribners, New York, 1955, p. 379. I owe my knowledge of this book, and the loan of it, to Professor G. F. Woods. As I read the proof I must now add how deep is the loss of students of Christian Ethics – and many others – by his untimely death.

Chapter Two

'NATURE AND NATURE'S GOD'

THE Declaration of Human Rights assumes that there is in man simply as man something which commands respect and imposes obligations on all other men and all organised societies, certain freedoms which must be guaranteed, certain rights which must be secured – that human beings are ends in themselves and must never be treated as means to anything else, such as privilege, profits or reasons of State, and that these are claims of universal validity. What is the ultimate ground of that assumption? For this looks something like an agreed morality.

Christianity, of course, will give its own answer. Man, it will say, is created in God's image, a moral and spiritual personality, child of God and heir of eternal life, redeemed by Christ and sanctified by the Spirit; and in Christ all humanity is ennobled. The Christian valuation of human life depends on God's gift to man and God's work in him rather than on his rational capacities or anything intrinsic to man himself. Human personality is sacred because Christ has taken our nature upon him and all men are precious in the sight of God. Man is seen, as it were, from God's standpoint – that is what is distinctive about the Christian doctrine. Wherever the Gospel is faithfully proclaimed it brings with it new ideas of human dignity, revolutionary in their implications, which are now being urgently expressed in the blizzards of change sweeping across Africa. ('Making the natives discontented' is indeed an essential part of the Church's mission, however little intended by the missionaries and however unacceptable to governments.) Human rights, Christianity will say, rest fundamentally on the faith that man is heir of a more than earthly destiny, transcending all his political institutions. And that is not marginal to its case but central to it, weakly though it may seem to be held today. Plato affirmed that the primary question of politics is that of the immortality of the soul. If anyone said that now in the House of Commons, Members would laugh or feel acutely embarrassed. Nothing, it would be thought, could be less relevant to the drafting

35

of any modern legislation. But it is of course in the end entirely crucial. If public welfare is the supreme law, overriding all personal rights and claims, then the way is open to totalitarianism, whether dictatorial or democratic, and the Caiaphases can plead that it is *expedient* that one man should die for the people – and with fatal ease get agreement from the Pilates. If a man, so weak and insignificant, is bounded by his three score years and ten, then the State is not only bigger and stronger than he is, it can seem to be more important and significant and the bearer of more lasting values. Rome is eternal: who dies if England lives? Reasons of State can always be made paramount. But all States and all civilisations die; and, if the Christian faith and hopes are true, then it is the individual citizen, not the State, who is permanent and immortal, and the State and all political institutions exist for him, not he for them.

It may be that the Charter would never have been drafted had it not been for diffused Christian influences. But it is not an avowedly 'Christian' document and indeed not many of the member-States in the Covenant are professedly Christian States. What, then, is the court of moral appeal for U.N.? On what foundation can human rights be based?

The American Declaration of Independence claimed to be founded on self-evident truths – that men as men have an indefeasible right to life, liberty and the pursuit of happiness. And these, which are described as 'natural' rights, are entrenched in the Constitution of the United States. (U.S.A. is almost the only society which was actually formed by a social contract.) If it were asked: What is their authority? Jefferson appealed to Nature and Nature's God. That was the language of the eighteenth century and it has a long history behind it. In order to understand the moral development of Western civilisation it is important to know at least something about that history.

No word used in ethical discussion is more ambiguous than the word Nature. In contemporary English usage it covers a wide variety of meanings, some of which are apparently incompatible: it is used to denote both what is and what ought to be. Nature can be contrasted with History, or the natural man with the spiritual,[1]

---

[1] 'Being by nature born in sin and the children of wrath we are hereby (in baptism) made the children of grace' as the Catechism puts it.

or natural events with supernatural; and in all these contexts it means something different. Nature can mean the total cosmic process through which God is disclosed in 'natural' religion,[1] it can mean what Wordsworth and the Romantics meant by it, and to-day not very much more than the open air. In the country a 'natural' means a village idiot. And all these uses have history behind them. In ordinary ethical discussion the word can be used in apparently opposite senses. We can speak of men as 'naturally' sinful or as 'naturally' good and even perfectible. We can say that it is 'only human nature' to be indolent or lustful or aggressive. ('Human nature, my boy, always has been and always will be.') Or we can speak of man's 'true' or 'better' nature – what he can be or is 'meant' to be or ought to be – as Christians would say, is intended by God to be. Here nature connotes the true law of his being, that in virtue of which he is really human, what he has it in him to become and, in becoming, to realise his humanity. This derives from the Greeks and particularly from Aristotle, who defined the nature of man (or of anything else) by relation to his 'end' or potentiality: the idea is essentially teleological. It is in this sense that nature is commonly used in the Western ethical tradition and it is in this sense that, as we shall see later, we can rightly speak of morality as natural, the law of the fulfilment of man's being, not something capriciously imposed upon him by external authority, whether divine or human.[2]

The two seemingly contradictory meanings of nature are combined by Hooker in a single sentence, in which he says that man 'is by nature little better than a wild beast, rebellious, obstinate and averse from all obedience to the sacred laws of his nature'.[3] The contrast can be seen in the different versions of the state of nature in Hobbes and in Locke respectively. For Hobbes human life in the state of nature is solitary, poor, nasty, brutish and short because of man's 'perpetual and restless desire for power after power' – that will to power which Christians call sin – that leads

[1] For very able and interesting discussion of Nature and Nature's God in the eighteenth century see Alan Richardson, *History, Sacred and Profane*, S.C.M., 1964, pp. 27, 78, 273.

[2] On this see Jacques, *The Right and the Wrong*, S.P.C.K., 1965, pp. 49, 70 and *passim*.

[3] Quoted by Basil Willey, *The English Moralists*, p. 110, who remarks that man is thus described as 'naturally unnatural'. If we get behind linguistic analysis, that is the profound and tragic truth about him – his existence contradicts his essence.

to the war of everyman against everyman. But, as generations of dons have pointed out, if that is the whole account of human nature it would never be possible for natural man to enter into any kind of contract, even on Hobbesian grounds of self-interest, and behave like a rational and social being. On the other hand, for Locke, the philosopher of the Glorious Revolution and Whig politics, the state of nature *is* rational and social. It is 'men living together according to reason'. And reason for Locke means 'natural revelation', the reflexion of what nature is and man should be. To follow nature was, for the eighteenth century, the way of virtue, happiness and freedom. Reason, which is the law of the state of nature, 'teaches all mankind, who will but consult it, that all being equal and independent no one ought to harm another in his life, health, liberty or possessions'. Here is the famous theory of natural rights, derived from the knowledge of Nature and Nature's God. In the state of nature all men are virtuous – the exact contradictory of the Hobbesian version; but though it is governed by the law of nature – what that is, I shall try to explain in a moment – yet there is, says Locke, this 'inconvenience' that everyman is still a law to himself and there is no legal or political system to guarantee to men their rights and their property. ('The great and chief end of men uniting in Commonwealths and putting themselves under government is the preservation of their property'!) Thus by a (mythical) social contract they agree to unite and establish a 'fiduciary' and essentially contractual state, which is answerable to the constituent members and forfeits its claim to their obedience if it violates their natural rights. Here is the ark of the covenant of Whiggery and the charter of American Independence.

But behind Locke, and indeed behind all 'democratic' political philosophy, there lies a profound theological principle, the idea of an ultimate law of divine justice prior to the laws of all earthly states and to which all political power is answerable (see pp. 222 ff.). Any law that conflicts with it is morally void and subjects are under no obligation to it. Locke's theory of government presupposes a laicised or secular version of the classical Christian doctrine of Natural Law as expounded by St. Thomas Aquinas, and to this we must now give further consideration. But it was Bertrand Russell who remarked, 'The view of the state of nature and of natural law which Locke accepted from his predecessors cannot be freed from its theological basis; where it survives without this, as in much modern liberalism, it is destitute of clear logical foundation'.[1] The theory of natural law, which has counted for so much in the ethical tradition of Christendom and in the structure of Western civilisation, is not in itself originally a Christian theory. Derived, to start with, from Greek philosophy it was thence elaborated by Roman jurists, and worked into an ethical doctrine by the Stoics, from whom it was taken over by the Church and, conflated with the Bible and Christian doctrine, was made the foundation of Christian moral philosophy in its authoritative, 'catholic' form. It has, of course, nothing to do with the 'law of nature' in the modern, scientific sense of hypotheses which are found to fit the facts in the behaviour of physical phenomena – which, in other words, are not really 'laws' at all.[2] Natural law in its ethical connotation *is* a law that must be or ought to be obeyed. It 'represents nature as the power which prescribes laws – laws which nature or God prescribe'.[3] It is true that Wordsworth in the *Ode to Duty* comes very near to the identification of the moral law with the physical laws of nature. (So for that matter, does the XIXth Psalm.) The law that 'preserves the stars from wrong' is in us the law of reason and conscience, 'stern daughter of the voice of God'. That was probably due, in the long run, to Stoicism, which identified nature with the divine reason, and as such the point belongs to a later paragraph. But it says something which, as we shall see, is of fundamental importance in Aquinas. In defiance of all the protests of modern philosophy, it insists that what is right, what *ought* to be done, is ultimately grounded in what *is*, and that is really inherent in Christian Theism. The eventual doctrine of natural law, however, started a long way further back than the Stoics.

When the Greeks first began to explore the world they were fascinated, as one can see in Herodotus, by the manifold variety of customs (*mores*) and the social and moral laws which they en-

[1] *History of Western Philosophy*, George Allen and Unwin, 1946, p. 649. On Locke see the whole section, pp. 642–665; also Ernest Barker, *Essays on Government*, O.U.P., 1956, pp. 87 ff., and his Introduction to Gierke's *Natural Law and the Theory of Society*, C.U.P., 1958, pp. xxxiv-lii I.

[2] See my *Questioning Faith*, pp. 103, 104.

[3] Bryce, *Studies in History and Jurisprudence*, Clarendon Press, 1901, vol. II, pp. 112 ff.

countered. But they also found some laws and customs which appeared to be common to all peoples everywhere. These, they concluded, must be by nature (*phusei*) implanted by nature itself in all mankind, and therefore prior to and more authoritative than the positive laws which existed 'by convention' (*Nomo*[1]). St. Paul was to say later, under Stoic influence, that the Gentiles do by nature the things of the law, having the law written in their consciences (Romans iii: 14).

Aristotle accepted the distinction between natural or 'common' justice, which does not depend on positive enactment and has a universal validity, and the 'conventional' justice of actual laws existing in Athens or any particular state. The corollary of Alexander's world-state was a common language, the *Koinē* – in which the New Testament books were afterwards written – and a common law, a *Koinos Nomos*. 'But the *Koinē* was an actual fact, the *Koinos Nomos* remained an aspiration. It was an ideal law which could only become actual if men were purely rational. Its principles were ideal principles. Among these ideal principles was that of equality.'[2] According to Zeno, the founder of Stoicism, all men as reasonable creatures are united and equal in their membership of the cosmic City of God,[3] the commonwealth of Nature and Reason. Thus 'by nature' slave and free are equal. (Aristotle had said that some men are 'by nature slaves' – there was no touch of a radical in Aristotle.)

As Rome began to expand into an empire, the Praetors found themselves trying cases – mainly, one imagines, commercial cases – between a citizen and a non-citizen, in which, therefore, one of the two parties was not amenable to the Roman law. If the citizen law (*ius civile*) of Rome could not be invoked, under what system of law could the case be tried? The answer they found was, under the law of nations (*ius gentium*), as a code of more general application – 'the universal element in antithesis to the national peculiarities to be found in the positive law of every state'. This is, in effect, Aristotle's 'common law', and Roman legal philosophy opened it out into the normative theory of natural law (*ius naturale*) as the common moral sense of mankind. 'Nature', for example, directs that parents should be supported by their children. Under *ius civile*,

---

[1] Cp. *Antigone* line 456: 'These are not of today or yesterday but live forever and no man knows whence they came.'

[2] Barker in Gierke, p. xxxvi.

[3] For the City of God, see pp. 121ff.

a slave may be merely a chattel, by natural law he is something more like a person.[1] In its essence, to quote Ernest Barker again, the *ius naturale* is 'the Stoic ideal of a common law of all humanity, which is a law of Reason and Nature'. It is permeated by the Stoic principle of equality; *omnes homines natura aequales sunt* – they are equal persons in the great court of nature. It is not a body of actual law which can be enforced in the courts. It is a way of looking at things, a spirit of 'humane interpretation' in the mind of the judge and the jurist, which may and does affect the law which is actually enforced, but does so without being actual law itself.[2] Cicero, however, was to write that 'there is a true law which is right reason, agreeable to nature, diffused among all men, constant, eternal, which . . . admits of neither alteration nor subtraction nor abrogation. The vote of neither Senate nor people can discharge us from our obligation to it . . . One law shall embrace all races over all time, eternal and immortal: and there shall be hereby one common master and commander of all – God, who originated this law'.[3] This is a strongly Stoic confession of faith. And here we have something like Locke's natural law prior to and the foundation of all government.

Aristotle had founded morality on the realisation by man of his true 'end' or nature, as all things seek for their end or 'good'. Morality is thus for him an aspect of the whole cosmic 'movement' or process, rooted in the structure of the universe, and is, indeed, conformity with that movement – the nature of things – on the part of man. (What none of the ancient thinkers seem to have realised is that man alone is conscious of that movement and able to respond to it or to defy it; and that it is just this unique fact which gives morality any meaning at all.)

All these streams united in developed Stoicism. The Stoics taught that all men partake in the divine reason, informing and ruling the Cosmos. (They never made up their minds whether the universe was 'one big machine' or 'one big soul' [*anima mundi*].

---

[1] It is true that *ius gentium* and *ius naturale* do not always coincide. The law of all known nations admitted slavery. The frontier is difficult to define and the jurists themselves did not define it exactly, but the general trend and tenor of their thinking seems to have pretty nearly been as stated above.

[2] op. cit., p. xxxviii.

[3] *De Republica* quoted by Gore, *The Philosophy of The Good Life*, John Murray, 1930, p. 138.

Zeno was a materialistic pantheist, and the Hymn of Cleanthes is through and through determinist.) Through this reason, controlling the passions, men could discern the true laws of life – the moral law – implanted by nature in the human mind, capable of rational demonstration, and binding at all times on all men. Thus virtue, the fulfilment of man's being, is found to consist in 'following nature', that is, obeying the natural law.[1]

When Christianity came into the Empire, the Church found much in all this that was congenial to it and seemed even to be speaking its own language. The idea of an immanent, universal reason informing and enlightening all mankind seemed to chime in tune with the Logos-doctrine and belief in the true Light that lighteth every man. Christian teachers early began to claim that the God of the Bible was himself the Author of the law of nature, which had been expressed for Israel in the Decalogue and was indeed reaffirmed by the Lord himself. 'So far from despising the best moral teaching given by Jew or pagan in their age, both [St. Paul and St. Peter] endorse it, while at the same time giving it deeper foundations and more far-reaching scope.'[2] In Christ the true way of life had been personified – this *is* life according to nature. Seen in those terms, it has been suggested, Christians can regard the natural law doctrine (in its Christian or 'catholic' form) as a declaration of the Lordship of Christ over all human life.[3]

The Apologists take natural law for granted. Despite his attitude to the pagan culture, Tertullian appeals for freedom of worship as a fundamental, natural right. (*Ad Scapulam* 2 as quoted in Encyclopedia of Religion and Ethics under Nature, Christian, p. 213 b.) Eventually the classical Christian statement was formulated, as everyone knows, by St. Thomas who, by an amazing *tour de force*[4] brought together the Stoic law of nature, Aristotle,

[1] But nature takes on a very rarefied and intellectualist meaning. It involves suppression of all the 'natural' emotions – pity, for example, was a sign of weakness. Stoicism became a doctrine of impossible self-sufficiency. Under the Empire it supplied the Opposition with a kind of escape-religion – an ark of refuge within which to live a self-respecting life in evil times.

[2] E.g. Selwyn on I Peter, p. 89. On this see Chapter Four.

[3] Vidler and Whitehouse, *Natural Law, A Christian Reconsideration*, S.C.M., 1964, p. 23.

[4] A *tour de force*, because the God of Aristotle has almost nothing in common with the God of the Sermon on the Mount. But apart from that, there is a radical dualism even within the Platonic-Aristotelian tradition in the Christian legacy. 'Throughout the greater part of its history western

Cicero and the Bible and the content of Christian revelation in one magnificent, all-containing synthesis, which may be called the charter of Christendom and indeed supplied the intellectual basis for a universal Christian civilisation. (See Chapter Six.) The natural law doctrine, thus formulated, survived the upheaval of the Reformation and is still the officially recognised basis of Roman Catholic moral theology. On the reformed side of the watershed, both Luther and Calvin use it in their own ways. In the Anglican

---

religion, in its more philosophical forms, has had two Gods . . . The two were indeed identified as one Being with two aspects. But the ideas corresponding to the "aspects" were ideas of two antithetic kinds of Being. The one was the Absolute of other-worldliness and self-sufficiency, out of time, alien from the categories of ordinary human thought and experience, needing no world of lesser beings to supplement or enhance his own eternal, self-contained perfection. The other was a God who emphatically was not self-sufficient or in any philosophical sense "absolute"; one whose essential nature required the existence of other beings, and not of one kind only but of all kinds which could find their place in the descending scale of the possibilities of reality – a God whose prime attribute was generativeness, whose manifestation was to be found in the diversity of creatures and therefore in the temporal order and the manifold spectacle of nature's processes.' [The reference here is to Plato's *Timaeus*; God is 'good' in the sense of perfect and self-sufficient, needing nothing, but also good in the semi-ethical sense of 'free from envy', and therefore must by the inner logical necessity of his own being create all that can be created.] 'The goodness of God is a constraining goodness; he is not, in Milton's phrase, "free to create or not" . . . since the characteristics of everything that is are inherent in the eternal Idea of it, neither God nor the creatures could conceivably have been or done aught but what they are and do.' [This idea that whatever possibly can exist, including evil things, must exist, underlies the eighteenth-century notion of the 'best of all possible worlds' and Pope's phrase Whatever is, is best – which is not merely moral cynicism but metaphysics.]

'With this theological dualism . . . there ran a dualism of values, the one other-worldly (though often in a half-hearted way) the other this-worldly. If the good for man was the contemplation or imitation of God, this required on the one hand a transcendence and suppression of the merely "natural" instincts and desires, a withdrawal of the soul from the world, the better to prepare it for the beatific vision . . . and it required, on the other hand, a piety towards the God of things as they are, an adoring delight in the sensible universe in all its variety, an endeavour on man's part to know and understand it ever more fully, and a conscious participation in the divine activity of creation.' Between the Middle Ages and the Enlightenment the latter emphasis is gaining ground. In the eighteenth century 'the idea of God was itself becoming predominantly this-worldly, tending towards a fusion with the conception of "nature", infinitely various in its manifestations and endlessly active in the production of different kinds of beings.' From Lovejoy's entrancing study *The Great Chain of Being*, Harvard University Press, 1961, pp. 314, 54, 316.

Church, Hooker depends entirely on it; Jeremy Taylor still takes it for granted, and in modern times William Temple based many of his ethico-social judgements on it. But with the break-up of the unity of Christendom with its single recognised court of moral appeal, there began to be formed, mainly in Protestant countries, what may be called a lay or secular version of it. (Grotius claimed that his thesis would be valid even if God does not exist.) In the eighteenth century the law of nature is becoming a revolutionary concept: it underlies both Locke and Rousseau. 'Reason', becoming critical and sceptical, destroys the foundations of the established order as something depending on 'rational' necessity, and leads to subversive political ideas. Reason becomes the prophet of liberation against every form of 'un-natural' authority. If reason teaches us to follow nature, it also teaches that man has a 'natural right' to life, liberty and the pursuit of happiness. *That* is the law of nature and nature's God. The American Declaration of Independence is much more a document of natural law in that secular sense than a 'Christian' document.[1]

But whether with or without its Christian framework the natural law doctrine still persists. Lawyers still speak about natural justice. U.N.O. still appeals to natural rights. Catholic moral theology still rests on this fundamental law in the nature of things in obeying which man fulfils himself, an expression of the nature of and will of God, which can be known by man as a rational being apart from any historical revelation. 'The participation in the eternal law by the rational creature is called the *lex naturalis*,' as St. Thomas puts it. Have we here the common ground of meeting for dialogue between Christians and Humanists – the foundation for an acknowledged morality? A fuller discussion of the Thomistic ethic will be found in a later chapter (pp. 128 ff.) and some of its limitations will be suggested. But the theory of natural law is not dependent on the form in which it was stated by St. Thomas; as we have seen, it goes back far behind him. Our concern at the moment is with the foundations of ethics rather than with a particular ethical structure. What we have to ask at the

---

[1] Lovejoy points out that Hume's sceptical assertion that reason is the slave of passions, i.e. influenced if not controlled by irrational (and as we now add, sub-conscious) forces, is common form in the prose and poetry of the seventeenth and eighteenth centuries and lies behind the checks-and-balances of the American Constitution. *Reflexions on Human Nature*, pp. 24 ff.

moment, therefore, is whether natural law is still a viable concept
and whether, indeed, there is such a thing at all. The *Oxford
Dictionary of Christianity* remarks with lexicographical finality
'that the Natural Law can be known by unaided human reason was
denied e.g. by Traditionalism; its dependence on God as the
author of nature is denied by Rationalism; and its very existence
by many modern philosophers'. It is, says Lord Radcliffe, 'one of
those conceptions which are at once too impalpable to destroy
and yet too enduring to be quite forgotten'.[1]

On the whole, the Protestant tradition has been violently
opposed to the whole idea, as smacking too much of salvation by
works and as minimising the corruption of man's will and reason
by sin and his need of grace to do anything that is good. Protestants have always, and rightly, been deeply suspicious of a moralistic or legalistic approach to the Christian life, even though, as
Herbert Waddams points out, 'there is a strong stream of natural
moralism in the Protestant churches', especially in this country and
U.S.A., 'and, as it is often not balanced by an adequate sacramental doctrine and practice, it is apt to be even more "natural" than
that of the Roman Catholics'.[2] And it is undeniable that the natural
law, when systematised and codified in the canon law and 'applied'
through an elaborate casuistry, can degenerate into an external
legalism and become the minimum standard of conduct that
Christians can decently hope to get away with – the fate which be-
fell the law of the Scribes and Pharisees. None of this, however, is
inherent in the notion of natural law itself. Some recent Protestant
writers go the length of rejecting not only natural law but any
attempt at systematising ethics on the ground that any system is
incompatible with the spontaneity of the Christian life.[3] The logical conclusion of such an attitude is to throw the whole weight of
every moral decision on the conscience and judgement of the individual, unsupported by any formulated experience – which is,
after all, what 'rules' really are. The crucial question that has to be

---

[1] *The Law and Its Compass*, Faber, 1961, p. 11.
[2] *A New Introduction to Moral Theology*, S.C.M., 1964, p. 48. He
quotes M.R.A. as 'An interesting phenomenon based on a natural morality, in which the Person of Christ and Christian teaching are optional
extras for its members'. This chapter (III) offers a very good discussion of
natural law, in Christian ethics.
[3] See, for example, the diatribe against Moral Theology in Lehmann,
Ethics in a Christian Context, S.C.M., 1963, pp. 287 ff.

decided is whether the Existentialists are right – whether every man is the creator of his own values – or whether there is an objective right and wrong which is morally authoritative for all men, prior to and the ultimate justification of all positive law and all systems of morality, and if so whether and how far natural law can now be said to embody or represent it? To Christians the theory is 'naturally' congenial. It consists with the whole body of Christian doctrine and it has pre-Christian Biblical antecedents. (Amos may be said to have been appealing to natural law in his denunciation of the atrocities and 'un-natural' crimes of the neighbouring peoples; Amos i: 2.) But can one believe in it if he is not a Christian? At the time when the law Christian was formulated, everyone believed in Christianity and in the divine origin of the world. Can it stand without the support of that belief? For what we are concerned with at the moment is not the specifically Christian form of it, but the basic notion of natural law in itself. 'It has', says Waddams, 'become clear in recent years that there are few if any principles of natural law on which all men are agreed. It is still possible to claim that the inherent and universal sense of Right and Wrong indicates that there are moral distinctions which men are meant to observe. But this sense cannot be made the foundation of any superstructure of moral law.'[1]

And perhaps that comes near the real truth about it. Perhaps the permanent value of the concept is not so much in yielding a moral code as in its insistence that morality is natural to man, not imposed upon him either by the *fiat* of a capricious deity or by priests, tyrants, or other kinds of 'establishment'. 'The theory of natural law is not in fact a code of moral rules, although many of its advocates and opponents think of it in this way. It is primarily an account of the naturalness of morals, although even when we say this we have to be on our guard.' (It does not mean, for example, an evolutionist theory of morals.) 'There is nothing in the concept of natural law to bind us to those aspects of mediaeval social theory or classical psychology which time has obviously invalidated. It is only when those modern sciences attack man's reason, freedom or intrinsic spirituality that those who base morality on natural law are bound to stand opposed to their findings . . . In teaching that morality is reasonable and is closely related to human nature, this age-long theory of ethics does give empirical

[1] Op. cit., p. 44.

and scientific disciplines an opportunity of incorporating their established findings into an account of the moral life which is valid for the modern world.'[1]

Natural law, in its metaphysical context, has been one of the safeguards of human dignity. The positivistic trend in modern thinking, whether legal, scientific or philosophical, has been, perhaps inevitably, reductionist in its evaluation of human nature. The result has been to dwarf man's moral stature, to threaten the primacy of personal values and to undermine the foundations of morality.[2] But that same trend will obviously develop a very critical attitude to natural law. For the latter was part of a total world-view in which the conception of nature was antithetic to that which prevails in secular thinking today. 'Hence it is that to its critics natural law theory has seemed to spring from deep old confusions from which modern thought has triumphantly freed itself while to its advocates the critics appear merely to insist on surface trivialities, ignoring profounder truths.'[3] In the course of his own critical analysis, primarily from the legal standpoint, Professor Hart complains that natural law theory tends to obscure or minimise the difference between the descriptive 'laws' of the natural sciences ('it is bound to freeze if the wind goes round to the north') and the moral law which is prescriptive ('you are bound to report for military service'). And this tends to confuse God's law for man – the law of the Lord which is an undefiled law – with the observed regularities of nature.[4] And this, as he most interestingly works out, derives from the teleological concept of nature which came into the stream from Aristotle. 'The events regularly befalling things are not thought of *merely* as occurring regularly, and the

[1] Jacques, *The Right and the Wrong*, S.P.C.K., 1965, pp. 70-71.

[2] 'This movement of thought all over the world towards a materialist or positivist view of the universe and away from a religious or even idealist philosophy has coincided with a real and very obvious retrogression from the humanism (in the sense in which Erasmus understood that word) of the XIXth century towards all the cruelties and atrocities of the present age. To me at least there is a close connexion between these two main movements in thought and practice – the conscious abandonment of religion and the idea of God, and the retrogression from humanity . . . They are, I believe, related to one another as cause and effect.' Lord Hailsham (sc. Mr. Quintin Hogg) in *Science and Politics*, Faber, 1963, p. 96.

[3] H. L. A. Hart, *The Concept of Law*, Clarendon Press, 1961, p. 182.

[4] Ultimately, of course, for the Theist, they are both, on their different levels, reflexions of the Being of God.

questions whether they *do* occur regularly and whether they *should* occur or whether it is *good* that they should occur, are not regarded as separate questions . . . what generally occurs can be both explained and evaluated as good or what ought to occur by exhibiting it as a step towards the proper end or goal of the thing concerned.' This cannot stand up to the 'scientific attitude' – though it might be thought that the scientific world-view is now moving steadily in the direction of purpose as its dominant concept. But the Aristotelian form of teleology is not essential to the natural law theory. What is really being objected to here is the confusion which we have already noted, between nature as what is and nature as what ought to be. But is this a fatal objection in the long run? Or may it not be the real strength of the theory? It has long been a dogma in moral philosophy that there is no passage from *is* to *ought*. No indicative statements can yield a true imperative. And everybody can see the force of that. Nevertheless, any theory of what ought to be, and therefore any moral judgements, must in the long run be firmly grounded in the way man is made and the way the world is made. No philosophy and no religion can alter the constitution of the universe: they must try to find out what it is and so to respond to it. That is the strength of the natural law theory.[1] A theory dependent on Greek metaphysics may well be unacceptable to the modern mind. But it can be set forth in a rather different way which avoids the abstractions of scholasticism, which can be deduced from actual experience and therefore admits of empirical verification.

The first lesson that has to be learnt about life is that we do not enjoy a freehold; 'we must abide our going hence ev'n as our coming hither'. We are tenants at will, not on our own conditions. We depend on powers that are not our own; we cannot dictate to them or impose our will upon them. We are creatures: 'he made us and not we ourselves'. If we are to continue to live at all we must accept certain conditions inherent in the way the world works. If we try to exploit the soil we die of starvation. God meets us first as sheer power – the resistance of the world to our whims – in a real sense,

---

[1] Underlying the synthesis of Aquinas is 'the resolution to discover the basis of right in the given, created nature of man and his world. His insistence that the ought is founded on the is . . . depends on the Christian belief that the Creator and Saviour are one, and that whatever salvation means beyond creation, it does not mean the destruction of the created.' Richard Niebuhr, *Christ and Culture*, Faber, 1952, p. 148.

the God of things as they are; and the fear of the Lord is the beginning of wisdom. Nature is only controlled by obeying her.
As man through obedience learns more about the regularities of
nature – the 'laws' of nature, built-in to the structure – it becomes
to him an intelligible order with which he is able increasingly to
co-operate, to bring more of its elements under conscious control
and to find enlarging possibilities of freedom and fulfilment in
living. Obedience is the way of freedom and self-realisation –
obedience, not to an arbitrary decree but to the way things are,
the structure of life. But if we try to defy that we destroy ourselves. God is not mocked. There is a law of consequences.
'Things are what they are and the consequences will be what they
will be.'

But the physical environment is not all. Men are related not
only to nature but to other persons and to their societies. (There
is no evidence of pre-social man.) There are moral as well as physical conditions, and these too are built-in to the structure of the
universe. Here too man has to discover and learn to obey certain
principles or laws which are inherent in and govern interpersonal
relationships and any workable form of social order. The moral
law is part of the way the world is made. What is 'good' is that
which enhances life by obedience to its inherent constitution,
what is 'bad' is what is out of relation to the structure of the world
and life as it is – theists, of course, will say, to the will of God.

I will walk at liberty, said the Psalmist, because I seek thy
commandments. The service of God, say Christians, is perfect
freedom. The moral law is not bondage but freedom. It presents
itself to us as law, or constraint, because of the contradiction in
ourselves, i.e. in religious language, sin. (See Chapter Three.)
As by learning and co-operation with the laws of nature, in the
physical sense, man achieves freedom from the sheer determinisms
of nature, so men realise their humanity (what they are) and become what they have it in them to become (what they are 'meant'
to be, their 'true nature') by response to the moral structure of
the universe. The moral law is the law of nature and the law of
nature is the way of life. The whole experience of the human race
corroborates that there are certain principles which lead to full
and successful living both for individuals and for societies, others
which lead to breakdown or dissolution. In the moral order no less
than in the physical there is inevitably a law of consequences. God

D

is not mocked. The wages of sin is death. If men ignore or defy
the natural law they will destroy themselves and their societies:
and that, after all, was the message of the Prophets.

Thus the two meanings of nature interlock. Both are grounded
in the nature of things itself. Moreover, increasingly in the modern
world what we know or can now hope to discover about man's
psychosomatic make-up (i.e. his nature as he is) is directly relevant
to his moral judgements (to what he ought to do or to be). The
universe is an interrelated whole. Both its physical and its moral
'laws' are expressions of the Being of its Creator. While they may
be and are in fact discoverable without any specific belief in God,
they point coercively to that belief, and it is in the long run only by
such belief that morality can be sustained or maintained. And for
those who believe in God, the moral law, transformed by a
transcendental relationship, is immeasurably deepened and extended.[1]

What the human race has gradually discovered about the laws
or principles of living if any society is to go on at all is embodied
in those tribal and social *mores* out of which morality, in the true
sense, is born. These *mores* differ between one tribe and another,
and a favourite recreation of ethnologists is to point out their
infinite diversity. Nevertheless there remains a constant – the
constant which was, as we have seen, the origin of the notion of
natural law (p. 40). In every society there are certain things which
are regarded as impious or shocking, certain things which *must not*
be done – violations of an order beyond the tribe, for which the
gods will exact retribution, such things as incest, murder or perjury, removing the neighbour's landmark and so on.[2]

[1] For these last two paragraphs and the next see Stephen Neil, *A
Genuinely Human Existence*. Constable, 1959, Ch. V.

[2] Professor Hart has sketched out a minimum content of natural law
(op. cit., pp. 180 ff.) based on the social will to survive. This mainly takes
the form of elementary forbearance, or abstentions – from violence, theft,
promise-breaking etc. – and they are based on certain fundamental facts
about men in primitive societies, e.g. approximate equality, vulnerability,
limited resources, a limited altruism and the like. The author states that
this empirical version of natural law is based on Hobbes and Hume (p.
254 note). He ends: 'these simple truisms . . . not only disclose the core
of good sense in the doctrine of natural law. They are of vital importance
for the understanding of law and morals, and they explain why the definition of the basic forms of these in purely formal terms, without any
specific content of social need, has proved so inadequate' (p. 194).

The specific forms of the things which must not be done will obviously be contingent on the facts and needs of the actual society – which accounts for the variety of *mores*. But the collective wisdom of mankind has agreed on certain positive norms or universals – respect for life, honesty, justice and so forth – which are recognised as binding and authoritative, and towards which men are conscious of *obligation*, feeling shame and guilt if they transgress principles recognised as unalterable, binding on all and demanding to be *obeyed*. (A law in the legal sense can of course be altered, but not the social rules or morality. It makes sense to say, Tomorrow it will cease to be illegal to park in Westminster; but none to say, Tomorrow it will cease to be immoral to drive dangerously and kill people. Cf. Hart *ad loc*.)

The sense of categorical obligation which, despite the variety of its *mores*, seems to be innate and universal in the human race, is the point where social custom or tribal tabu passes into morality. Every form of the so-called naturalistic fallacy – that is, the attempt to define ethical words (right, good, ought) in terms of something else (e.g. happiness) – will be found under scrutiny to be fallacious. There can be no definition of ultimates. Words like good and ought denote ultimates.[1] Ought is unique and irreducible. Values are not 'subjective' and relative. Obligation is objective and self-justifying. (There is no real answer to the question, Why ought I to be good?) Values are transcendent and independent of individual choices and preferences. Yet we cannot conceive of values as existing ghost-like in a conceptual stratosphere, like Platonic 'Ideas', waiting to be acknowledged. Values are meaningless except in relation to mind and spirit. And along that line the argument will lead, if it is followed up to its conclusion, to belief in a 'personal' and righteous God. There morality passes into religion.[2]

[1] 'Every world-view, religious or irreligious, is based upon a principle of meaning, a vision of truth, which is accepted by a kind of faith as the key note to reality as a whole . . . All artistic creation is a striving after absolute beauty. All moral striving seems to presuppose an absolute and perfect Goodness that is never realised in men's conduct but that haunts them and beckons them on. Thus the aesthetic and moral experience of men, as well as their religious experience, points to a transcendent Reality and Good beyond this world.' G. F. Thomas, *Christian Ethics and Moral Philosophy*, Scribners, New York, 1955, p. 100.
[2] See for example, H.P. Owen, *The Moral Argument for Christian Theism*, Allen and Unwin, 1965; A. E. Taylor, *The Faith of a Moralist*, Macmillan, 1937; Gore, *The Philosophy of the Good Life*, John Murray, 1930, Chapter VIII, and the very impressive last chapter of Hailsham's *Science and Politics*.

Chapter Three

WHAT IS MAN?

I

WHEN men of my generation were at Oxford we were taught that Ethics depends on Metaphysics – that what man ought to do must be grounded in the purpose and meaning of the universe, and accordingly that our moral judgements presuppose the view we take about the whole of things. Metaphysics is a dirty word now, and anybody who mentioned it in Oxford might risk being deprived of his degree – it would be far more subversive than Tract XC! Most philosophers seem now to assume that metaphysics of the old type – resting, as it did, on *a priori* concepts – is now finally dead beyond recall, and tend to disclaim for themselves any ambition to interpret the meaning and purpose of the universe. Abandoning its earlier pretension to survey all time and all existence, philosophy has accepted the humbler role of clarifying the meaning of propositions, and its wings have therefore been drastically clipped. Certainly moral philosophy has long since withdrawn from any attempt at exploring the ultimate implications of Good and Evil and even, indeed, from enquiring what it is that makes an action morally right or wrong, to confine itself, as we have already noted (p. 32) to analysing the structure of ethical statements. No one who has read Professor Hare's book[1] will undervalue what can be achieved by this or the light which can thus be thrown on our moral judgements. Yet the major premiss remains unexamined – What, in the end, *are* right and wrong, and can ethical statements be called true or false – as opposed to merely stating our own preferences – in the sense that they either do or do not correspond with realities in the nature of things itself?

But morality is far too important to be safely left to moral philosophers. One may feel inclined to agree with Mrs. Warnock that 'if moral philosophy had always been based on a mistake,

[1] *The Language of Morals*, Clarendon Press, 1952.

52

perhaps the best course would have been to stop doing it'.[1] There may yet be a revival of metaphysics, so urgently needed by Christian theology, and there are some welcome signs on the horizon. The day is probably past when a philosopher could sit down on his chair (or, like Descartes, in a stove!) to think up in his head a vast conceptual system and explain everything in the world in terms of it. Metaphysics tomorrow will want to be more empirical. But it must still be true that a valid judgement about what is morally right or morally wrong must depend on our understanding of human nature and so – in the end – on the way we think the world is made: what ought to be must be grounded in what it is. Nothing at any rate can be morally right which either defies or fails to do justice to the actual constitution of human nature. Christians can happily endorse the statement[2] though of course there is something more that they will add to it – that the 'end' of man is simply to be human, or, as it might be otherwise expressed, to be what man has it in him to become. What is good is that which enriches and fulfils, what is bad is that which impoverishes or injures the realisation of human nature; and the answers will turn on the views which are taken of that. At this point Christian ethics are likely to differ from those which are based on other presuppositions. But no religion or moral ideal can change the fundamental structure of human existence. Christianity has its own interpretation of the facts, but the facts are what they are, and if it does not meet them and answer them, or if, as some object, it does violence to them, then it cannot be the religion for all mankind nor can the Christian ethic claim validity. Grace fulfils nature, it does not destroy it;

[1] Mary Warnock, *Ethics since 1900*, Home University Library, p. 78 – a bleak record of sterility in ethical thinking. The reference is to a famous paper 'Does moral philosophy rest on a mistake?' by H. A. Pritchard, whose lectures I attended in 1911 and who examined me in Greats.

[2] 'The opening sentence of St. Thomas's moral theology expresses a truth which we Christians today have almost entirely forgotten . . . that morals deals first and foremost with *man*, but its truth is to explain what man should be like – the ideal of man – and that consequently Christian morals should foster the Christian ideal of man. In mediaeval Christianity this truth was taken for granted. But it soon came to be overlooked, and already, two generations after St. Thomas, Eckhart had to remind his contemporaries that people should not concern themselves so much with what they should *do* but rather with what they should *be*. Later on, owing to a variety of causes, moral theology came to lose sight of this view of things altogether.' Pieper, quoted by Vann, *Morals and Man*, Fontana, 1960, p. 108.

for the Giver of grace is the Author of the Creation. But it is through grace, through God's work in man, that we best understand what 'creation' means. Man is the key to the structure of the universe.

It has been the temptation of Christian theology and perhaps not least of moral theology to move in a world of abstract ideas and ignore the natural basis of human experience. But all social and moral life has its roots in nature. Civilisation, however 'artificial' and sophisticated it may become, is yet ultimately dependent on nature and can only exist by respect for the laws of nature. No more than religion, therefore, can ethics survive in a reservation labelled ideals, or in isolation from a total world-view. The question is whether we try to interpret the world by man's moral and spiritual experience – which is after all every bit as much a fact as any findings of physics or biology – or whether we are to start with a cosmology which must be built mainly out of the natural sciences and then try to find support and justification in it for man's moral and spiritual experience. The former is the procedure of Christian thinking, pledged as it is to a personalist philosophy and claiming Christ as the incarnate LOGOS, who reveals in man how the world is made. The latter is that of contemporary Naturalism, and has landed it in an impenetrable *cul-de-sac*.

It is commonly said that traditional explanations of the nature and destiny of man and his place in the scheme of things have broken down, and among these most notably the Christian. But to this it may be replied that none is so hopelessly and conspicuously bankrupt as the modern, enlightened, 'scientific' worldview.[1] There is not in fact any necessary connexion between a scientific approach to nature and a mechanistic theory of the universe. For various reasons, however, it has happened that contemporary thought in the natural sciences has taken over into its own system, and erected into an all-embracing philosophy, the mechanical conception of the universe derived from the seventeenth and eighteenth centuries, when the world was conceived as a vast machine. In such a cosmology there is no room for purpose. At the time that was not clearly realised. It was indeed from the Clock-

---

[1] 'Nothing is so evanescent in history as the philosophic theories that flourish among the *illuminati* of all times, in the bright sunlight of the latest scientific discoveries, and nothing can be more easily dismissed by later periods as mere speculation'. Richard Niebuhr, *Christ and Culture*, Faber, 1952, p. 96.

maker analogy that the Deists and near-Deists of the period derived
their 'proofs' for the existence of God. 'Evidences', in the eighteenth century, were drawn from nature, not from theology. It was
argued that the total scheme was purposive on the ground that it
appears to be constructed in such a way as to serve useful ends –
often described in quite childish terms. But, as Birch has recently
pointed out[1] 'a purposive system cannot be described simply in
terms of the mechanical relation between the parts'. Because a
machine serves beneficial ends, it cannot be argued that the
machine is purposive. The machine, after all, did not design itself;
the purpose, if any, is not in the mechanism but in the mind and
will of the designer. Moreover, nineteenth-century evolutionism
and Darwin's theory of natural selection have shown how many
mutations and adaptations are in fact disastrous and eliminating
rather than beneficial in their effect, and in the whole evolutionary record Biology, which increasingly makes use of mechanical
and physiochemical categories, can descry and exhibit no sign of
purpose. The old-style natural theology has indeed been torpe-
doed by Darwinism. The twentieth-century scientific outlook
is dominated by physics and astrophysics and is therefore inevitably mechanistic and materialistic in its total world-view. The
result of all this is a positivistic philosophy which conceives the
world as a vast impersonal system of mechanical, mindless and a-
moral forces in which there can be no place for mind or spirit, in
which man is an alien, friendless and alone in a universe that knows
and cares nothing about him. All that is characteristically human
and indeed constitutive of human life – our aesthetic, moral and
spiritual experiences – can be no more than illusion or epi-pheno-
mena. (It is a sound rule to assume that any sentence which contains 'nothing but' contains a fallacy. See p. 61.) Heraclitus taught
that fire was the primal reality. The twentieth-century mind would
tend to say: There is no fire, there is only a burning. For it, reality
is process – space-time, by which we are all being eaten up.

This is the great twentieth-century myth which is also the
terrible twentieth-century nightmare. But how paradoxical and
absurd it is! Here is man, constructing a world-view in terms
which leave no room for himself in it and can offer no account of
his own existence. But if it leads to such a grotesque conclusion,
must there not be something wrong with the premises?

[1] *Nature and God*, S.C.M. Paperback, 1965, p. 53.

For the purposes of laboratory experiment and for the technical applications of science the mechanistic hypothesis is necessary and it has triumphantly vindicated itself in dealing with those aspects of reality which are patient of quantitative measurement. The theist will say that these quantitative aspects, with their (at least) apparent determinism – though there is no passage from them to God, who must be known, if at all, through other channels – reflect some element in the Being of God, and indeed that the regularities of nature are the condition of spiritual freedom. For if we were not able to assume that like effects will follow like causes, we could make no plans and carry out no purposes. But the quantitative aspects of reality are not the only components of reality nor are they the only facts to be interpreted. It has also qualitative aspects. There are, for example, men and women. And the most important things about men and women, what indeed makes them men and women, are not quantitative at all, but qualitative – their interior life and experience as spirits. Human beings indubitably exist and the universe has somehow given rise to them. What kind of universe, therefore, will it be? 'That man is possible in this world means that the world has properties which a world in which man is not possible does not have.' As William Temple frequently remarked, that the world has produced a creature who knows the world is a fact which tells us a lot about the world.

Surely we ought to start the other way round. If man wants to understand his world, if he wants to determine his own status in it, we must start, surely, from what we know best. And we all know much more about spirit than we know about matter – whatever that may be. Of spirit we have all a direct experience for we all of us, within limits, know ourselves, whereas 'matter' is but an inferential construct. We must start from ourselves as distinctively human creatures.

As Birch says, in the book already mentioned, 'We must begin not with the electron or the amoeba, nor with the universe, but with man. The most directly accessible clue we have to the nature of the universe is neither the electron nor the amoeba, but man. What is man? That is the relevant question to ask. It is man's self-awareness that leads him to ask the question. His answer determines his answer to the broader question that includes it, what is the nature and purpose of the universe? . . . What matters to me most is not mass, velocity and the like but my own experience of value and purpose, all the qualities of friendship and love. It is precisely these qualities that the mechanistic theory of nature leaves out.'[1] Old Testament scholarship reminds us that the story of creation in Genesis, which has the law and the prophets behind it, is derivative from the central theme of the Bible – man's relation to God and God's work in man. Dr. Birch goes on to explore what may be implied in that, in words which bear closely on what is said above. 'It makes sense of man to see him as dependent on God for his qualitative life, the life of mind and spirit. The question which we are then led to ask is whether the whole universe is in some analogous way dependent on God for its being? This would of course have to include man in his physical being as well as his qualitative being. The concept of creation is that this is the nature of the universe and all that is in it. The universe and all that is in it can only be understood in relation to God. If we reject the concept of the universe as contrivance and no more, this seems to me the one valid alternative open to us' (p. 27).

So, far, therefore, from being a mere anomaly in a world of blind, mechanical forces in which there seems to be no room for spirit, the spirit of man may prove to offer the clue to it – and that suggests the vindication of Humanism. So far as it goes Humanism is right. It stands for man's dignity and unique prerogative. Can it, however, hold that position on those naturalistic assumptions to which, on the whole, it now seems to have succumbed, or on any ground short of Christian Theism? Humanism derives from two sources, one of them being Greek and the other Hebrew. The two streams flow together in Christian Humanism and the Christian theology of man. But the two traditions are complementary, each requiring infusion from the other.[2]

---

[1] Op. cit., p. 60. 'Consciousness itself is a phenomenon no doubt capable of being studied scientifically but nevertheless of a nature which, on purely logical grounds, excludes a purely materialistic conception of any universe which contains it . . . The thing which says in regard to the reality it studies, including itself or its fellows, "I know, I believe, I deny, I understand" or still worse, "I love, I admire, I detest", is not a thing which can be described simply in terms of molecules, hormones, ionised particles or electrical activity.' Lord Hailsham (sc. Mr. Quintin Hogg), *Science and Politics*, Faber, 1963, p. 108.

[2] The strongly 'humanist' emphasis in the report on the Doctrine of Man by the Lambeth Conference 1948 – which has since been subjected

The debt to Hellenism is obvious. As the sky-god and the Olympian worships defeated – at any rate officially – the aboriginal dark gods and nature-worships, man was set at the centre of his world. Man, said the Greeks, is the measure of all things; and this is what secular Humanism stands for. The Greek contribution must never be undervalued, as it tended to be, for example, by the Puritans. Yet man was regarded as a closed system, self-sufficient, self-justifying and self-explanatory, and there was the ultimate failure of classical Humanism. The ideal of *Humanitas* broke down, until Christianity came in to revive it (see pp. 122 ff.). Man cannot for long believe in himself unless he can also believe in something more than man. And, as I argued more than thirty years ago in my book *The Relevance of Christianity*, and has since been seen in the history of our time, Humanism unsupported by belief in God tends to become human-all-too-human and too easily drops to the level of sub-humanity.

Meanwhile, in another culture, the Bible, in its sustained polemic against nature-worship, had withdrawn man from a merely 'natural' context and affirmed that the place where he belongs is History. What it has to say about man's prerogative dignity is memorably summarised in the eighth Psalm and in the phrase 'made in the image of God'. But the Bible is concerned not with man in his innate or independent qualities, but with man as creature, dependent upon God and in his responsibility before God – a person in his confrontation with God. This, which may be called Theocentric Humanism, is fundamental for Christian thinking, and the brilliant characterisation of the Old Testament stories may remind us how richly and vividly 'human' it can be. Yet the essential gift of the Hebraic spirit is ethical and religious concentration; and it cannot be denied that Protestant Biblicism has tended to be hard and narrow and to breed a rather unlovable type of character. It needs for its completion the art and science and the wide cultural interests of Hellenism. Yet without the support of a conviction rooted in something beyond man himself, the latter will find it hard to survive at all. Any adequate doctrine of man requires both.

---

to criticism – was a reaction against the 'savage and inhuman theologies' of neo-orthodoxy.

II

What, then, is man and what do we know about him? There is, of course, no such thing as man as a universal abstract noun, there are men and women in all their inexhaustible variations. But there are certain constants in human nature underlying its manifold expressions, as there appear to be, broadly speaking, certain agreed norms of human character, and these are what make human beings human. We start fron no *a priori* doctrine, we start from factual investigation and then ask how are the facts to be interpreted? In such an enquiry into the actual facts Christians and others can go a long way together. But Christians can be content with no findings which ignore what can be known through Jesus Christ who is, as they hold, the one complete man, the one 'genuinely human existence'.[1] The New Testament speaks of Christ as the Second Adam – the fulfilment of what man is meant to be, who reveals both God to man and man to himself. The traditional phrase, not a man but Man, is no doubt in that verbal form untenable. Jesus Christ was not an abstract noun. But anybody can see what was intended by it. And the claim will have to be made that in the long run the human situation is inexplicable and the human moral predicament insoluble apart from the answer given by Christianity. But, while comment is free, facts are sacred, and the Christian cause is very ill served indeed if the facts are wrested so as to fit the comment. The Christians' God is the God of things as they are.

There can be no need at this time of day to dwell at any length on the basic fact – our involvement in the natural order and the physical structures of the universe, alike organic and inorganic, and in their determining necessities. Man is a creature, not the lord of creation, who exists and can exist only in dependence on powers that are not his own. Though he may be 'caught up into the third heaven' (II Corinthians xii: 2) his roots strike deep into the soil that raised him. He depends for his existence on the earth-mother, subject to the conditions of nature and the final sentence of mortality. However religious or moral a man may be, if he cannot get what he needs to eat he perishes. If he defies or ignores the conditions which nature imposes man will destroy

[1] This is the title of the striking study by Stephen Neil already referred to, p. 50.

himself. No religion and no moral principles can alter these fundamental realities, though both have too often been tempted to forget them. It is man's recognition of dependence on powers beyond
and greater than himself, and his need for their succour and support, that may be the matrix of primitive religion.

Civilised man has learnt, and is every day learning more, how
to control nature and impose his own will on the external world.
Christians hold that the image of God in man includes at least a
reflexion of the Creator and that God has entrusted to man by
delegation some share in his creative work in a still unfinished
universe (cp. the 'dominion' over nature given to man in Genesis
i: 28). But that does not mean that nature can, with impunity, be
exploited for man's own profit or convenience, or to suit his own
short-term calculations. And there are, in fact, very drastic limits
to what man can do without disastrous consequences in disturbing
the balances of nature and the subtle network of interrelationships
by which life on our planet is maintained. A book like *Silent
Spring* is an urgent warning, and ecology may have nasty shocks in
store yet, to say nothing of the results, still unpredictable, of radio-
active fall-out in the atmosphere. There are, moreover, elemental
forces beyond human control altogether. Apart from such things
as volcanoes and tidal waves there are the implacable demographic facts, the 'population explosion' for example, which simply
dictate terms for human action. And we know, too, more than our
predecessors knew about the determining factors which are operative in the biological and genetic field, and are so largely constitutive of character. Here one has only to mention DNA – an understanding of which Lord Snow has laid down as a test of what is
meant by being educated![1] Broadly speaking, moralists have been
prone – and this is not least true of Christian moralists – to underestimate the extent to which life has to be lived and moral decisions
made in a framework of events and processes which are beyond
human control and, accordingly, how restricted is the range of our
freedom. Realistic ethics must take full account of all this. The
'state of life' to which God shall be pleased to call us and within
which we are to do our duty, includes far more than the job or the
social standing. It includes the total situation – geographical,
historical and economic – in which men and women at any time

[1] This brought a quip in a letter to *The Times* that if you don't understand DNA you will not find yourself in D.N.B.

are, and not least their own innate constitution, whether physical or psychological. As Niebuhr says, 'there are limits of creature-liness which man cannot transcend and inexorable forces of nature which he cannot defy. . . . Every social decision is modified and circumscribed by natural circumstances and historical tendencies beyond the control of human decision'.[1]

As the product of biological evolution, man carries with him, physically and mentally, the indelible legacy of his pre-human origin. The oceanic tides of his earliest home still affect the rhythms of human physiology. His mental and emotional constitution has a long history behind it and never ignores or cuts itself loose from its 'natural' and innate endowment; and any relevant ethic must allow for that. He does not however retain them unchanged: in man himself they are radically modified. We cannot derive ethics from biology (see p. 157). Man is more than an animal who has learnt to speak and to use tools more cleverly than the apes. He is more than a biological phenomenon. The human mind derives from the pre-human; but the human mind, once it has emerged, is something entirely distinctive and unique. Once true man has appeared upon the stage then, though the whole process is continuous and we cannot argue for such a discontinuity as was implied in the 'special creation' theory, a new and essentially creative fact enters the evolutionary series – for man will now be able, within limits, to control the course of his own evolution. No amount of know-ledge of where man started from can tell us the most important thing about him – what he is now and whither he is going – what he has it in him to be or is 'meant' to be, what is, in the teleological sense, his 'nature'. If man is no more than a biological fact, if he is completely and totally determined by physical (and social) deter-minants, if his aesthetic and moral intuitions are 'nothing but' conditioned reflexes – tricks of nature to secure survival – then no question of ethics can arise. But of men as we know ourselves that is simply not true. We are concerned with facts not with theories.

From the Greeks onwards, of course, there has been a theory – now commonly labelled as 'naturalism' – which identifies man with nature so completely as to rule out what is distinctively human in him and reduce his mental and spiritual qualities to resultants of physical and material forces. This is potent in popular thought

[1] *The Nature and Destiny of Man*, Nisbet, 1941, vol. I, pp. 59, 73.

today as well as in more sophisticated quarters. There is no need
to deny that at certain levels human behaviour can be simply re-
flex. To save an intolerable waste of energy certain routines have
to be developed, certain patterns of action built up, eating, shaving,
driving a car and so forth, in which no deliberate choices are involved and indeed no conscious awareness of what is being done
or how it is done. If a man stops to ask, Am I doing this the right
way? he will probably kill himself or grind his gears. It may be conceded that behaviourism is, so far as it goes, a true account of certain aspects of human conduct. But not of those with which ethics
is concerned. And it certainly will not take us the whole way. The
mere fact that someone has constructed it shows that man is not
completely immersed in or determined by material forces. And it
will be found that all forms of naturalism, as of modern economic
determinism, are inherently self-contradictory.

Sooner or later every first-year student in philosophy will an-
nounce to his tutor, 'The truth is, there is no such thing as truth'.
and maintain that this great idea is true. But if what he says is true,
then it is not true. Similarly the man in the street declares that
scientific knowledge is the only knowledge. But the statement presupposes that it is not true. If it were true how could anybody know
it? For it certainly is not scientific knowledge. So, if man were 'nothing but' a natural fact he could not be telling himself that he is
no more than that, or asking himself whether he is more than, or
what is his relationship to, the natural order. He would not have
formed the concept of nature and could not be aware of any distinction between himself and his natural environment. If he were
completely immersed in the time-process he could not be aware,
as he is, of the flux of time. All forms of naturalism are self-defeating. They have to assume that at any rate one man, the philosopher
propounding the system, is outside and exempt from the conditions for which he claims universal applicability; and the whole
rigid system breaks down.

The Marxian dialectic of history has thrown a flood of light
which has great importance on the social and moral realities of history, and so too has the Freudian analysis on the springs and
motives of character. Some of the newly-born social sciences can
provide invaluable information about the behaviour of men in their
societies and the forces which tend, as a generalisation, to operate
in various social contexts. But when scientific analyses of this kind

are blown up into an absolute metaphysic for which human action is 'nothing but' a by-product of force external to itself and regarded as explicable, without remainder, entirely in terms of secondary causation, then they do more than collide with theology, they by-pass man and never come to terms with him. Ethics must welcome the findings of the sciences and everything they may have to tell us about the way in which human behaviour works. But not all the sciences together can tell us what constitutes a human being. They cannot answer the question What is Man? There is that in man which cannot be contained in any closed system of forces, whether biological or economic. Human action is caused by the human will and that is something altogether distinct from anything that exists in the natural order. Man's brain, his nervous system, his muscles are the secondary causes of what is done. But the real cause or first mover is not any of these, it is the man himself, giving effect to a freely chosen purpose. When, for example, I sit down to write 'there is a mental component to my action, which is the purpose which I have in mind when I set pen to paper. That purpose is the real cause of what I do'.[1] Human action steps forth out of nature into an order of self-determination, an order of personality or spirit, in which man lives not by compulsions from behind him but by value and purpose, summoning him to realise what he has it in him to become. (Christians will say that in the long run it is Jesus Christ who shows what that is.) If life is real, values are real. We go on living because we think it is good to live.

There is in the end only one way in which facts like these can be adequately accounted for – that man is part of nature and yet transcends it. That is his greatness and that is his tragedy.

For it is not only his bigger brain and other related bodily characteristics by which *homo sapiens* is differentiated. It is his interior mental experience, for which the former provide the physical basis. Speech, in itself a social acquisition – for we learn our humanity from one another – enables him to form rational concepts and so to reflect on events without and within and to bring order into his experience. It does more than that. It enables him to communicate with his fellows and to share their thoughts and purposes. It makes cultural tradition possible and thereby the accumulation of experience. Human evolution will now proceed through the social and cultural inheritance – in other words, it will

[1] Birch, op. cit., p. 52.

proceed in history rather than by merely physical selection – or in other words in the biological series. Man can respond to and delight in beauty. He is capable of moral discrimination. 'If we look at human beings in general . . . it is likely that the most important thing about them will appear to us, as it did to Kant, Hegel and Bradley and to Sartre, to be their capacity for acting spontaneously and choosing between alternatives; for making and keeping resolutions, for regretting their decisions and rationally changing their minds, for feeling guilt and feeling pride in their achievement.'[1] But what this means is that man is self-conscious. He is aware of and able to reflect upon himself and his own thoughts and purposes, able to stand, as it were, outside the self and know the self as the object of its knowledge. For not only does man transcend nature, still more importantly, he transcends himself. This is what it means to be personal or spirit. And this is the most certain fact in human experience.[2]

When they ask what it is that makes a man a man, what is the distinctively human thing about him, nearly all the classic philosophies have tended to say that it is his *nous*, his reason. This, it has been held, is the image of God in man; as the Cambridge Platonists were to say, this is the candle of the Lord in him. This is what lifts man above the animals. Reason is what man shares with God. That is true enough, no doubt, so far as it goes. But the answer is not entirely satisfactory. For one thing, it is in danger of leading to the Greek and Stoic theory of the 'divine spark', and so in effect of regarding man as part of God in virtue of his reason. For another, it tends to ignore or to play down the non-rational factors in our make-up – the emotions, the surging, clamouring 'vitalities', instincts, desires, and insatiable appetites, if not, in the long run, even the will to live.

For Kant, all the natural, vital forces in the life of man and

[1] Mary Warnock, op. cit., pp. 205, 206.
[2] 'Every other animal but man is a complete representative of his species; man remains the unfinished animal . . . ever reaching out into the unknown. Man's growth, therefore, is not completed by his biological fulfilment as a mate and a parent; nor is it completed by his death. Man's nature is a self-surpassing and self-transcending one; his utmost achievements are always beginnings and his fullest growth must always leave him unsatisfied . . . above his instinctive and automatic activities lies a whole stratum where purpose and meaning have full play. A meaningless life and a purposeless life belong to the not-yet-human.' Mumford, *The Condition of Man*, Secker and Warburg, 1944, p. 7.

indeed, for that matter, the empirical moral agent himself, are excluded from the field of ethics. The Stoics and those who derive from that tradition have attempted to anaesthetise or suppress all the disturbing emotions and appetites and even the 'natural' human affections. (The 'wise man' will not grieve when his child dies.) 'Apathy', 'motionlessness', was the ideal. There seems to be something 'inhuman' about that. And there is. It rests on a faulty analysis of human nature, and results, accordingly, in a very vulnerable ethic. The ethic of this tradition implies, in effect, that the further you get away from the body the more truly human and moral you will be.

That is a legacy from Greek philosophy. With its notion of the two levels of reality – the eternal changeless world of pure forms and the lower, contingent world of changing things ('becoming') – it was always suspicious of 'matter', and too easily fell for the suggestion that the body is always dragging down and corrupting the pure, rational soul. Therefore the seat of evil or sin is in man's physical nature, in his body. But that is too easy altogether. The real moral problem lies in the fact that the seat of evil is in the mind and will. (The 'sins of the flesh' are really sins of the spirit.) Unfortunately that disastrous dualism did penetrate into Christian thinking and not least into its sexual ethics. (The doctrine of the resurrection of the body was partly, at least, a protest against it.) The theory is in itself false to the facts, and it can claim no support in the Bible. 'The Bible knows nothing of a good mind in an evil body.'[1] Indeed the biblical doctrine of man is necessary for the proper understanding of man – 'to correct the interpretations of human nature which underestimate his status (naturalism), depreciate his physical existence (idealism) and fail to deal realistically with the evil of human nature (liberalism and humanism)'.[2] The Christian and biblical doctrine of creation implies that the ground of his spiritual being is also the ground of his physical 'vitalities'. That is not where the contradiction lies. The contradiction lies within man himself, at the centre of his being as personal, and in his defiance of God.

III

What is distinctively human about a man, even more than his

[1] Niebuhr, op. cit., p. 8.
[2] Ibid., pp. 140, 141.

E

rational endowment, is that he is a person, a spirit, and therefore both free to work upon the determinisms of nature, ever reaching out beyond himself towards satisfactions never completely realised, and able to choose both the evil and the good. (A world in which morality is possible must be a world in which free choice is possible, in which some relative measure of independence has been committed to dependent spirits; and this will be found to have important bearings on any approach to the problem of evil.) 'Neither naturalism nor idealism can understand that man is free enough to violate both the necessities of nature and the logical systems of reason.'[1] He is able both to create and to destroy and it is the tragedy of human history that man cannot create without destroying.[2] Human life is at war within itself – that conflict was the essence of Greek tragedy.

Man lives by values beyond himself – he does not, as the Existentialists affirm, create his own values as he goes along – and can find no enduring satisfaction in material, perishable goods – man does not live by bread alone. He is ever reaching out beyond himself. Wanting the sun and the moon and the stars (cp. the symbolism of Joseph's dream in Genesis xxxvii: 9) and thinking himself the king of infinite space, yet all the time he is bounded in his nutshell, involved in the flux and finitude of nature and always threatened by the last enemy, so that his freedom, and indeed his nature as spirit, may come to seem illusory. It is this fear of meaninglessness and death which generates in men that anxiety of which so much is being heard today and which underlies so much mental illness. But anxiety is the root of sin.

Because of this fundamental insecurity men are always trying to build up false securities, pretending to be and behaving as though they were, the centres round which everything else must revolve, and so collide both with the limiting facts – inducing inferiority complexes for which they compensate by aggressive attitudes – and with other spirits, all behaving the same way. Since every finite centre of consciousness claims to be or pretends to be infinite, we men clash with and prey upon one another. Thus we forfeit our birthright of freedom, developing inner conflicts and resentments and being in moral bondage to ourselves. This is the contradiction at the heart of us. The fundamental and

---

[1] Niebuhr, op. cit., p. 138.
[2] Ibid., p. 11.

radical moral problem of the human situation lies here. There is probably no word that is less acceptable to the 'modern' mind than the word sin. But the essence and meaning of sin is that self-centredness, with all its consequent rationalisation, self-justification and self-righteousness, which perverts and corrupts all our thought and action, spoils our relationships with one another and vitiates our morals and our religion. (It was the 'good' people not the 'wicked' to whom Christ had the sternest words to say.)

All this means that no simple moralism and certainly no mere moral exhortation can meet our need or make goodness possible, any more than reason can by itself supply the dynamic of moral action. But yet no analysis less radical can claim to do justice to the facts of the empirical human situation – it is one of the points at which Humanism falls down. This is the 'Fall' and here we approach the terrain of Grace and the Christian Gospel of redemption.

Man is neither an animal nor a god. He is a spirit yet an embodied spirit. He is part of nature yet he is not confined by it. He is free yet he is limited and dependent. As spirit he cannot find his home in nature. There is that in him which 'feels immortal longings' yet he is part of nature and not pure spirit. Man is indeed the Great Amphibium, whose problem arises from his habitation on the frontier between nature and super-nature. What, then, *is* man and what is the law of his nature? What does it mean to become truly human?

The Christian interpretation of man's state is that it is explicable only in its relation to that spiritual environment on which it depends and by which it is transcended, and that man will never be complete or satisfied or freed from his own interior contradictions till his true relationship to it is achieved. (In religious language, man is made for God and 'our heart is restless till it find rest in him'. Alone among the creatures man is a worshipper, seeking fulfilment in that which transcends his finitude.) That is man's true 'nature', what he is *meant* to be. In all his moral and spiritual experience a man is in contact with and is sustained by that transcendent spiritual environment apart from which he does not exist as spirit, just as in all his physical experience he is drawing upon that natural environment apart from which he cannot exist as organism. In his recognition of moral obligation he recognises its ultimate claim upon him and in that confrontation he knows himself as a person – that is the heart of the Biblical doctrine of man. In reverence for and obedience to that claim he realises the law of his true nature.[1] In refusal he violates his nature so that he becomes estranged from his true being, and involves his relations with other men in anarchy. For what from the moral standpoint is injustice is for religion rebellion against God. The ultimate law of man's nature is Love, that is to say, the 'reconciliation' or achievement of harmony between life and life. For the Christian, the measure of that is the Cross of Christ.

When Christians say that God is Love they mean, as Niebuhr has finely said, that the ultimate ground and source of all that exists is the source of the harmony of life with life.[2] This is the meaning and purpose of the universe. Love is the fulfilling of the law. 'The whole conception of life revealed in the Cross of Christian faith is not a pure negation of or irrelevance towards the moral ideals of the "natural man". The ideal is involved in every moral aspiration and achievement . . . Moral life is possible at all only in a meaningful existence, obligation can be felt only to some system of coherence and some ordering will. Thus moral obligation is always an obligation to promote harmony and overcome chaos. But every conceivable order in the historical world contains an element of anarchy. The obligation to support and enhance it therefore can only arise and maintain itself on the basis of a faith that it is the partial fruit of a deeper unity and the promise of a more perfect harmony, than is revealed in any immediate situation.[3]

The Platonic tradition in Christian philosophy tends to identify God with Reason, that is with the principle of form and rational order in the cosmos, that, indeed, which makes it a cosmos. Only in virtue of that can we think coherently or introduce order into our thought and experience. But the world as we know it is not pure rational order. It is full of unreconciled antagonisms. Life preys

---

[1] 'Morality as the experience of the moral imperative is a function of man as man. Without it he would not be man . . . The moral imperative is not a strange law imposed upon us but it is the law of our own being . . . Morality is the self-affirmination of our essential being.' Tillich, *Theology of Culture*, Galaxy Book, O.U.P. New York, 1964, pp. 134, 136.

[2] Op. cit., p. 157.

[3] Niebuhr, *An Interpretation of Christian Ethics*, S.C.M., 4th edition 1948, p. 115.

upon life. Wills clash with wills. As we have seen, man as free spirit introduced anarchy and disorder. We are not at unity within ourselves. Our need is for wholeness, which Christians call salvation. But we cannot be made whole in isolation.[1] The need is for an all-embracing harmony in which our divided selves can be unified in right relationship with the world, with other personal centres of consciousness and with the infinite spiritual environment. But it must be a creative harmony, not a static pattern or regimentation such as would be imposed by pure reason, and is rightly described as 'rationalisation'. That creative harmony is called Love and it is the essential being of God as made known to man in Jesus Christ. In him the end and meaning of human life and of the universe out of which it comes – how man is made and how the world is made – and thus of the basic structure of morality, is revealed in the one human Life which was perfectly and completely human because it was perfectly in response to God. That Life is the source of the Christian ethic.

[1] St. Paul saw that the hope of redemption through Christ embraces the whole order of creation (Romans viii: 18 *seq.*).

Chapter Four

WHAT *ARE* CHRISTIAN ETHICS?

WHEN the Christian religion first appeared it did not come into a primitive society in which it had to begin with the foundations. It came into a highly developed civilisation with a highly developed system of thought and morality and a rich humanistic culture, contained within the framework of Roman law. In a real sense, Christianity was a fresh start – a seed instinct with a new creative life. But it was not sown in an empty world, and like any seed it had to make its body out of the soil in which it had been planted. Born out of the Hebrew, Biblical tradition, Christianity from the early days took over whatever was sound in the Graeco-Roman legacy, to transform and revitalise it from within. As we have seen, Western civilisation was formed by the blending of the two traditions. From the sixteenth century onwards the two streams have flowed apart and in different directions. The crisis of Christianity today and the moral confusion of the West may both be said to result from the isolation of the Christian faith from contemporary culture.

Christianity has never said, or if it has it ought never to have said, that there can be no good outside itself. Christians believe in God too much for that. They believe that Christ is the incarnate Logos and the true Light that lighteth every man – words which have to be given their full force. That carries with it the belief that the moral education of the race, the accumulated store of human wisdom, is itself the work of the eternal Christ and the gift of the Spirit of God in the hearts of men. Arguments to discredit Christianity are sometimes drawn from 'anticipations' of it to be found in non-Christian religions.[1] But if there were none, if it did not correspond to the deepest needs of mankind the world over, how could it be the universal religion? God did not begin to be God

[1] Cp. Gibbon's famous sneer 'The Logos. B.C. 360 taught in the School of Alexandria, A.D. 97 retold by the apostle St. John.' *Decline and Fall*, ch. XXI.

70

when that Baby was born two thousand years ago. So too here:
if Christian morality were something that had been revealed *in
vacuo*, if it did not gather up into itself all men's partial and frag-
mentary insights, how could it claim to be universally valid? But
it does claim that. It claims to be not merely the code of a voluntary association or the etiquette of a religious club, still less a body
of negative regulations that dwarf or maim human possibilities,
but the way to become genuinely human, the way of life and fulfilment for all mankind. Christ came not to destroy but to fulfil.
The fundamental business of the Church in a day of moral confusion like the present is not to denounce people's immoralities.
It is, rather, to help hard-pressed men and women to recover faith
in God through Jesus Christ – and that will certainly not be done
by preaching at them.

Of course there was much that was decadent and evil in the
ancient civilisation, as in our own. There was something rotten in
Hellenistic society in that period – in its sexual corruption and in
its sadistic cruelty.[1] Anybody who reads the literature of the time
and then comes from it to the New Testament must be conscious
of an antiseptic quality, as though a window had now been thrown
open in some fetid, fever-ridden room so that sunshine and clean
air were streaming into it. 'The night is far spent and the day is at
hand.' One can hardly exaggerate the sense of liberation and
healing and vitality, of being translated into an open universe of
opportunity and responsibility. 'All things are being made new.'
Something new and healing had come into the world, proclaimed
in the preaching of the Resurrection. The New Testament presents
to us that new thing. And it is not so much a system of ethics as a
transformed quality of life.

But while it strongly insists upon the contrast between the
Church and its Hellenistic background – a contrast, as it says, between life and death – yet not everything in that background was
evil. There was indeed much that was good, and the Church had
many sensitive points of contact; otherwise how could it ever have
communicated? Christians and others could both take for granted
a common stock of basic moral ideals – so much so that later imagi-

[1] 'To explain the triumph of Paul and Augustine, one must read the
description of Trimalchio's feast in the *Satyricon* of Petronius Arbiter.
What had the Roman made of the body? Corrupted meat. And what of the
soul? A polluted Dream.' Mumford, *The Condition of Man*, Secker and
Warburg, 1944, p. 44.

nation invented exchanges between St. Paul and Seneca. Some familiar passages in the Epistles are apparently drawn from popular Stoic manuals (see p. 79 ff.), and the Church must have appeared to the onlooker as one among other contemporary societies for the reformation of public morals. St. Paul had declared, with a splendid courage, that the moral law which Christians acknowledged was written in the hearts of the Gentiles, and the early Apologists, following that lead, were prepared to endorse the idea of the law of nature as a kind of universal morality; and this had, they claimed, been set forth in the Decalogue engraved (the story said) on tables of stone, a permanent and authoritative morality resting upon the declared will of God, not simply the tribal *mores* of the Israelites. This made it in the true sense a *law*, the Commandment of God which must be obeyed. It was not a capricious, arbitrary *fiat*. It was not good because God commanded it, he commanded it because it was good. God is good and he cannot deny himself. It is the expression of his own being and the law of God is therefore the law of life.

The Western Church, inheriting both the Jewish Law and the Roman legal tradition, has tended to emphasise too one-sidedly the juridical character of the Christian ethic.[1] The attitude of the mediaeval Church, as reflected for instance in the Penitentials, seems to be far more judicial than pastoral. It knows an awful lot about sin, but how much compassionate concern does it show for sinful men and women? The whole trend of this legal emphasis, formulated in an elaborate casuistry, was inevitably towards salvation by works, by an external (and minimal) conformity to a code of prescribed or prohibited conduct. This led in its turn to all manner of moral subterfuges, which gave casuistry its bad name, and at last to the whole unsavoury apparatus of indulgences, pardoners and all the rest of it.

Against all that the Reformers made their protest. The heart of the Reformation at its best is the understanding that man can be 'justified' not by wisdom or conduct but by faith in the grace and forgiveness of God through Christ – which was rightly claimed as essentially Scriptural doctrine.[2] But, contrary to the popular

[1] The able Encyclopaedia article (by H. H. Williams, afterwards Bishop of Carlisle) finds in this juridical character the distinctive note in Judaeo-Christian ethics. *E.R.E.* Ethics, Christian.

[2] The Reformation was far more deeply coloured than it realised, or historians have realised, by the late mediaeval system against which it was

mythology, the last thing that the Reformers wanted was religious
liberty. What they wanted was liberty to impose their own systems.
There was precious little liberty in Geneva, or in Puritan England, or in Massachusetts.[1] There were antinomian sects on the
extreme left who knew no authority but the inner light. But the
main streams of the Reformed tradition held fast to an absolute
Christian morality, a Christian law, God-given and authoritative.
But where was the authority to be found? If not in the Church,
then in the Bible.

G. M. Trevelyan wrote in a well-known passage that no one can
understand the English character if he has not a working knowledge of the Bible. For centuries our fathers have been brought up
to lead a godly, righteous and sober life by reading and meditating
upon the Good Book. 'If it is in the Bible it must be right.' Some
of the sectaries went to the length of saying 'If it is not in the Bible
it must be wrong'. The result of that has been to create little anti-
quarian enclaves like the Mennonites in Pennsylvania, who have
not heard the news of the death of Moses. But our fathers drew from
the Bible a strength and integrity for which we can never thank
God enough. God's word was a lantern to their feet and a light to
their paths. From it they could learn what they ought to do. Here
was 'the most precious thing that this world affords' – moral direction given by God himself – an infallible manual of Christian
conduct.

But – we have no longer got an infallible Bible. To many,

---

ostensibly a revolt. Though it claimed to be a return to Scripture it soon
developed its own form of scholasticism, and the 'articles' of the reformed
confessions tend to be more punditry than Scripture.

[1] For a fascinating sociological analysis of the Godly Discipline see C.
H. Hill, *Puritanism and Society in Pre-revolutionary England*, Secker and
Warburg, 1964, Ch. VI. 'The nonconformist congregations were all that
there was to replace the local communities as custodians of moral standards once the villages had been disrupted by enclosure and growing
class divisions.' The discipline 'welded the new rising middle classes in
organisation and helped them to throw off the yoke of the feudal nobility.
It brought a new kind of layman into the government of the Church, inevitably the "better", the "industrious sort" of men, who would be elected
elders . . . Such a disciplinary system would have more faithfully reflected
the social structure of England and would have given a predominant influence to the man of new wealth.' For a similar approach to Sabbatarianism see Chapter V. The new employing class disapproved of Saints' Days
because so many holidays interrupted industry; but they did need to secure
a guaranteed weekly rest-day for their workers.

therefore, the very foundations of morality seem to have been undermined.[1]

No Christian is likely to doubt that the Bible offers him a divinely-given moral guidance, but the modern Christian cannot find it that way, by approaching the Bible as though it were a textbook in which we had merely to look up the index to find the answer to any moral question. If we treat it literally and legalistically we shall never hear what the Word of God is saying to us. We can solve no moral problem by the quotation of isolated texts. That can, indeed, be dangerously misleading. Notoriously, you can justify *apartheid*, or slavery, or polygamy, or wars of extermination, or almost anything, by quoting texts out of the Old Testament without any sense of historical development or relation to Christian standards of judgement. No doubt Christians have sometimes been prone to become fixated in the Old Testament, as though the social patterns of the Patriarchs were to be regarded as permanent moral archetypes.[2] In like manner today one can still hear arguments based on appeal to Old Testament precedents for the retention of the death penalty or for the savage treatment of homosexuals because they are required by the law of God. But once Biblical literalism has been abjured, arguments of that type are no longer valid. Does that mean that we can no longer appeal to Scripture – or at any rate to the Old Testament – for any authoritative Word of God which can speak in the moral perplexities of our own time? Can we no longer claim that in the Bible we are given a declaration of the moral law? We certainly can, but not quite in the same terms as those of the pre-critical way of using it.

[1] In his lecture printed in *God, Sex and War*, Fontana, 1964, Prof. Burnaby goes the whole length. 'If we are content to do without an infallible Church and have no longer an infallible Bible to put in its place, we can no longer look for guidance to an infallible Christ' (p. 108). What he means primarily is that we cannot be sure in any particular instance that we have the *ipsissima verba* of Christ himself; and the modern Christian has got to accept that, though there is surely about some at least of the Sayings, even after two translations, a characteristic, authentic ring which makes them recognisable anywhere as his own voice. But Burnaby's lecture proceeds at a far deeper level than that of textual criticism, and I should venture to describe it as a major contribution to Christian ethics. See also p. 88.

[2] Cf. the quotation from I Peter iii: 6, in the exhortation in the (1662) marriage service. Sarah obeyed Abraham, calling him Lord. What, one might ask, did Abraham's slaves call him?

The message of the great Hebrew prophets – figures who are unique in human history – with its magnificent challenge to social righteousness, to do justice and to love mercy, was the expression of the Being of God and the way of life for men and nations. That message can never be superseded, and there never can be any going back on it. It marks a decisive moral 'breakthrough'. Since Elijah and Amos and Isaiah the world can never be the same again. Moreover, the great Old Testament stories now preserved in the historical books have all been worked over in the light of the prophetic tradition and reflect it. 'Behold, to obey is better than sacrifice and to hearken than the fat of rams.' Saul and Samuel, David and Nathan ('thou art the man'), Ahab and Naboth's vineyard, these and many other immortal stories are a permanent challenge to the Christian conscience and can never cease to be directly relevant to human conduct in all times and places. They bear witness to the law of God and its final, absolute moral obligation. 'I am the Lord thy God: thou shalt have no other gods but me.' And what God *is*, the prophets declare, is Righteousness.

But nothing in the Bible will tell us exactly what we ought to do now, in the circumstances of our own time and place. The witness was given, it must be remembered, within then existing situations. The prophets were not speaking in a vacuum, nor were they addressing themselves consciously to unimagined future civilisations. Their message was immediate and topical, addressed to given historical situations and the circumstances of their own time and place; and the modern reader cannot clearly appreciate it without some knowledge of its historical context such as is provided for him in the commentaries. The Old Testament, as a sociological document, exhibits man and his social institutions with the corresponding moral demands that they make upon him, in his successive stages of development – from the primitive nomadic tribe to pastoral and agricultural settlement, and thence to the beginnings of urban life, trade and commerce, monarchy and empire – and to all of them it speaks the Word of the Lord. What we have to say to ourselves as we read it is, 'If this was God's Word to men and his will for men in those circumstances and situations, what is it for us, if we would be obedient to it in our situation and circumstances today?'[1] And that entails far more than

---

[1] On this see Alan Richardson, *History Sacred and Profane*, S.C.M., 1963, pp. 78, 226, 249 and elsewhere.

quoting texts. It entails an effort of faith and wisdom and insight, the imagination to put ourselves in their place, and so under the guidance and judgement of the Word of God. It entails, moreover, reading the Old Testament from a more historically-minded standpoint than our predecessors were always able to bring to it. The Old Testament points to One who was yet to come, who is indeed the subject of the whole Bible and the key to its interpretation. If we read the Old Testament as Christians, with a conscience illuminated by the light of Christ, that may involve the frank recognition that in some of the things which the ancient Hebrews believed to be God's command they were mistaken or – at the least – the children of their own age. The ruthless extermination of the Amalekites, or the hewing of Agag in pieces before the Lord, never can have been the will of God, the Father of our Lord Jesus Christ. They confused the exclusive claim of Yahweh with vindictiveness towards those who did not believe in him.[1]

If not the Old Testament then, what of the New? And above all, what about Jesus Christ himself to whom the New Testament writers bear witness? Surely here is authoritative guidance, plain and direct commands about Christian conduct which we have simply to study and try to obey? If we ask what the Christian ethic is, this is surely where we can look for it and find it.

The early Church, meaning by that the Church soon after the close of the New Testament period, would have had no hesitation in agreeing. The general assumption of writings in that period – the *Didache*, for example, or the Epistle of Barnabas – is that Christ was the author of the law constitutive of the Christian society. They tend to present a picture of the Two Ways, two ways of living, the bad old way and the Christian way. The new way is governed by the new law, laid down through the life and teaching of Jesus Christ. Christians are people who live, or should live, under the imperatives of the Christian law. Here the Christian life and the Christian ethic are presented in naïvely moralistic terms, as they are, or were, in Liberal Protestantism and the pre-war twentieth-century Social Gospel. There are undeniably traces of such an outlook inside the New Testament itself (p. 86). But that is not its characteristic emphasis. Nor is the matter quite so simple as that.

[1] In Ezra this becomes indistinguishable from racial discrimination.

'If Christianity', said Blake, 'were ethics, then Socrates was the
Saviour.'

Like the Christian religion itself, the New Testament is ethical
through and through. Yet it is not a manual of Christian ethics.
It may truly be said that its *primary* concern is not with ethics at
all but with religion. The ethics flow out of the religion, as the
religion expresses itself in ethics – the two are indissoluble and
correlative. Yet without the religion there would be nothing. What
essentially the New Testament is about is redemption and forgiveness through Christ bringing men into new relationship with
God. Out of that there flows an interior transformation, a radical
transvaluation of values, a changed attitude to life as a whole –
to God, to the world, to the self and to other people – a refinement
and deepening of character and that distinctive quality of spirit
for which the New Testament shorthand is *Agape*. The Gospel is a
Gospel about God and this is what the New Testament sets forth.
The Gospel is always verified in action and in men's relationships
with one another. It has thus far-reaching ethical implications.
But it is not in itself a code of ethics. The New Testament is certainly not a blue-print for twentieth-century Christian behaviour.
Its books were not written to be 'holy scripture' nor intended for
twentieth-century eyes to see. They have proved in the Providence
of God to be written, as the collect says, for our learning. But they
were not written in order to teach us, they were written for those
who first read or heard them. They are all, therefore, historically
conditioned; and this will be clear so soon as it is realised what these
New Testament documents really are. This will explain their
apparent limitations. Yet the creative life which they reflect is the
permanent dynamic of Christian ethics, subject to no historical
conditions and valid for Christians in all times and places.

Once he has given up reading it legalistically, the modern reader
is sometimes disappointed at finding in the New Testament so
little that seems to apply directly and immediately to the ethical
questions that we have to ask today. Its ethical teaching seldom
goes beyond the field of personal and domestic conduct, and it
seems to have little concern with the larger questions of civic and
social responsibility. And even within this closely limited area it can
seem at some points to be positively misleading – that is, if it is
taken *litteratim*. For example, it seems to take slavery for granted,
and a rather archaic attitude to women. But one has to remember

the actual situation of those for whom these books were written, as a tiny and uninfluential minority in a vast, despotically governed empire. (See p. 114.) When it comes to the life and teaching of Christ himself there may be the same sense of limitation. There is nothing here about economics or sociology or race-relations, or the urgent questions concerning peace and war. How, it is sometimes asked, can he be claimed as the final and absolute moral authority if he is silent about such things as these? Are not Christian ethics now outdated? About so much in the highly complicated industrialised society of today have we not now to 'look for another'? And of course, in a certain sense of the words, we have. We cannot derive directly from the Gospels any detailed regulations or set of rules which can be 'applied' as they stand to the political and industrial problems of the twentieth century. For these, as I have already emphasised (p. 31), we have to seek information from other sources – from natural law (if we believe in that), the factual findings of the social sciences and the best moral philosophy we can get. And in fact, as we shall be seeing in a moment, the early Christian teachers themselves did just that.

All this, however, is part and parcel of the whole principle of concentration, the so-called 'scandal of particularity', implied in a historical Incarnation. Jesus was a Jew of the first century. Within that framework and its limitations he lived and prayed and taught and died and rose again. Nothing can make him a man of the twentieth century – if we try to do that we shall make a fictitious Christ. Within that framework God is revealed to men, not in 'mankind' in general but in this Man – ultimate reality in this one particular, universal truth in this one Man's life and teaching. (According to St. John, he said I am the truth, rather than I teach you the truth – I am the Way and the Truth and the Life.) Jesus Christ did not tell us everything. What he told us was the one thing needful. What he gave us was the one pearl of great price which gives their value to all other pearls – the disclosure of what life really is, life in its essential quality and meaning – in New Testament language, eternal life – when it is in the right relationship to God. That is the core and heart of Christian ethics, and that is what the New Testament is about.

What is distinctively Christian in Christian ethics is that which derives from the Lord himself. But Christianity in the course of history has taken into itself as it was bound to do, whether by inheritance or by acquisition, much ethical material from other sources; and all this it has carried along with it to form the total corpus of Christian ethics, the morality of the Christianised West. All of it stands under Christ's judgement and must be constantly brought to the test of the Gospel. Some of it is still indubitably sub-Christian. The task of the Church in every generation is to bring the traditional body of Christian ethics into closer confor- mity with the mind of Christ. That will demand a great deal of Christian insight and – no less – a strong tincture of Christian realism. What help can the New Testament give us?

The Apostolic letters – the 'Epistles' – were not meant as formal theological treatises. They are the correspondence of missionaries with the churches of which they had been the founders or for which they felt some special 'concern'. They are by intention and in treatment topical. They are dealing with various problems and difficulties, whether theological or pastoral, of which the writer had become aware, in the life of these young Christian communi- ties. (The letters *from* the churches, asking questions or replying to the epistles, have not survived.) Through them we can get a glimpse of these little groups – and it is the first sight we have of Christianity – as they try to 'build up' the Church in these local centres. They show us what Christianity meant to them, or at least how the Apostles interpreted it, both as a response to the Gospel and as the way of living which was implied in that, in their relation- ships with one another and – so far as they could not avoid it – with 'the world'. These are therefore obviously key-documents.

In the main, the Epistles are laid out on the same pattern. The ground-plan contains two compartments, like the chancel and the nave in our ancient churches, two rooms for two different pur- poses; and these correspond to the now well-known distinction between the *Kerugma* – the apostolic preaching, the content of the Gospel itself – and the *Didache* – the instruction of converts in the practice of the Christian life. In the first section, the problems of the local Church (not all of which, of course, we can now recover) are referred back to the ultimate Christian principles and the nature of Christianity itself. This, the major theological section, unfolds, from one angle or another, the fundamental realities of the faith – God's redemptive action towards man manifested in the Cross and Resurrection, forgiveness, sanctification, rebirth into

newness of life within the redeemed community. In the second section – to which the transition is sometimes made by the pregnant
word, Therefore – the writer gave practical directions for living
the Christian life – for Christian ethics – in the actual first-century
situation. Now in all the Epistles, as C. H. Dodd points out, these
sections appear to be built to a common pattern. They are all written in the same style, in a recognisably different kind of Greek,
they are closely similar to one another, they contain very much the
same material, and they seem to depend on some underlying documents from which they are giving extracts. They may be drawing
on some form of 'catechism' (*Catechesis*), some current manual
of the Christian life provided for the converts from paganism.
They closely resemble the Jewish 'domestic codes' and the current
Stoic handbooks of morals, and there is at least a high probability
that they are in fact partly derived from these sources. 'Neither in
the Epistles nor in the Gospels is there any suggestion that no
moral excellence is to be found outside Christianity' – it would, as
I have said, be incompatible with Christian orthodoxy to suggest
that. The earliest Christian teachers were availing themselves of
the best moral philosophy they could find.[1]

What kind of conduct do they enjoin on Christians? Here 'enjoin' is the operative word. For with all his insistence on Christian
liberty and for all his polemic against the Law, St. Paul does not
talk about Christian ideals or suggest that Christian morality is
permissive. He issues authoritative orders. He speaks about the
commandment of the Lord Jesus and he frequently speaks of his
own commands, in the name of our Lord Jesus Christ (e.g. II
Thessalonians iii). The idea current in some Christian circles that a
binding moral law is incompatible with the spontaneity of the
Christian love-ethic can find little encouragement in St. Paul.
Christians are to bear one another's burdens and so fulfil the law
of Christ (Galatians vi: 2). Love fulfils the law, it does not abro-
gate it. (See pp. 89 ff.)

First of all, then, the Christians are enjoined to abstain from the
grosser pagan immoralities – the catalogue of vices, which recurs
in a number of different points in the New Testament, reads like

[1] For this paragraph see Ch. I of Dodd, *Gospel and Law*, C.U.P., 1941,
on which I am leaning heavily in this whole section. For a detailed study
(Greek text), see Essay II in Selwyn's *I Peter*, Macmillan, 1946. See also
Kirk, *The Vision of God*, Longmans, 1932, pp. 124 ff.

more or less stock material, and is said by scholars to resemble closely corresponding lists in some of the Stoic manuals – and to set themselves to cultivate the opposite and characteristically Christian virtues. (For the lists, see for example Galatians v: 16–24, Colossians iii: 5 ff., I Corinthians vi: 9–11, Romans i: 28 ff., II Timothy iii, etc., and perhaps Mark vii: 21, 22, I Peter iv: 3 ff.) This much, surely, might have been taken for granted – or so we might think if we did not know something about the moral scandals in Corinth. It is terribly easy to be more religious than our non-Christian neighbours, but less moral. Some of the clergy decry 'mere morality'. Yet in a society like ours, no less than in the world of antiquity, it may require miracles of grace to keep even the elementary rules.

Secondly, they prescribe Christian behaviour in family and domestic relationships – husbands and wives, parents and children, masters and servants (i.e. slaves) – and the duties of Christians towards one another and to Elders and other officers of the Church, not leaving out the financial implications. (E.g. Romans xiii and xiv, I Corinthians *passim*, II Corinthians ix, Galatians vi: 1–10, Ephesians v and vi, Colossians iii, I Thessalonians v: 12 ff., II Thessalonians iii: 6 ff., I Peter ii, iii, v, James v: 13 ff. and many other passages.) Thirdly, they deal with the duties of Christian citizens, about which St. Paul took a very positive line. These include respect for civil authority, obeying the laws – and paying your rates and taxes! (Romans xiii: 1–7; cp. also I Peter ii: 11–16. On this see pp. 115 ff.)

All this may seem at first sight to be rather formal. Yet it exhibits a rugged ethical sanity. Even now, pastors and spiritual leaders know how fatally easy it is for converts, caught up in a thrilling spiritual experience, to think that the ordinary daily duties are too 'small' and 'unspiritual' to bother about, and how sadly often very religious people – not least, professionally religious people – can behave intolerably in their own homes. To converts from the Hellenistic world it was always a danger to think that being 'spiritual' meant to ignore the material and physical and imagine that deeds done through the body were things indifferent to the soul's salvation. It was much, then, that they should be reminded to treat their wives with fidelity and compassion, to accept the responsibilities of parenthood – yet not so as to make their children hate them (Ephesians vi: 4). It was no less important that they

F

should be commanded not to idle their lives away in 'religious' stargazing, waiting around for the day of the Lord to come, but to get on with their jobs and earn their livelihood. St. Paul claims Christ's authority for the saying: If a man will not work neither let him eat (II Thessalonians iii: 6 ff.) This means, presumably, that he must not expect to be supported out of the common fund, or it may, perhaps, mean that he must not be admitted to 'eat' at the table of the Lord – if he shirked honest labour he must be excommunicated. In the ancient world it was only the Jews and the Christians who did not regard manual labour as degrading. But of course, as soon as you stress the importance of work or talk about the dignity of labour you 'put ideas into the heads' of 'the workers', as the Puritan movement was later to discover; and the Church has not always been prepared for that. Luther panicked at the peasants' rising, for which his own teaching had been so largely responsible. The record of the Church in this country, from Lollardry onwards, can hardly be called immaculate. 'Justice' has been too easily interpreted as the preservation of the existing order (see p. 133).

This teaching owes a great deal to its Jewish ancestry, to what has been described as 'the Old Testament and Talmudic concern with secular moral order. Lacking a belief in an after-life, Judaism is, after all, *the* worldly religion; it centres on patriarchal authority, the intricacies of family piety, and its ten commandments are a social code. At the core of it all are twin concepts of respect and responsibility.'[1] But the good pagan could have agreed with most of it. For what we have here, it can be fairly said, is just the fundamental morality of domestic and social obligation, the morality of 'my station and duties'. And it is set out in a mainly traditional form, in terms of a paternalistic society. It is the best morality of its own time. It accepts, on the whole, the subordination of women – though it was, in the long run, to make that impossible. Although it stresses the mutual obligations of masters and slaves to one another – and there was the seed of a moral revolution, for it meant regarding the slave as a *person* – yet it does not question the institution of slavery. What we have here is natural law ethics – the morality, so to speak, of all good men – sweetened already by Christian faith and experience, yet fundamentally common to all

[1] From a book review by A. Alvarez in *The Spectator*, July 9th, 1965.

mankind and embodied, for Jews and Christians, in the Decalogue. This, Christianity has never abrogated. Indeed it must always take this for granted, as Jesus himself certainly took it for
granted. But into this body of common moral ideas there comes
like a sword-thrust out of the New Testament the distinctively
Christian interpretation of life to penetrate and transform it
from within, bringing into it a new depth and delicacy, and
challenging even the best and highest morality with an ethic of
unattainable perfection.[1]

In the New Testament we can watch this happening, and can
trace two dominant motifs in the process.

The first is the expectation of the *Parousia* which is thought,
at least in the earliest books, to be imminent. It has been held that
because it was believed – and possibly our Lord himself had believed – that in the lifetime of that generation Christ would 'come',
in power and great glory, to wind up the process of history and
establish the messianic reign, therefore the New Testament is
concerned with no more than an 'ethic of the interim', for the
brief period which still remains. But closer examination does not
support this. Certain traces of that can no doubt be quoted, as,
for example, St. Paul's strange remark about 'having wives as
though you had them not', his reason for which is that the time
is short (I Corinthians vii: 29–34). But that is not the characteristic
emphasis. In what may be the earliest of his letters St. Paul warns
the Church in Salonica not to become paralysed and futile while
it waits for the great event to happen but to get on quietly with
the daily work (II Thessalonians; cf. – much later – I Peter iv: 7).
And indeed he was continually insisting that what really mattered
about the Christian life was not over-heated emotional excitement
– speaking with tongues was one manifestation of it – but moral
stability and constructive effort such as would help to 'build up
the Body of Christ', the actual organised Christian community.
(Love 'edifies', is essentially constructive.) So far from suggesting
a kind of moral indifferentism, what the Parousia-expectation did
was to 'sharpen the edge of all moral values'. If civilisation was
really about to stop, then what were the things that mattered most
now? Our age, though for very different reasons, is being forced

---

[1] In his well-known book *The Two Moralities* A. D. Lindsay perceived
this essential point, but proceeded to give a two-tier presentation of it.
For the two-tier ethic in St. Thomas see pp. 131 ff.

to ask the same question, and the answer it gives is, material comfort. That was not the answer that the Christians gave. It meant, they said, that physical security and the preservation of life were not absolute values. Life and Death began to take on new meanings – what the pagans called life the Christians called death, and the Christians had 'passed from death unto life' (I John iii: 14 and *passim*). In current theological writing 'eschatological' is a blessed word, conveying almost nothing to the layman, which provides an escape route from the real problems of history and of actual Christian conduct. But the sense of living 'at the last hour' on the frontier between 'this age' and 'the coming age' was indeed pregnant with ethical implications. If Christ was 'coming', if he was always coming and, as someone has put it, coming into everything, then everything, all existing social structures, are under his judgement and waiting for his redemption. There is no situation to which he is not relevant, none with which Christians can remain contented, none of which he is not the Judge or as to which he has not the final word.

Thus the day-by-day ethical decisions are set in the dimension of eternity and seen against the transcendent background of the ultimate purpose of God revealed in Christ. Moral obligation means Christian loyalty, obedience to the will of God for Christ's sake, and to disobey is not merely 'wrong', it is *sin*. 'What for morality is social injustice is for religion rebellion against God.' Here ethics passes into that which transcends ethics.

All this brought into Christian conduct a new range – a new length and breadth and height and depth – and a transfiguration of all traditional values. Here on earth we have no continuing city. We are in this world as a colony of heaven, pledged to live, in the routine duties of citizenship, by the life of the world to come. Christians were baptised into the new age. They 'showed forth the Lord's death till he come'. Christ was raised from the dead by the glory of the Father that henceforth they should walk in newness of life, that they should 'put on the New Man, who after God was created in holiness'. One can hardly exaggerate this sense, revealed almost everywhere in the Epistles, of living under a new dispensation, of experience infinitely enriched and deepened, and of still unrealised possibilities. They could never say that they had reached the goal, they were pressing onward. They were pilgrims. Christian ethics are always *in via*. They can

never be simply keeping the rules. 'When you have done all that
is commanded you, say, We are unprofitable servants' (Luke
xvii: 10).

But of course the ultimately decisive fact which was to trans-
value all the traditional values was that which is constitutive of
Christianity – the presence of Christ in the life of the *Koinonia*.
Always implicit in that new relationship to God and to one another
through Christ there were the seeds of a social revolution. Sharing
together in the Spirit of Christ, men and women found more in one
another, came to mean more to one another as personality was
enhanced and deepened, and so to claim more from one another.
What you regard as due to a man depends on what you think a
'man' is and what possibilities he has within him. And for that,
Christian experience gave new *data*. If any man is 'by nature a
slave', a thing, then no human rights will be conceded to him.
(Rights inhere in personality.) But if a man is a fellow-member of
Christ, redeemed by grace and an heir of the kingdom of heaven,
can there be any limit to what is due to him?

Thus traditional moral valuations come to be transformed from
within. A new depth and refinement is imparted to them. Natural
human and social relationships are now lifted on to a higher plane.

Thus in the relations of married life and parenthood Christians
are first ordered to be faithful to the ordinary, accepted, 'decent'
standards; but the words are then added 'Only in the Lord', and
those words were to make the entire difference. They involved a
new spiritual relationship which was to redeem and transfigure
the state of marriage. There is no attempt to disguise or to de-
precate either its biological basis or its sociological and legal framework, or even its contemporary etiquette – veiling of women,
silence in church and so forth, ephemeral though we can now see
that to have been. But something new and distinctive is brought
into it, so that marriage becomes henceforth not merely a contract or (as in Roman law) bound up with property, but a union of
spiritual personalities who are partners in the Spirit of the Lord
Jesus, and a sacrament of the 'mystical union which is betwixt
Christ and his Church'.

In a similar way, the Church accepted slavery as a social and
legal institution – it was not in its power at that time to do anything
else. Yet within the Community of the Holy Spirit there could be
neither slave nor free. In law, a slave was his master's property and

Christian slaves were told that they must accept that and try to verify their Christian calling inside those crippling limitations – Onesimus had done wrong to abscond. But in the Church he is a brother in Christ; and for Christian masters surely that meant – as St. Paul hints broadly in writing to Philemon – that the legal nexus was morally intolerable. Here too, therefore, something new comes in out of Christian experience which was, in the end, to make slavery unthinkable – though it took the Church 1,800 years to realise it. (The mediaeval monasteries *owned* slaves [serfs].)

Here we can see the signs of 'the real thing' – that new quality of thought and living which came into the world with Christianity. It was not so much a new moral code as a revolutionised attitude to life which implied a new scale of valuations and so a new attitude to all morality. St. Paul called it the fruit of the Spirit, and some years before that Jesus had warned people that the fruit is not to be had without the tree. Grapes, he had said, do not grow on bramble bushes. Essentially what the New Testament communicates is neither a systematic theology nor a codification of morals but the Christian experience of life itself – what it came to *mean* in the light of Christ, what it can become when the Spirit takes possession of it. The Apostles do not seem to have thought of him as primarily the teacher of a new ethic – even though St. James and St. Matthew probably did (p. 76). There are few direct references to his teaching. Although, as C. H. Dodd has worked out,[1] his recorded words are implied more often than the few overt quotations might suggest, the primary emphasis is on what he *did* as Redeemer and Author of new life, and on the 'Imitation' of his character – which is not the same thing as 'doing the things that Jesus did'. 'Let this mind be in you which was also in Christ Jesus, who humbled himself obedient unto death.' 'Ye know the grace of our Lord Jesus Christ, who though he was rich for our sakes became poor.' 'Christ suffered for you, leaving you an example that you should follow in his steps.' Christians are to forgive one another as God for Christ's sake has forgiven them. All this implies a new tenderness and compassion, humility and purity of heart, a new sense of mutual responsibility, and above all, perhaps, a new forgivingness, than which there is nothing more morally creative.[2]

[1] Op. cit., pp. 47, 39, etc.
[2] The collect for Easter II in the Prayer Book probably gives the true

Agape, the unique and distinctively Christian quality and the source of all Christian acts and graces, is, in itself, fundamentally religious rather than a precept of ethics. Its motive is response to the Gospel. 'We love because he first loved us.' Christians are to treat one another as they themselves have been treated by God. We are only capable of it, as Dodd says,[1] or can even understand what it means, 'because we are first its objects'. The spring and the living heart of the Christian ethic is Christ himself as the transforming power, 'formed', as St. Paul said, in the lives of men. The famous chapter I Corinthians xiii is more than a hymn in praise of *agape*. It is a verbal portrait of the Christ-life. When the official portrait was published, that is to say, when the Gospels were written, it was seen to have described the authentic Person.

The Gospels come out of those communities. They reflect the faith and experience of the churches and the way of life as Christians had received it. Here is the Source from which it has all flowed. But the Gospels are not a collection of ethical maxims. In the composition of the synoptic Gospels, a record of some of the characteristic teaching, already in circulation in some of the Churches, is interwoven by Matthew and Luke into the basic narrative of the facts as it had been presented by Mark. Their fundamental concern is not with ethics. Their fundamental concern is with Christ himself, as he was in his life and in his death. The teaching is the expression of the Man – the Man through whom God had been brought near, the Man in whom (as St. John said) was life, and the life was the light of men. What manner of man had he been and what had he taught? One thing was clear. The whole story was inexplicable and the teaching very nearly unintelligible apart from his relationship to God, the central all-commanding Reality of what he was, of his thoughts and deeds and words. (The Humanist suggestion that Jesus was 'morally right but religiously mistaken' defies all psychological probabilities.) God was for him *the* decisive fact and all human life is seen

---

scriptural balance. 'Almighty God who hast given thine only begotten son to be unto us both a sacrifice for sin and also an example of godly life, give us grace that we may always most thankfully receive that his inestimable benefit and also daily endeavour ourselves to follow the blessed steps of his most holy life.'

[1] Op. cit., p. 10.

in the light of that fact. Thus his first message was Repent, which meant not merely repentance of 'sins' but a re-orientation of the self, a new outlook, a new approach to life. 'Change your minds and believe the Good News.' People would have to repent of their 'ideals', of their moral standards and their religion too. Jesus makes our ideals look shoddy. He makes us not only penitent for our failures, he makes us feel ashamed of our best. This radical, revolutionary perfectionism, inherent in all Christ's thought and teaching and essentially religious in origin, is the *differentia* of the Christian ethic. But withal he was super-naturally 'human' and understanding of 'ordinary people'. He was criticised for being the friend of sinners – perhaps he liked them rather than the righteous persons – and for keeping disreputable company – something which no 'good' man would do. Here is another hint that forgiveness is very close to the heart of Christian morality: the Christian ethic is part of the Christian Gospel.[1] William Blake said that there is nothing in Christ's moral teaching which was not already in Aristotle. Christ was not a teacher of moral virtue, what he taught was the forgiveness of sins. Wildly exaggerated though that remark is, may it not be pointing in the right direction?

Our Lord stood in the prophetic tradition. He spoke with authority, not like the scribes, who were professional students of authorities. Thus saith the Lord, *I* say unto you. He was urgently proclaiming the reign of God. One might say that the content of all his teaching is obedience to the laws of God's kingdom – the laws of the way life is made and the world is made. These include the normal, 'natural' processes presupposed in the parables of growth, and the 'right' ordering of daily life in men's relationships with one another; they include the ultimate self-dedication of Calvary. The laws of the Kingdom are the laws of God's being. The right way of living, the right way of doing things, is that which corresponds with reality – with the structures of life as God designs it, the way of obedience to the will of God. The Kingdom is the kingdom of right relations.

To love God with the whole mind and soul and strength is to be rightly adjusted to life – and that, of course, includes more than ethical values – and therefore to other people, to the neighbour. So the second commandment is 'like unto' the first, follows from it and is the ethical expression of it. As the ethics are grounded in his

[1] See Burnaby in *God, Sex and War*, pp. 118 ff.

faith in God, so it is only in deeply ethical terms that the service of God can be understood. This was in the prophetic tradition, but he knew even more about God than the prophets did.

Like the prophets, therefore, he was critical of the religion prevailing among his own people and – in the perpetual irony of the Gospel – most critical of that which was best in it. The Pharisees were the religious progressives. He had more in common with them than with any other party and in the debate about the Levirate marriage he implied that they were right as against the Sadducees (Mark vii: 18 ff.). Yet he said that the word of God had been 'made void' under the overlay of Rabbinical casuistry. His criticism of the Scribes and Pharisees was that a legalistic approach, identifying obedience to God's will with external conformity to a code, had emptied morality of its real meaning. Even worse than that it could breed religious prigs who imagined that they had fulfilled the law's demands and so were justified in the sight of God – and that led to self-righteousness and moral blindness. 'If the light that is within thee be darkness, how great is that darkness!' ('I'm sure I've never done nobody any harm.') A young man did once solemnly tell Jesus that he had kept all the commandments from his youth up. Formally, that may not be inconceivable. He may never have actually murdered anyone or robbed the till or borrowed his neighbour's wife. But that is not at all incompatible with a hard, unloving and self-righteous temper. Obedience to God implies a righteousness which exceeds the righteousness of the Scribes and Pharisees.[1]

Our Lord was a Jew. He accepted the Jewish Law. He did not claim to have superseded the Decalogue. 'If thou wouldest enter into life, keep the commandments.'[2] But what was meant by keeping the commandments? He was always pressing back to their real

[1] 'In Hell all is Self Righteousness; there is no such thing there as Forgiveness of Sin; he who does Forgive Sin is crucified as an Abettor of Criminals and he who performs Works of Mercy in any shape whatever is punished and if possible destroy'd, not through Envy or Hatred or Malice but through Self righteousness that thinks it does God service, which God is Satan. They do not Envy one another, They condemn and despise one another; Forgiveness of Sin is only at the Judgement Seat of Jesus the Saviour where the Accuser is cast out . . .' *The Note-Book of William Blake*, Nonesuch edition, MCMXXXV, p. 134. (Capitals as in the text.)

[2] Our Lord did not cite the Two Great Commandments as a new ethic which he was recommending. He said they represented what was fundamental in the Jewish Ethic. See T. W. Manson, *Ethics and the Gospel* (posthumous), S.C.M., 1960, pp. 60, 61.

meaning, their true religious implications. 'It was said by them of old time . . . but I say unto you.' Not that what men of old said was mistaken, but that there was latent something more profound which they had then imperfectly understood and Rabbinical Judaism had obscured. He was always with penetrating insight calling people back from the external code to the inner springs of motive and character. Hatred and contempt are the real murder; illicit desire is the real adultery.[1] It is from within, out of the heart of man, that evil deeds and corrupt thoughts proceed. So too the good man brings forth good out of the good treasure of his own heart. He seems indeed to have been far more concerned with what people *are* than with what they do. What matters most is the quality of the tree. The tree will bear its characteristic fruit.

This was not the teaching of a new ethic. It was a critique of the traditional ethic, which he accepted and sought to deepen and purify. He had not come to destroy but to fulfil. He did not provide a new set of rules. He did not tell people exactly what to do. Even the magnificent 'Go and do thou likewise' did not tell the man precisely what to do. He might never encounter a man that had been coshed. It might mean healing the wounds in his own family. But he was to be 'going out of his way' to help if he genuinely wanted to love his neighbour. The point, surely, of some at least of the parables is to analyse a moral situation and then leave people to make up their own minds. The Sermon on the Mount is not legislation which can be 'applied' as it stands to a pluralist, twentieth-century society which has to find some way of dealing with bandits and murderers and armaments. The nearest approach to a code, as Kirk wrote, which can be confidently ascribed to our Lord – the Beatitudes in St. Matthew's version – is a code not of actions but of dispositions.[2] And the same surely is true of the whole Sermon. It is not legislation for Christian posterity. It is a description of, and it enjoins, those qualities of mind and character which make for and are themselves the fruit of God's reign in the thoughts and wills of men. Be merciful because God is merciful. There is indeed only one precept which is absolutely binding on Christians and it is one that no Christian can obey – to be perfect even as our Father

---

[1] But as Manson well insists, the point here is not so much the assessment of sinfulness as the injury done by the evil thought to the neighbour.

[2] *The Vision of God*, p. 132.

is perfect. What is set before us is an attitude to God, to life and to moral obligation.

There is not very much, it seems, in the recorded teaching which had not been anticipated or cannot be paralleled in the Old Testament or in other sources, little that was, as we say, 'original'. There seems to be not very much that was original in the Shakespearean plots – except Shakespeare. What is 'original' is the Lord himself – his piercing insight into moral reality, the strong, creative thinking enshrined in his unforgettable and deathless sayings, his unconquerable faith in God and intuition into the possibilities, and indeed the very meaning, of Goodness which shines forth from his recorded speech, was verified in his recorded deeds and exhibited in his life – and in his death, which is the supreme manifestation of *agape*. He was uniquely the Man for others because he was uniquely the Man for God. To behold him is to behold Goodness Absolute under human and historical conditions.

Love is the fulfilling of the law, but no disciple will ever have fulfilled it. There are always depths below depths, still unexplored. The Love-commandment implies a constant criticism of all ethics, including Christian ethics. Whatever standards and moral insights Christians have attained there is still yet more to be realised. The Christian ethic is not a completed system, it is cumulative, dynamic and creative. This ethic of unattainable perfection has to be obeyed and translated into action in the loyalty of our responses to the relative situations in which we are. What it lays upon us is 'the obligation to reproduce in human action the *quality* and *direction* of that act of God by which we are saved, may be in quite lowly and unspectacular ways' (Dodd, op. cit., p. 74) – some humanising of the criminal law, some remedial social legislation, some humble attempt at the realisation of neighbourhood.[1]

[1] Niebuhr, *An Interpretation of Christian Ethics*, S.C.M., 1948, p. 23. 'The moral effectiveness of the religious life depends upon deeper resources than moral demands upon the will. Whenever the modern pulpit contents itself with the presentation of these demands, however urgent and fervent, it reveals its enslavement to the rationalistic presuppositions of our era. The Law of Love is not obeyed simply by being known. Whenever it is obeyed at all, it is because life in its beauty and terror has been more fully revealed to men. The love that cannot be willed may nevertheless grow as a natural fruit upon a tree which has roots deep enough to be nurtured by springs of life beneath the surface and branches reaching up to heaven.'

Like 'the letter' an Absolute Standard 'killeth'. If we have no
more than a sublime Example there is nothing left for us but despair. But Christianity offers us more than that. It is not admira-
tion for a dead hero. It is life in the Spirit of the Living Christ.
The innermost meaning of the Christian ethic, is the Christian
life and character in action – the life which is growing up into
Christ, sustained by the grace of God through prayer and sacraments within the community of the Holy Spirit, and bringing forth
its characteristic fruits. 'As the branch cannot bear fruit of itself
except it abide in the Vine, no more can ye except ye abide in me.'

But if all this is true, how far can we still be justified in talking
about the Christian moral *law*?

Chapter Five

'LOVE AND DO AS YOU LIKE'?

'LOVE and do what you like,' said St. Augustine, and could hardly have said anything more dangerous – or should one say, more authentically Christian? The phrase is now in general circulation and is part of the stock in trade of the emancipated. To left-wing Christians it gives support to the argument for 'situational' ethics. To the secularist or non-Christian humanist it is one more stick to belabour Christian morals. Here is one of the highest Christian authorities, one of the makers of the Western Church, and he didn't believe in 'all those silly rules'! Because of his views about unbaptised babies, his obsessional reactions to sex and his terrible gloss on 'Compel them to come in', Augustine has long been dressed up as the bogey-man, who made Christianity what it is said to be – guilt-laden, anti-humanist and repressive. It would be an ironical paradox indeed if he is now claimed, on the strength of those six blessed monosyllables, as the patron saint of what is called the 'new morality'!

The words may serve as a text for some discussion of the relation between law and love, legalism, so called, and Christian freedom. Is the Christian ethic a matter of 'law' at all, or is that inconsistent with its real ethos? But this will be found to involve further questions – for example, about the authority of conscience, about moral objectivity and subjectivity, and about the translation of principles into situational decisions.

Love and law seem to be incompatible. Love is spontaneous, law constrains. Is there not, indeed, an inherent contradiction in being 'commanded' to love at all? The question must have occurred to many Christians and it is now being asked, in varying forms, both in Christian circles and beyond them. There are one or two obvious points to be made to start with. Of course 'the ideal of love transcends all law'. But love is not an emotional inclination, it is a direction of the total self, that is, in everyday language, of the will. It is a deliberately chosen attitude with which the self seeks to be

identified. It may run counter to our inclinations – it may be that
we heartily dislike our neighbour. Love, as Christianity understands it, is a matter less of emotion than of will – though it does
not, like Kant's moral imperative, override or rule out the natural
affections (cp. Matthew cii: 9–11). The command to love is addressed to the will. For the total self is not love-directed. Love presents itself to us as law because of the interior contradictions and
recalcitrance of human nature. The command to love, like the
moral law itself, is 'the claim which the essential nature of man
makes upon him in his present sinful state. The virtue which corresponds to the essential nature of man therefore appears to sinful
man in the form of law – the "good which I would but which I do
not" '.[1] If the self were really identified with its true being, love
would no longer present itself as law. If we did love God with all
our heart and mind – and this is what Augustine is talking about –
then 'Do as you like' would be a sound directive, though directives
would then be no longer needed. What we liked would then be
what God wills for us. We should want to do what now we know
we ought to do. We should 'love that which God commands and
desire that which he doth promise'. That, however, is not where
we are now. The ideal presents itself to us as law. Moreover, love
must embody itself in action. But love is a principle, not a set of
rules. 'It does not specify a certain kind of act, it requires many different kinds of acts appropriate to the needs of different situations.'[2]
The 'law' of love does not mean regimentation or any wooden conformity to a code, restrictive of Christian spontaneity. Indeed, as
we shall see later, moral freedom, like political freedom, is freedom
under law. But that question is part of the very much wider debate,
which ranges far beyond Christian ethics in itself.[3]

One current objection to the Christian ethic is that its claim to be
based on a revelation makes it arbitrary and authoritarian (see p.
15), and therefore denies the rightful claims of reason. Any ethic
acceptable to 'adult' man must, it is said, be rational and self-
justifying, discerned by reason and rationally defensible. A 'revealed' ethic merely says 'I'm telling you'. This is really a hang-

---

[1] Niebuhr, *Nature and Destiny of Man*, I, p. 289.
[2] Thomas, op. cit. p. 386.
[3] Any speaker or writer has to decide whether 'ethics' is singular or
plural. Should he say 'ethics is' or 'ethics are'? I follow the normal English usage of treating it, like physics, as singular. Nobody would say
'physics are'.

over from the eighteenth century and its obsessional preoccupation
with the contrast between reason and revelation. But that cannot
be made an absolute distinction. Revelation must be accepted by
the mind, i.e. by reason, or it is not revealed, and it therefore
requires the fullest use of reason. (Faith and reason are not two
different things, as though faith could be a substitute for knowledge, but two different approaches to reality which are complementary to one another. All knowledge, in fact, starts from an act
of faith, faith at least that something is there to be known, and
that reason can find out something about it.) Moreover, any alleged
revelation must be judged by the Christian to be good before he
accepts it as revelation. When a thing is seen to be good, reason is
satisfied. A revealed ethic does not mean an ethic which is not in
itself rationally defensible – that theme may be said to run through
the whole of this book as it runs through the whole catholic tradition.

The rational 'autonomy' of ethics cannot mean, surely, that
ethics can exist independently of all moral experience. Nor can
reason alone motivate moral action. 'No rational moral idealism
can create moral conduct. It can provide principles of criticism and
norms, but such norms do not contain a dynamic for their realisation.'[1] The rightful claim for rational 'autonomy' – a claim that
Christianity does not question – is that reason should not be asked
to submit passively to any extrinsic religious or moral authority,
but should freely derive its ethical norms and judgements from
its own reflexion on human moral experience – which is the raw
material of any ethic. It is not an abdication of rationality to give
serious consideration to the moral experience of Christians. What
the Christian ethic may fairly ask its critics is to stop arguing over
'revelation' and try to assess its ethical truth and value.[2]

The authority which the Christian ethic claims is thus not arbitrary or capricious. I have been trying to show, in the preceding
chapters, that the Christian ethic does not rest on a *fiat* but that it
expresses the true law of man's being – the way man is made and
what he may become. Of that Christ is the absolute incarnation.

But the popular protest against Christian ethics is not to be met
by these academic arguments. Few of those who demand moral

[1] Niebuhr, *Interpretation*, p. 216.
[2] For these two paragraphs see G. F. Thomas, op. cit., p. 375, on which
I have drawn freely.

emancipation will so much as have heard the name of Immanuel Kant. It is part of the general climate of opinion. People today are not going to be put upon. There is a general reaction against authority, against all kinds of establishments and censorships, and by consequence an inevitable reaction against any form of authoritative morality, any appeal to an absolute moral law, as an unjustifiable imposition. There is no need for Christians to be shocked by this. Indeed there is much in this attitude at its best that Christians ought rather to honour and respect. One of the finest things in the life around us is the search for a personal 'structure of meaning' in a fragmentated and depersonalised society, a longing for personal wholeness and integrity – which in Christian theology is called salvation – the desire of men and women to be themselves, not spares in a stock of interchangeable parts. This is surely something that Christ himself would approve. But it leads them to say that they mean to manage their own lives, to discover their own morals for themselves and not to be governed by 'other people's rules, even when they call them God's law'.[1] Even if it takes anti-Christian form, this should not be regarded as an 'unChristian' attitude. All men are called by God to be themselves. Yet selves do not exist in isolation, they are formed through their interpersonal relationships. Nor can any man attain moral freedom except by taking the law of God for his own law. If we were to use the psychological jargon, the Christian reply would be that the superego is not, as Freud held, the enemy of the ego, preventing a man from realising himself, but the medium through which the self is realised.

Again, both in the homes and in the schools there is a changed approach to all questions of discipline and moral education. The Victorian sense of duty may have died and obedience seems to the young a dingy virtue, even if it is virtuous at all. But the stern paterfamilias of the period and the old-style schoolmaster have gone with them. Moral education breathes in a different atmosphere. It is now much less a matter of imposed rules – these orders are to be obeyed or else – than of mutual discussion and consultation ending in a more or less voluntary acceptance. This too is all to the good from the Christian standpoint. Potentially it is a far more Christian approach than demanding passive conformity to a

[1] H. A. Williams, *The True Wilderness*, Constable, 1965, p. 52.

code, and more conducive to that responsible freedom which belongs to the essence of Christian living.

But there is undeniably another side to it. The danger in a 'permissive morality' is that it may lead, as it too often does, to saying that moral standards are optional or can be assessed in terms of inclination – do this if you feel like that, but of course not otherwise; and that is to part company with morality, for the moral judgement implies an imperative claim. Further than that, it is cruelly unfair, in so far as it throws an intolerable burden on the immature and uninstructed conscience, which is left at the mercy of external pressures, while all the time the hidden persuaders are engaged in an organised conspiracy to exploit all that is weakest in young people and entice their least creditable motives. Here again, then, it becomes apparent that the abandonment of objective standards, that is, of an inflexible moral law, so far from making for freedom, makes for slavery – as can be seen in too many homes today. Either through irresponsible indulgence, or through their own moral confusion and insecurity, parents are too prone to withdraw from trying to offer their children any moral guidance – or, as some would say, to 'impose our ideas on them' – and send them out into a dangerous world 'to find out for themselves when they are grown up'.

No sane person, however, would send a boy, knowing nothing whatever about chemistry and without any guidance or instruction, into a laboratory and tell him to get on with it and find out things for himself – if he did, he would wish he hadn't at the funeral. The boy has got to make his experiments but within a defined field of reality – what we call the laws or principles of chemistry. He has to know something of these before he starts. Through the experiments he finds out more about the truth and validity of the laws.[1]

All moral decisions are experimental. They have to be made in particular situations with the materials actually at hand. But they are informed by knowledge of the principles. Hare suggests an illuminating analogy. Before he takes a car on the road a man is required to undergo driving-instruction. He must learn something about the way a car works, how to control it, how to start and stop it (when to say Yes and when to say No), what kind of treatment it needs to function efficiently, and what kind of behaviour will make

[1] Hare, op. cit., p. 76.

G

him a good driver, the rule of the road, the principles of safe driving. That is to say, he is taught the kinds of action appropriate in various situations. When he gets into the traffic on the A1, he will have to make his decisions for himself in the light of the principles which have been imparted to him. Principles can be taught but not decisions. A driver may know the book of words by heart but that will not tell him exactly what to do in any particular situational crisis. But it would be mad to 'go to the other extreme and leave it to him to find his own way of driving'.

When it comes to life and conduct as a whole, the rule of the road is the moral law, 'that settled body of principles which is the most priceless heritage that any generation can leave its successors'. The principles have not changed but the road has changed. In the rapidly changing society the decisions made by the pre-war generation – the actual content of what it is right to do in response to the concrete situation – may not necessarily be right for their successors, who tend therefore to say that the principles were false, that the pre-war morality is outdated. The content of any ethical decision must be, it would seem in the nature of things, contingent. It is the right or the wrong decision in the given situation to which it relates and is 'relative' to that situation. But that does not mean that morality is 'subjective' or that there is no objective moral law. The objectivity of the moral standard is, therefore, so far from being incompatible with some variability in implementing it, in what it may require to be done, that it may be said positively to require it. Otherwise it would be merely an empty schema. Yet if the principle were not objective, if it were not, in some sense, 'there' antecedently to our decisions, then all acts would be equally good or equally bad, if indeed good and bad had any meaning; and nobody in fact believes that this is true.

It looks, indeed, as if the great debate about moral absolutes and moral relatives, objectivity and subjectivity, may be found in the end to revolve round the difference between principles (or 'laws') and decisions. At any rate the parents' dilemma does, as Hare points out, throw a great deal of light on it.

'The objectivist says, "Of course you know what to do; look at what your conscience tells you and if in doubt go by the consciences of the vast majority of men". He is able to say this because our consciences are the product of principles which our early training has indelibly implanted in us, and in our society these principles do not differ much from one person to another. The subjectivist says, "But surely when it comes to the point I have to decide for myself, or I shall be a mere traditionalist or conventionalist." The plea of the subjectivist is quite justified. It is the plea of an adolescent who wants to be adult. To become morally adult is to reconcile these two apparently conflicting positions by learning to make decisions of principle; and it is to learn to use "ought" sentences in the realisation that they can only be verified by reference to a standard or set of principles that we have by our own decision accepted and made our own. That is what our present generation is so painfully trying to do.'[1] Contrast the connotation of 'morally adult' in contemporary fiction and entertainment!

To Protestantism in most of its forms the mention of law starts a chain-reaction. It awakens echoes of the ancestral voices – salvation by works, legalism, grace, justification by faith and all the battle-cries of the war for spiritual liberation. Law, it protests, can have no place in the Gospel. Christianity is not that kind of religion. The Christian life is faith that worketh by love, and that is essentially inward and spiritual, not outward or carnal obedience to law. Works done before the grace of Christ are not only not acceptable to God, but 'we doubt not but that they have the nature of sin" (Article xiii). Faith and love must never be tainted with 'legalism'. Christ is the end of the law to all believers. These were the protests of the Reformation, symbols of the faith for which the fathers died and the liberty with which Christ has set us free. They are needed in every Christian generation. But if these convictions are formalised into systems, they may lead to such suspicion of ethical judgement as to empty the Christian life of its moral content, because it is almost bound to remain indifferent to those relative moral discriminations which can only be made through 'law' and rational criticism. Luther placed 'a perfectionist private ethic in juxtaposition to a realistic, not to say cynical official ethic'. How in that case can there really be a Christian ethic? All this comes fatally near to a pietism which breeds a 'fugitive and cloistered virtue' (Milton the puritan might well have agreed).

May it be ventured that there is some confusion here? Love

[1] Op. cit., pp. 77, 78.

is the fulfilling of the law. In a real sense love transcends the law.
But can that be rightly interpreted as meaning that the recognition of moral obligation is somehow derogatory to Christian
Agape? Brunner appears to be wanting to go that length. 'Duty
and genuine goodness are mutually exclusive.' 'The chief emphasis
of Scriptural ethics lies not in victory over lawlessness but in the
fight against legalism . . . freedom means release from the "ought",
Duty and genuine goodness are mutually incompatible.'[1] On that
Niebuhr's comment is that 'there would be little goodness in history by that standard'.[2]

St. Paul, for all his polemic against the law, expected the converts to keep the law, and outside the lunatic fringes of antinomianism no Christian leader has ever said anything else. (I am
not, of course, suggesting that Brunner does!) No Christian seri-
ously supposes that we can dispense with the fundamental principles as they are embodied in the 'law of Christ'. But to call that
legalism is quite misleading. Legalism means something different.
It means the attempt to elaborate the law in a code of detailed
regulations, valid at all times and in all circumstances, and to
claim for these regulations the same sanctity and the same permanence as is rightly claimed for the fundamental law. And that
may succeed, as our Lord told the Pharisees, in making the law
itself of none effect. Surely there just cannot be a list of actions
which all Christians everywhere must do, placed as they are in
many different countries in many different stages of development,
in an infinite variety of circumstances, in unique and unpredictable situations. We cannot equate the decisions with the principles
– the kinds of action which Christian love requires. And this, it
would seem, is the real issue here. It is not a question of law
versus love. It is between what is constant and what is contingent.
'The old morality', says the Bishop of Woolwich, with whom I
should find myself closely in agreement here, 'rightly calls us to
remember the eternal foundation in which all human life is
grounded: "I, the Lord, do not change; therefore you, O sons of
Jacob, are not consumed" (Mal. iii: 6). It becomes brittle and
unbending (and therefore weak precisely where it thinks it is

[1] *The Divine Imperative*, pp. 72 ff.
[2] *Nature and Destiny of Man*, II, p. 197 note. See the whole discussion
of the 'defeatism' of the Lutheran dualism, pp. 192 ff. 'The Sectarian conception (e.g. Milton's) of the relation of the Gospel to social problems is
right and the Reformation is wrong.'

strong) when it transfers the constancy of the foundation to the permanence of the super-structure.'[1] Here again, behind the smoke of the arguments and emotional words like 'absolute' and 'relative', most Christians would probably agree. Not many, when once they have understood the point, would really wish to equate Christian conduct with conformity to the letter of a code, as though it were governed by a legal text. 'The error of traditional absolutism at this point has been to identify the universal principles with specific rules or standards which have been formulated by men of a certain culture. The result has been to treat those rules or standards which are relative to time and place as if they were absolutes . . . The absolutes of which we are speaking are general principles rather than specific rules. Moreover, the formulation of those principles can never be regarded as final and must be revised again and again.'[2] The Christian ethic, in other words, is a growing thing, not a static and irrelevant anachronism. It is always inherently and in its very nature at once a new commandment and an old commandment (I John ii: 7, 8). It can never accept a stereotyped formula. There is nothing at all subversive in saying that; it is but to say what the Lord said himself – that there is more truth to be learnt yet, that the Spirit will show us things to come, and that life requires willingness to lose it. Accordingly, so far from being shocked or passing resolutions to keep our courage up, when Christians to whom new insights have been given, or who find themselves called upon to act in unprecedented situations, try to give effect to the ultimate principles in forms hitherto untried and unconventional, we ought, rather, surely to welcome it and be glad about it. The Christian ethic is that kind of ethic. Yet every moral reformer in his time has probably been accused of antinomianism, of corrupting the youth or, like the Lord himself, threatening the Temple and the Law.[3]

The experiment may, in a given case, have been wrong; but it was not wrong in being experimentalist. The onlooker may find

---

[1] *Christian Morals To-day*, S.C.M., 1964, p. 18.
[2] G. F. Thomas, op. cit., p. 465.
[3] 'Any ethic which is genuinely Christian will always be open to the charge of destroying the law and the temple. Jesus faced this charge; Stephen faced it; Paul faced it. Antinomianism is always a false accusation, but I should immediately suspect that there was something sub-Christian about an ethic which did not provoke it.' Robinson, *ad loc.*, p. 22.

it hard to understand just why the man acted as he did. But that is no justification for moral censure. Nobody can understand from outside exactly what the situation was within which, or on which, the other man had to act, simply because it was *his* situation, and therefore included not only the outward circumstances but also his own personal history and all the motives, conscious or unconscious, inclining him to decide the way he did decide. Judge not, therefore, as we would not be judged. We may never know just how another man is placed. Life is so complex and human motives so opaque and often inscrutable to others, that we have no right to pass on fellow-Christians or, for that matter, on anybody else – our glib, standardised moral condemnations. (An act may be subjectively virtuous – done from good motives and aiming at a good end – and yet rightly be judged to be a bad act and may turn out to have disastrous consequences; so too good may result from bad motives. It is no human judgement but God's alone 'to whom all hearts be open, all desires known and from whom no secrets are hid'.)

Both the need for experiment and its fallibility bring us back yet once more to the same point. Without a Christian law we are morally blind, but without spontaneity in action we are not responsible moral agents in the liberty with which Christ has set us free.

There will be times when it is crystal-clear what the immediate situation needs and what is the right Christian reaction to it. Then love can act, as we say, spontaneously without internal debate or calculation. But such times are rare. We may not too lightly assume that any or every act of 'self-giving', irrespective of all other considerations, is a valid manifestation of Christian *Agape*. Normally, there will be conflicting claims, long-term calculation of consequences, wider questions of Christian social strategy and all manner of difficult assessments which must be taken into the account. This internal debate is the operation of conscience. When a man has done everything he can to decide what is the right thing to do in the light of his conscience – and his common sense, not always the strongest point in religious people – then, in the long run, he has got to do it. The one sacrifice he must never make, which can never be acceptable to God, is the sacrifice of his integrity. 'Here I stand, I can no other.' Yet 'Follow your conscience and you will always be right' is an extremely dangerous pre-

scription. Some Christians are conscientiously convinced that
apartheid is inherent in the law of God. Christians have roasted
others over slow fires in obedience to the dictates of conscience –
which was wrong because it assumed a wrong theology; it was
warped by belief in a sub-Christian God. Conscience, in other
words, must not be claimed as in itself the infallible Voice of God.
It requires discipline and education.

Bishop Butler gave a magnificent description of the sovereign,
regal office of conscience presiding over and issuing its commands
to the interior constitution of human nature. 'There is a superior
principle of Reflexion or Conscience in every man which distin-
guishes between the internal principles of the heart as well as his
external actions; which passes judgement upon himself and them;
pronounces determinatively some actions to be in themselves just,
right and good, others to be in themselves evil, wrong and unjust
. . . It is by this Faculty, natural to man, that he is a moral agent,
that he is a law to himself . . . a faculty in kind and in nature supreme
over all others and which bears its own authority for being so . . .
You cannot form a notion of this Faculty, Conscience, without
taking in Judgement, Direction, Super-intendency. To preside
and govern, from the very œconomy and constitution of Man,
belongs to it. Had it Strength, as it has Right, had it Power as it
has manifest Authority, it would absolutely govern the world.'[1]
Now, to be a man is to be self-transcending, to be aware of the self
and to pass judgements on it (see p. 64). But conscience is not
a separable faculty, any more than reason is a faculty. Reason is the
total man reasoning. Similarly, conscience is the man himself
engaged in moral debate and judgement, and can therefore claim
no infallibility. And it is evident that what it tells him – even when
it tells him to defy society – must be to a large extent informed by
the social and moral tradition which he inherits. The education
of the Christian conscience is by sharing in the life of the *Koinonia*,
with its gathered moral wisdom and experience, its traditions and
teaching, its treasures of love and holiness, and – through all that –
by growth in sanctification and transformation towards 'the mind
of Christ'.

To know the good, said Plato, a man must *be* good. Make the
tree good, said Jesus, and its fruit good. Christian conduct proceeds from Christian character. But the closer a man has come to

[1] *Sermons in the Rolls Chapel*, 4th edition, 1749, no. II.

Jesus Christ, the more daring, creative and 'unconventional' are his moral decisions likely to be – and for that, full liberty ought to be accorded to him. An institutional Church must be very careful not to identify the mind of Christ with conventionality in moral judgement. That would mean unchurching some of the greatest saints – and indeed the Lord of the Church himself.

'The Old Testament stands for law and the New for love: the Jewish religion (or alternatively, the pre-Reformation Church) was legalistic; Christianity (or alternatively, the Reformation) brought men moral freedom.' There are phrases like these in many popular utterances, but they are too rough and ready and too uncritical. Has the New Testament nothing to say about the law and the Old Testament nothing about love? There is legalism enough in the priestly code; but what else can anyone say about St. James? There are traces of legalism in St. Matthew (contrast, for example, xviii: 21, 22 with xviii: 15–17) and notoriously there is plenty in *The Two Ways* (The Didache) and other books of the sub-apostolic period.[1] We must not fall for that over-simplification. Both Testaments insist on law – the law of Yahweh and the law of Christ – as the regulative norm of the common life in the two societies out of which they come. In both the law proceeds ultimately from love. Behind the law stand the prophets – Hosea and Jeremiah as well as Amos – and their message about the covenant-relationship initiated by God's 'loving-kindness', their constant reminders of what God had done – how in his love for his people he had delivered them and brought them in safety into 'this good land'. It was *that* God whose law Moses taught them and the

---

[1] An almost classical case is at viii: 1. Our Lord said, When ye fast be not as the hypocrites . . . This appears as, 'Let not your fasting be with hypocrites, for they fast on the second and fifth day of the week, but you must fast on the fourth and the sixth' (Wednesday and Friday). Kirk's comment was (*Vision of God*, p. 130) 'Our Lord's great effort to purify the whole conception of fasting has degenerated into a sectarian wrangle about dates . . . This is the sort of thing that legalism can lead to – putting trivial questions of propriety or ecclesiastical usage on the same level as Justice and Mercy or insisting that they are part of the eternal law of God. Churchmen know how all too often local or temporary, and frequently undesirable, regulations or ceremonial usages have been bound on men's shoulders as having catholic (universal!) authority . . . But the saying The Sabbath was made for man . . . surely covers all ecclesiastical rules that cannot be traced to Dominical origins.'

law was the framework of the community-life under the Sovereignty of the Lord God. Judaism could certainly not have survived without it, and certainly could not have survived the Exile,
during which the law was developed and elaborated. The Torah,
Manson wrote, 'was not primarily the formulation of a series of
categorical commands and prohibitions with appropriate sanctions,
though such an idea is part of its meaning. It is rather a body of
instructions regarding man's place in God's world and his duties
to his neighbour. The Torah is the divine guidance as to the right
way in which man should behave as subject of the heavenly King.'[1]
The Psalms, and especially CXIX, reveal what the law could mean
to the devout, not as a burden but as delight and joy. 'Lord, what
love have I unto thy law: all the day long is my study in it.' 'The
law of thy mouth is dearer unto me than thousands of gold and
silver' – and when a Jew has said that he has said something!
It provided a symbol and guarantee of the presence of God with
his people 'in a strange land' when the Temple-symbol was no
more.[2] But because it was that, and because the Exile, during
which the Rabbinic learning was being amassed, was such a
traumatic and searching experience, the aim came to be seen as
building a 'fence' to protect the people of God from being con-
taminated, or even submerged, by the surrounding heathenism.
Thus it tended, as perhaps in the long run any elaborate codification must tend, towards negative avoidance of evil rather than
towards a positive and dynamic realisation of creative goodness.
Holiness tended to mean separation. But 'Ye shall be holy for
I am holy' meant a very great deal more than that; it meant the
illimitable claim of Goodness, and what that can mean the Lord's
life revealed. Jesus showed what holiness really does mean – an
outward-going purity of spirit which brings with it life, hope and
healing.

It is quite unfair to suggest that the Rabbis concentrated
attention on the external act and were unconcerned with the interior motive. The Sayings of the Fathers and other sources provide far too much evidence to the contrary. Yet this immense corpus of the law, covering every detail in life, had to be presented in

[1] *ad loc.*, p. 29.
[2] The Reformation, seeking to substitute Bible for Mass, had to teach
people to find their focus of common life not in one big building but
round one big book. Some of the results have been markedly similar
in the two cases. Bibliolatry can hardly avoid becoming legalistic.

an elaborate code; and codification seems to involve the 'tendency to judge by externals and in the mass, without due consideration of circumstances' (Kirk). It tends, too, to a painful scrupulosity – the perpetual, anxious question Am I right? which makes religion a self-centred affair. Conversely, it tends to make people satisfied with an uninspiring ideal of blamelessness: and because it may be formally possible to avoid the violation of a code by carrying out all the prescribed actions, it can make people into awful prigs who keep the law and are only too well aware of it – and hope that God is aware of it too. (The Pharisee and the Publican.) But above all, in this mass of legislation where every detail matters as much as another, all sense of proportion gets lost. As our Lord said, with his eye for the ridiculous, they 'strain at a gnat and swallow a camel'. Answering the question What really matters? Where can we find any standard of moral reference? Jesus quoted the two Great Commandments. These are what all the law and the prophets come to. Everything else must be tested and judged by these. These alone are of absolute validity. All the laws of the Decalogue are valid, they express God's will and purpose for mankind within their own field of applicability, but they may be overridden by the higher law, and by it they must be tested.[1]

That, as we have seen (p. 90), was not a new ethic, it was his criterion, so to speak, of all ethics. But in him that word was made flesh and he lived it. And when he gave his own 'new commandment', it was to love *as I have loved you* (John xiii: 34) – and that is absolute, final and inexhaustible. All that is distinctively Christian in the Christian ethic comes back to that. It is the perfect realisation of Goodness, absolute for all men at all times, infinitely manifold in content. It is on those terms and in that sense that the Christian ethic can claim to *be* Morality (see p. 15).

'If the Christian ethic is anything at all, it is a living, growing thing. "Love as I have loved you" is not to be construed solely in the past; if there is anything in the Christian religion, "I have loved you" is true of the past, the present and the future. "I *have* loved", in the perfect tense, means that it is a past thing which continues into the present until the end of time. Further, just as

[1] 'God's command does not vary in *intention* but it varies in *content* according to the conditions with which it deals.' Thomas, op. cit., p. 137. Thus as Brunner puts it, the various commands of the Bible are expositions or 'paradigms' of the one command – to love. *The Divine Imperative*, p. 134.

the power and inspiration of the Christian ethic is represented in a living Person and a living Body, so the achievement of the Christian ethic is always something new and original. Christian ethics is certainly not a slavish obedience to rules and regulations. It is active living, and therefore has the power to go to the heart of every ethical situation as it arises. It has the power to see what response is called for in terms of feeling, word and act, and the power to make that response and to make it creatively and effectively. In short, Christian ethics is a work of art.'[1]

It is sometimes asked whether the Christian ethic is deontological or teleological – something done from sheer sense of duty, or for the end or good which it seeks to realise. (The distinction, I think, cannot be made too sharp. Recognition of moral goodness or value seems to bring with it a claim or obligation.) Whatever the formal answer may be, to the Christian, at any rate, within the context of discipleship and Christian faith, the question itself seems to mean very little. As the law of Moses stands within the Covenant and is given, according to one form of the narrative (Exodus xxxiv) after the Theophany of God 'full of compassion and gracious, plenteous in mercy and truth', so the Christian ethic is *response* – 'that ye should do as I have done to you' (John xiii: 15). That is the motive of Christian obedience.

Note: Paul Ramsey's *Deeds and Rules in Christian Ethics* (Oliver and Boyd, 1965) was published after the MS of my book had left my hands. But it throws much light on the debate between 'legalism' and 'spontaneity' discussed in this chapter, and attention ought to be called to it here. Ramsey takes up a suggestion of Frankena's that 'if Christian ethics is a possible theory of normative ethics it may or will or must take two forms, which he calls *act-agapism* and *rule-agapism*. These are two possible views of how Christian love best exhibits itself in practice'. Ramsey protests that 'no social morality ever was founded, or ever will be founded, on a situational ethic'. But, he says, Frankena's analysis should at least remove some of the acrimony from the debate and help to clarify the real questions of ethics. 'For one thing, a rule-agapist should no longer accuse the act-agapist of being a "materialist", a "relativist" or "subjectivist" or a compromiser when he is only

---

[1] Manson, op. cit., final paragraph.

an act-agapist. And the proponent of Christian "situational ethics" should no longer accuse the proponent of rule-agapism of being a "legalist" lacking in "compassion", when he only believes that Christian compassion can and may and must embody itself in certain rules of action.'

Chapter Six

THE CHRISTIAN SOCIETY

I

CHRISTIANITY is a religion of redemption and the Church is in the world to redeem the world. It follows therefore that Christian obedience can never be completely fulfilled in the purely personal and domestic ethic to which, on the whole, the New Testament is confined. The Church must develop a Christian Social Ethic; and this cannot be done directly from the Gospel; any such attempt must end in sentimentalism. ('If only people would love one another there would be no more poverty or war and everything in the world would be all right.)' No Christian doubts that the love-commandment is relevant to social and moral life in all circumstances and at every level, even to the 'little less or little more' of relative justice and common or garden 'decency'. But the notion that the perfectionist ethic of Christian Love can be 'applied' *directly* to any imaginable social order, corrupted by sin – i.e. the will to power – falls very far short of Christian realism. Nor, in any case, does the love-commandment tell us how it is to be carried out in any concrete social situation or in any actual judgement or decision. The Gospel enjoins on us to heal the sick, but it does not tell us how to cure cancer or how to make an accurate diagnosis. Love bids us care for the poor, but it does not provide the social techniques by which alone, in a complex society like ours, that can be carried out. Love requires justice between man and man, but what that implies at any given stage of social development, or by what machinery or through what institutions it can be best effected, cannot be learnt from the Sermon on the Mount. All this is too obvious to need elaborating. And right from the beginning, as we have seen, the Apostles and teachers of the Church availed themselves of the best moral philosophy they could find. So it has been all through Christian history, and we today shall be under the same necessity, though we need, of course, not only moral philosophy (so far as that can now be said to exist) but also the

physical and social sciences. Christian moral judgements in the
social field are bound to involve many technical factors about which
Christians, simply as Christians, will not have the necessary information and need therefore to rely on expert advice – which may
be drawn from non-Christian sources. 'A prophetic religion', says
Reinhold Niebuhr, 'which tries to re-establish itself in a new day
without appropriating what was true in the Age of Reason will
be inadequate for the moral problems which face our generation.'[1]

No historical situation is permanent. While the fundamental
moral principles of a Christian ethic are permanent and unchang-
ing, the *content* of Christian moral judgements and the specific
forms of Christian action will clearly differ in differing social
contexts; and not least with the differing relations between the
church and the culture or the society within which, at a given time,
it lives. Christians today are not immune from the danger of
identifying a Christian society with a previously existing relationship – a 'synthesis' – which belongs to past history – so that their
thinking is still too much geared to a situation that no longer exists.
There is no one pattern laid up in heaven, archetypal in all times
and circumstances, of what a Christian civilisation means. (At
various periods people have imagined that there is some one form
of 'Christian' architecture. The eighteenth century thought it
must be 'classical', the nineteenth, imitation Gothic: the deplorable
results are still with us.)

There have always been some absolute, radical Christians –
Tolstoy is the obvious name to quote – for whom any co-operative
contact with the secular civilisation of their day spelt betrayal and
contamination. Civilisation itself, they held, depends on legal and
political institutions which are incompatible with the law of Christ.

This seam runs all the way through Christian history and is
found outcropping in almost every period. That protest is undeniably always needed and without it we should be infinitely the
poorer. But as a *rule*, mandatory on Christians, it can only be called
fatally misleading. Most of us are self-righteous enough already
without fomenting spiritual pride by regarding ourselves as the
'true' and 'real' Christians. We need continual warning against
mere worldliness. But God has set us in this world to live and he

[1] *An Interpretation of Christian Ethics*, S.C.M. 4th edition, 1948, p.
173.

calls men as Christians in their history – in their own social and cultural situation, as Romans, Germans, Africans or Englishmen. We cannot divest ourselves of that situation without ceasing to be the men we are; and no man, in fact, can serve God in a vacuum. Even if it were possible – which it is not, for a man draws even his speech from his culture – to seek to abjure the world altogether is an abdication of moral responsibility and a shirking of the tension inherent in an incarnational religion. For fundamentally this negative radicalism rests on a sub-Christian theology. It breaks down on the relation of Jesus Christ to God the Creator and the Lord of history.[1]

How, then, is Christianity related to the civilisation in which it is embodied? Ernest Barker once described that question as the profoundest question of history.[2]

The immediate and enduring result of the Lord's life and death and resurrection was the emergence of a new society – the Community (*Koinonia*) of the Holy Spirit. To be a 'Christian' – at first a local nickname, subsequently adopted by the Church – meant to be a member of that society. To be 'in Christ' is to be in the Koinonia – a community gathered out of the 'world' (the social and economic complex), which tried to live as a self-contained society, entrusted, as it believed, with the one true faith, called to holiness and the law of love. What was to be the relation of that community to the wider community in which it lived – the vast Roman

---

[1] The Radicals' 'rejection of culture is easily combined with a suspicion of nature and nature's God; their reliance on Christ is often converted into a reliance on the Spirit immanent in him and the believer; ultimately they are tempted to divide the world into the material world governed by a principle opposed to Christ and a spiritual realm guided by the spiritual God. Such tendencies are evident in Tertullian's Montanism, in Spiritual Franciscanism, in the inner light of the Quakers and in Tolstoy's spiritualism. At the edges of the radical movement the Manichaean heresy is always developing.' Richard Niebuhr, *Christ and Culture*, Faber, 1952, p. 91. This book may fairly be called a classical study of the questions which we are now discussing and, like others, I am heavily indebted to it. I shall be referring to it again later. For Tolstoy, see pp. 68 ff.

[2] 'Modern philosophy, even when it is far from orthodox, is largely concerned with problems, especially in ethics and political theory, which are derived from Christian views of the moral law and the catholic doctrines as to the relation of church and state' . . . 'To understand the Scholastics we must understand Hildebrand, and to understand Hildebrand we must know something of the evils against which he contended.' Bertrand Russell, *History of Western Philosophy*, George Allen, 1946, pp. 326, 327.

imperial organisation controlling the daily lives of all its citizens, and with an idolatrous worship at the heart of it? How could they sing the Lord's song in a strange land? Here was 'a sociological situation of a hitherto unfamiliar kind'.[1] How did the Christian community approach it?

There is no evidence to support the thesis that the origin of the new Christian movement was a kind of proletarian revolution. No doubt it is true that in the early days the membership of the Christian society was drawn largely from the lower classes (cf. I Corinthians i: 26), the underprivileged and not least the slaves, who found within it a fellowship and a status denied by the legal and economic nexus, as the victims of the industrial revolution in England were later to find in the Methodist classes and chapels – a fact which has had far-reaching social consequences. But the first believers were not 'proletarians'.[2] Our Lord and the Apostles belonged to the class of small owners and family shipping firms. Any working man today lives on a standard which would have seemed luxurious wealth to them; but they were neither propertyless nor wage-slaves. They were peasant smallholders and they were self-employed. The first economic experiment of the Christians – the so-called communism of Acts ii: 44 and iv: 32 ff. – was a communism of consumers and presupposed the possession of private property. The first adherents were probably humble folk but already, within the New Testament period, the Corinthian church included the city treasurer (Romans xvi: 23) and Luke/Acts is dedicated to an Excellency. Pliny reported in the reign of Trajan that in his province of Bithynia 'many of all classes' had become Christians.

But in any case, this Marxian approach totally misconceives both the origin and the nature of new community. Both were in truth essentially religious. What created the Church was the Resurrection and the Presence of Christ in the hearts of the believers,

[1] John Baillie, *What is Christian Civilisation*, O.U.P., 1945, p. 6. This short book is still of great value; but it was published twenty years ago and *our* situation has changed a good deal meantime. I think that if he were still with us John Baillie might wish to give reconsideration to some of the judgements he then expressed.

[2] The Church no doubt took into itself what Toynbee calls the 'internal proletariat', the spiritually and culturally dispossessed, of the Empire. But that is not quite the same thing. There was in fact little free employed labour in ancient society. But, as always, the existence of slave-labour was creating a vast population of 'poor whites'.

re-experienced in depth at Pentecost. What united, vitalised and directed it was a common faith and a common expectation. It was intimate, personal and Christ-centred. The Disciples, first of all in the upper room and then, as believers were added to the Lord and the missionary expansion began, in the various 'churches' in Europe and Asia Minor, were drawn together simply by their religion – their common allegiance to Christ as Lord, their mutual sharing in the Spirit, united at once with Christ and with one another, and their experience of Christian love.

'The grace of our Lord Jesus Christ and the love of God and the community of the Holy Spirit' – that might have been written over the doors of their meeting-places, for it exactly describes what they were for. What constituted the new society and what primarily it offered to share with others was not any kind of 'social Gospel' but a vital, rich and profound religious experience. The horizontal relationship depended on individuals' vertical relationship; and accordingly Christianity, like Stoicism, was potentially world-wide and universal. That came to be realised as time went on.

Yet it was not a *purely* 'spiritual' community. The believers, whether ex-Jews or ex-pagans, were now cut off from their previous social backgrounds and inherited cultural associations – had indeed, as they said, passed through a kind of death – and translated into a new way of life with nothing but one another to depend upon. Socially, they were left, as it were, in mid-air. They were no longer either Jews or Gentiles, they were, as Diognetus was to put it in the second century, a 'third race' – in our sociological jargon, a new subculture. They could not hope to survive in a hostile world or resist the pressure to fall back into their own past without the support of an organised society, a 'temple' (a visible structure), a 'Body', in which they could share in a common life together.[1] St. Paul attached highest value to those 'gifts' which tended to the 'building up of the Body' and sustained the organic life of the society. Gradually there began to be developed the elements of an official Ministry – the New Testament shows us only the earliest stages of it – as the organ of unity and of continuity. There were corporate funds and a common table.

---

[1] That is why the Jewish food-laws, which seem to us relatively unimportant, presented them so early with a major problem. They created the same obstacle to fellowship and a shared life as, for example, a caste-system.

H

From the start, the Church had assumed responsibility for the economic support of its poorer members – the Love-command-ment could not require less than that – and by the fourth century, if not earlier, had developed a network of welfare-services, which the Emperor Julian tried in vain to imitate on a neo-pagan instead of a Christian basis.[1]

This was but one sign of its ethical creativity. Yet that did not, at any rate intentionally, flow out beyond the Christian community to make any impact on the surrounding world. It was channelled almost entirely on a closed circuit. For the Church itself, as seen in the New Testament, was virtually a self-contained system – a society within a society. For the mighty imperial civilisation round them the Christians felt no responsibility. The aims and ambitions of a godless empire had nothing to do with the heirs of the Kingdom of God. They were therefore conscious of no obliga-tion to attempt any reform of the social order, even if these tiny minority groups, many members of which were not even Roman citizens,[2] could conceivably have done anything about that, under an increasingly despotic Caesarism. 'Those that are without God shall judge' (I Corinthians v: 13). In Christ there could be neither Jew nor Greek, man nor woman, slave nor free. Within the Koino-nia all alike were equal. In their social contexts and daily occupa-tions these same people were altogether unequal. A slave could hold office in the Church; in the world, under Roman law, he was a chattel. But this situation the Christians took for granted. The existing structures of human life – rich and poor, masters and slaves – were just there, whether so ordained by God's creation or, as Christian theology was to suggest later, permitted as conse-quences of the Fall. They made no attempt to alter or 'reform' them. (For the Thomist attempt to deal with this anomaly, see p. 132.)

The Christians had their own business and vocation. They were called to be 'an elect race, a royal priesthood, a holy nation, to shew forth the excellencies of him who called them out of dark-ness into his marvellous light' (I Peter ii: 9). Holiness was inter-preted as separation – an idea which still survives in the modern

---

[1] See Harnack, *The Expansion of Christianity*, I, Ch. III.

[2] This is true of the New Testament period – see for example Acts xvi: 37, xxii: 25; later on Caracalla (A.D. 211–217) conferred citizenship on all provincials.

Church, but now needs very critical examination. This therefore becomes the normative ideal. 'Come ye out from among them therefore, my people, and be ye separate, saith the Lord, and touch no unclean thing' (II Corinthians vi: 17, 18). That referred directly, at Corinth, to the risk of pollution involved in mixed marriages and in contact with sacrifice in the pagan temples, but it seems to have been the general governing principle. The world, as St. John said, 'lies in the evil one' (I John v: 19), and Christians were people who had been called out of it into membership of the holy community; the less contact they had with it, the better. This was not altogether feasible in practice.[1] Christians must earn their living in the 'world', they must buy their food in the ordinary market, they might be involved in cases in the courts, and I Corinthians is a 'classic' document for Christian life in a mixed society. But St. Paul's concern in his pastoral advice was how to preserve the purity of the Church, rather than how the Church could discharge any duty it owed to society at large. Such an idea would not have occurred to him.

There was, however, one inescapable fact to which Christianity had to define its attitude, and that was no less than the imperial Government. The Church could not exist as a society, any more than the society which contained it, without the protection of Roman law, the Roman guarantee of the corn-supply – few cities in the ancient world had food in hand for more than three weeks – or the legions standing on the frontiers. And as to that, the rather sharp dualism which is so evident in the Johannine books is not to be found elsewhere in the New Testament. St. Paul, who knew what the Christian mission owed to the Roman roads and the *Pax Romana*, took a positive attitude towards the State as the source and guarantor of the *pax terrena* without which the Christian society would perish. (In this, he was followed by St. Augustine later.) He strongly urged the duty of civic obedience and unquestioning loyalty to Caesar (Romans xiii: 1–7). The Caesar when he wrote that was Nero.

But of course there was always another side to this. At the heart of the Roman society was Emperor-worship – the idolatry of organised power which is still the anti-Christ in the world today – and with this the Christians could admit no compromise. Thus seen,

[1] Where did they send their children to school? See William Boyd, *The History of Western Education*, A. & C. Black, 1964, Ch. III.

the State embodied and personified all that was in opposition to the law of Christ. It could not be regarded as something good in itself – many must have thought that St. Paul had gone too far; it could at best be something that God permitted because of or as a punishment for sin. This ambivalent attitude towards the State as at once an order of God's creation and a necessary evil due to the 'Fall', runs all the way through Christian history.[1]

From the time of the Flavian Emperors onwards the Church was in theory an outlawed society and to be a Christian was to be guilty of treason.[2]

Whenever active persecution flared up, then it was inevitable that the State should appear to them under the image of the Great Beast, the Satanic opponent of the reign of Christ, the incarnation of the power of evil. *Regnum Caesaris regnum diaboli.* Relative detachment from the social environment then becomes naked opposition to it. 'What has Athens to do with Jerusalem?' At such times the radical or 'exclusive' Christians, of whom Tertullian is the most often quoted, disclaiming all kinds of involvement in or obligation towards Roman society, must have seemed to many to be the realists, who accepted the sheer facts of the situation. Was there anything else that the Church could do at such times than to bear its witness, 'to be the Church', to renounce the world along with the flesh and the devil, and to wait in faith and patience for the Lord's coming? The Church under outlawry and persecution, as it has been and is again in our own time behind the two 'curtains' if not elsewhere, driven back, as it must be, within its own lines and confined there by legal barbed wire as well as by economic deprivations, can have very little freedom of manoeuvre. In such a case it is doing its work greatly through common worship and fellowship in suffering, keeping the Christian faith alive at all. We must recognise that humbly and with deep respect. But that is not at all same as saying that in face of an unresponsive, indifferent or even actively hostile society in a secularised climate of opinion, the Church today should retire within its own lines, marking off a reserve called Sacred or Religious and trying to live in a churchy world of its own, turning the Church into a kind of club for those

[1] For further discussion see Ch. X on God and Caesar.
[2] For the possibility of prosecution 'for the name', not simply for criminal offences, see I Peter iv: 15, 16. But notice that even so Christians are bidden to honour the King; ii: 13 ff.

who enjoy that kind of thing. Religion that is not embedded in the common life too soon degenerates into religiosity, and an inward-looking Church is a dying Church.

II

It might be supposed that Constantine's conversion would have brought a radical change in the relationship. A new day was dawning – but what was going to happen? What could come of this paradoxical alliance, in which Constantine, deified as Roman Emperor, was acclaimed by the Church as Apostle and near-saint? Was there now to develop a 'Christian Empire'? Or would the Empire swallow the Church, using it, as the Emperor probably meant, to revivify and restore the imperial system and secure the fulfilment of the Roman dream? The alliance was from the first full of tensions and the two allies were really at cross-purposes. The Church was quick to use the new liberty and the endowments which were lavished on it to consolidate and strengthen its own position. The bishops become territorial magnates. The clergy become a powerful clerical caste. Prominent laymen are raised to high positions. It was easier now, and on the whole safer, to be a Christian than not to be a Christian – and it is the commonplace of all the history books how all this tended to infect the Church with worldliness and a compromising temper.[1] Constantine may have believed quite sincerely that Christianity as the true religion would bring moral and spiritual health to an empire which had no faith to live by. He would not have been human had he not expected that the Church, in its gratitude for his princely favours, would support and buttress the imperial throne. But the Nicene definition gave the bishops a new independence and spiritual authority. Constantine may have talked about 'My bishops' and have thought of them as largely his own officials, but they could be disappointingly independent. It was not long before St. Ambrose could inflict a public humiliation on the Emperor Theodosius at Milan.

The Church had been a State within a State. Now, with its very fast increasing numbers and its more highly developed organisation, more or less coterminous with the Roman world, it

[1] The Monastic movement was to a large extent, in the early stages, a protest against the worldliness of the institution. Papal strategy later contained it inside the institution.

became more like an empire within an empire, or rather an empire side by side with an empire, spread over the same geographical area, under the same imperial constitution, yet largely autonomous and self-contained. There were in fact two parallel societies in no organic relation to one another. How that relationship came to be defined is the key to the history of the middle ages.[1]

But the Edict of Milan initiated a movement which could only end in the 'Christian Society', the mediaeval *Corpus Christianum*. The whole trend is steadily moving henceforth in the direction of a Christian empire. The position could not remain where Constantine left it. Theodosius, who had been baptised as a 'catholic' (i.e. not an Arian) in the third year of his reign, seems to have been genuinely convinced of that and set himself to embody the true religion in the legal framework of the imperial code. 'As the real prototype in history of the "Christian prince", he was profoundly concerned to work out the logic of his position, and it is this fact . . . which determined the scope and character of his effort to bring about a radical readjustment of existing relationships between the temporal and the spiritual powers.'[2] He dropped the title of *Pontifex Maximus*, hitherto borne even by Christian Emperors, and later, by an ironic paradox, to be transferred from the Caesars to the Popes, and proceeded on a course which was to end in the complete subordination of the temporal to the spiritual power. An enormous volume of 'Christian legislation', embodied now in the Theodosian Code, did not merely confer upon the Church new privileges and immunities, or attempt to amend existing Roman laws – particularly those concerning the family – in what were claimed to be 'Christian' directions: it was a deliberate attempt 'to "realise", within the framework of the Roman system, the forms of a Catholic state'.[3]

[1] 'It is strange that with all Jerome's deep feeling about the fall of the ancient world, he thinks the preservation of virginity more important than victory over the Vandals and Goths. Never do his thoughts turn to any practical measure of statesmanship; never once does he point out the evils of the fiscal system, or of reliance on an army composed of barbarians. The same is true of Ambrose and Augustine. Ambrose was a statesman, it is true, but only on behalf of the Church. It is no wonder that the Empire fell into ruins when the best and most vigorous minds of the age were so completely remote from secular affairs.' Bertrand Russell, *History of Western Philosophy*, p. 363. But what about men like Gregory the Great?
[2] Cochrane, *Christianity and Classical Culture*, p. 324.
[3] Cochrane, p. 328.

It was a decisive moment in history when by the Edict of Thessalonica (A.D. 380) the profession of Catholic Christianity was defined as the condition of citizenship. To be a Roman was now to be a Christian, and an orthodox, Catholic Christian at that. Later decrees made various specified forms of heretical doctrine criminal offences. To be a Christian was now to be a Roman – to believe what the Emperor and the Roman See believed. And this was later to have momentous consequences. Nor was Christianity now to have any rivals. Within a very short time there followed edicts aimed at the total extirpation of paganism. The cults were proscribed and became 'illicit religions' just as Christianity had been in the centuries of pagan ascendancy. They were disendowed and their properties were confiscated. It was punishable to take part in pagan worships. The various colleges of priests were outlawed. The ancient pagan calendar was withdrawn and for it was substituted that Christian calendar – completed when, before the end of the century, the Feast of the Nativity was instituted to supplant the Mithraic Birthday of the Sun – which the western world still observes today. Paganism, it seemed, was now finally dead. The pagan gods had failed to save the Empire and the Empire, now become Christian, had killed them – or so, at any rate, Theodosius hoped. (Of course it was not as simple as all that. Old gods do not die, they go underground. Paganism has never in fact been extirpated, either in the Mediterranean lands or in northern Europe or in the English villages.) The grandiose structure now seemed complete – an organised, monolithic Christian Empire, with built-in legal guarantees, united in one orthodox faith and worship, supervised by a powerful, State-supported hierarchy; and the Christian frontiers almost coincided with the frontiers of Western civilisation. It foreshadowed the mediaeval dream.

But how much reality or substance had it? Was this in any real sense the 'Christian answer'? How far could the Empire rightly be called Christian? Can it be said that under the new regime any new significance or dignity had been imported into human life? Was the lot of the ordinary citizen beginning in any way to become more tolerable? Was freedom being enlarged or justice deepened or public abuses and corruptions purged, or naked power brought under moral criticism? Those were surely the questions that Christians ought to have asked. But what they had got in fact was not so much a 'Christian' society as a legal fiction.

'Theodosianism', wrote Professor Cochran⌣, 'betrays a fatal confusion of ideas. For to envisage the faith as a political principle was not so much to Christianise civilisation as to "civilise" Christianity; it was not to consecrate human institutions to the service of God, but rather to identify God with the maintenance of human institutions,[1] i.e. with that of the *pax terrena*. And in this case the *pax terrena* was represented by a tawdry and meretricious empire, a system which, originating in the pursuit of human and terrestrial aims, had so far degenerated as to deny to men the very values which had given it birth; and was now held together only by sheer and unmitigated force . . . While, therefore, under governmental pressure, the empire rapidly shed the trappings of secularism to assume those of Christianity, it remained pagan at heart and was, to that extent, transformed merely into a whited sepulchre . . .'[2]

But the Christian Empire was already tottering. Men had assumed that Rome was eternal – that she 'sat as a queen and no widow and should in no wise see mourning' (Revelation xviii: 7); but that illusion could not survive much longer. In the east, Justinian and his successors could still maintain a Byzantine State-church which persisted, somehow, for nearly 1000 years and still survives in a secular form in the Kremlin.[3] In the West, Rome had already lost control. Wave after wave of Barbarians broke the frontiers; and less than a century after the Edict of Milan, Rome was sacked (A.D. 410) by the Goths under Alaric and outlandish troops marched through the capital so lately dedicated to Christian worship. The shock of that disaster can still be felt by anyone reading the literature of the time. And indeed it shook the world out of its orbit. Rome has been sacked again and again since then but the shock was never so cruel as at that time, when the mouth of the bottomless pit seemed to open, and the Roman dream to be ending in a nightmare. For not only had the eternal city fallen; it had fallen in the hour of Christian triumph. Was it in spite of that triumph or because of it?

---

[1] As some in our own time have been tempted to stage a recall to Christianity as a political bulwark against Communism.

[2] Op. cit., pp. 337, 338.

[3] (Russian Christianity stems from Byzantium.) 'That is why the modern Russian does not think that he ought to obey dialectical materialism rather than Stalin.' Bertrand Russell, op. cit., p. 13, note 2. (The book was published in 1946.)

The pagan Old Guard, of course, had the answer ready: This is what comes of deserting the gods of our Fathers and surrendering to an upstart, anti-social, fundamentally subversive religion. It is those Christian 'Reds' who are the guilty men who have undermined the foundation of society. The government ought to have kept them all locked up. And after all their Christ has proved to be powerless. Christianity has been tried and it has failed. Our one hope is a revival of the old faiths. (But it was far too late for that now. Once a culture has been even superficially Christianised it can never find its way back to paganism. The choice is between Christianity and Secularism, as the twentieth-century West has been finding out.)

But for the believers the question must have been agonising.

If to be a Christian meant to be a Roman and to be a Roman meant to be a Christian, did not that imply that Christianity was bound up with the Roman 'way of life'? And if so, could it survive its dissolution? That question is being asked again in our own time.[1]

No less profound or far-ranging were the questions now crying out for answer. They were faced in one of the world's greatest books, written in Africa by St. Augustine, whose thought was to exercise a tidal influence on the whole subsequent course of Western history. Very few books other than the Bible have been so pregnant as *The City of God*.[2]

The City of God is the tale of the two cities – the earthly city and the city in heaven. But right from the start it must be understood that these are not simply the Empire and the Church. The tempting but fatal equation of the Church with the Kingdom of God has no sanction here. Whatever later centuries have read into it, this book is not about Church-and-State relationships: the

[1] The British people have not yet recovered from the psychological trauma inflicted by the loss or transference of their Empire. But the life of the indigenous churches in Asia and Africa shows triumphantly how wrong were the cynics who thought that Christianity in the dependent countries was little more than the ceremonial aspect of the *Raj* and would fall with it.

[2] There is a very good summary and discussion in Ernest Barker's Introduction to Dent's one volume (abridged) edition in English (John Healey's Elizabethan translation). Because of the abridgement, the references do not always tally with other complete translations. For exciting discussion of the political results and implications of St. Augustine's thesis see J. N. Figgis, *Political Aspects of St. Augustine's City of God*.

Church is not the same thing as the city of God, and the earthly city is not the same as the State. Nor has it any direct concern with the Papacy. All such themes are as yet anachronistic. St. Augustine is not discussing the frontiers between two institutions or jurisdictions. It may fairly be said that the ground-theme of the book is the ultimate opposition of two faiths, two rival and irreconcilable philosophies – the Christian reading of human life and destiny and secular Humanism as expressed in the classical ideal of *Humanitas*. 'Two loves made the two cities' – two attitudes to life, two value-systems. 'Love of self in contempt of God has built the earthly, love of God in contempt of self the heavenly. The one glories in itself, the other in God.'[1] Despite its great and splendid achievements – and the Christian is bound to acclaim them as real achievements, part of God's education of mankind – classical Humanism had proved itself unable to carry the structure which it had built. The disasters befalling the Empire on all sides and from which it had not the reserves with which to recuperate, showed that the philosophy on which it rested was morally and spiritually bankrupt. Augustine was the child of the Roman culture. 'In a world, the moral and intellectual foundations of which appeared to have been shattered, he clung doggedly to a faith that however "vicious" or defective in principle, the secular effort of mankind had not been wholly in vain; and he was determined not to resign himself, like so many of his contemporaries, to the cult of futility.'[2]

For the Christian thinker, the whole ambitious experiment had been sterilised by a false philosophy. That philosophy had interpreted human life as though it were absolute and self-sufficient, self-justifying and self-sustaining. It worshipped the Creature instead of the Creator. (St. Paul had ascribed to that central fallacy all the moral corruptions of his own period; Romans i: 25.) It had nothing but itself to believe in, and now it had finally ceased to believe in itself. Along that road there was no human future. 'By his presentation of the law of Christ as the creative principle and the *ordo* alike of the physical and the moral universe, Augustine's philosophy offered a faith to live by, a dynamic of progress and emancipation which would outlive the fall of a dying empire. In the course of it he uncovered the two

[1] Book xiv, 28: in the Dent edition, Book XII, 16.
[2] Cochrane, op. cit., p. 384.

concepts which are specially constitutive of the "modern" world, namely, Personality and History."[1]

The City of God owes a great deal to Plato. The question it asks is in principle the same question as Plato had asked in the *Republic* – What is it that constitutes a true society? And Augustine's answer is deeply coloured by Platonism. It is indeed in principle the same answer: the ideal or perfect society would be one in which all men are seeking their real 'end' or 'good'. The difference lies in the Augustinian or Christian conception of the 'good' – nothing less than the knowledge and love of the living God. The sub-title of the *Republic* is Concerning Righteousness: which is expressed, said Plato, when every citizen fulfils his own function and keeps his appointed status. (This, as has frequently been pointed out, comes dangerously near a caste system. But the notion persisted all through the Middle Ages [see p. 133] and it is what Shakespeare means by 'degree'.) But everyone will discharge his proper function, there will be a city of right relations, Plato had argued, only when the whole city is organised and ruled by the vision of that final good which all men are seeking, however mistaken may be their pursuit of it, and in which alone true 'happiness' can be found, the idea of the good, that is, Goodness in itself.[2] But philosophers alone can discern that. Plato was thus led to his famous paradox that the city ought to be ruled by philosopher-kings, who would so organise the society that everyone wants what the élite knows he ought to want. (This is strongly clericalist or theocratic and is almost the exact contradictory of the 'democratic' or secular ideal.)

The city of righteousness is an ideal city, laid up, says Plato, somewhere in heaven. The City of God is an actual society. Though not visibly present in the world in any institutional embodiment (for it is not identical with the Church), it is composed of the true servants of God, gathered out of every people and nation and tongue, who respond by faith to his gifts of grace, reborn from self-love (sin) into the love of God who is man's true end and in whom is 'peace' and bliss. It, too, is a city of right relations, obeying the 'order' of God's will for the universe, that order which is

---

[1] Cochrane, op. cit., p. 456.

[2] The Latin translation of *Dikaiosune* was *Justitia*, and this fact has introduced a legalist tinge into Western theology and ethics. Ernest Barker's translation was 'right relations'.

inherent in the creation, without which indeed there could be no universe, though in man it has been disorganised by sin. In Christ – the Logos by whom all things were made – perfect order is manifest; and he has brought redemption from sin. (This rests on the ultimate Christian theology: Creator and Redeemer are one God.) Earthly societies share, in their degree, in that order; they have some measure of justice in them or they could not be societies at all. No earthly society, therefore, is wholly evil. It reflects something, at least, of the Being of God. As St. Thomas was later to express it, though it does not conform to the absolute law of God, it is justified by a 'relative' natural law. The State has its place in the divine economy. Willed by God 'as a remedy for sin', it provides that measure of earthly peace and justice, that protection for the weak and restraint of violence, without which no society could continue and no moralisation of power could be achieved. The city of God 'uses the peace of Babylon', which is thus, as it were, in the providence of God, the servant and 'colleague' (*Coadjutor*) of the heavenly city.

On earth the two cities intermingle. But all societies in this troubled world (including the Roman Empire) are relative, contingent and perishable. God's city abides. 'The city of God remaineth.' It is moving forward to its consummation in that peace which is the eternal peace of God – 'the perfectly ordered and wholly perfect society enjoying God and one another in God'.

Thus earthly societies have their divine sanction. Within their own limits and despite their self-centred will to power, God's law is at work in them. What is disappointing is that for Augustine, if I have not failed to understand him, the relation between them and the City of God seems at the end to be simply eschatological. He does not seem to think that the citizens of the heavenly city have any responsibility for consecrating the earthly city to God's purpose as a better servant of human life as the Christian religion understands it. To the secular world he appears to be able or willing to attach no more than an *instrumental* value as the earthly condition for the city of God – and, maybe, for the contemplative life (see p. 132).

That may be regarded as a limitation which he shared with all his Christian contemporaries, and which was to persist into the 'ages of faith'. Yet it was a far less crippling limitation than the secularising of the Christian hope or equating it with the 'Roman way of life'. He gave the Christians a faith and a confidence which was not exposed to the accidents of history but could yet give a meaning to the course of history. And there is now no greater contribution that the Church could make to secular society than a re-affirmation of the eternal hope which gives significance to man's years in time.[1]

St. Augustine died in A.D. 430, while the Vandals were besieging his see-city, soon to destroy Roman rule in Africa – and the Moslem invasions were not very far behind. It was no more than forty-five years later that the Western Empire came to an end. After the resignation of the last Caesar – the unfortunate boy Romulus Augustulus, virtually deposed by Odoacer – there was never again an Emperor in the West. Roman rule was rapidly breaking down, as destruction and anarchy swept across the provinces – what happened in Britain was happening everywhere else – and ordered civilisation sank in chaos.

Yet men refused to accept the unthinkable. The mystique and the majesty of Rome had left an impression that was ineffaceable. The universality of the Roman name – Spaniards, Britons, Gauls, Syrians, Africans, all alike called themselves Romans – and the unity of a world-civilization under Roman administration and Roman law, seemed now to be part of the very nature of things. The Barbarian conquerors felt a sense of awe before the material monuments and the culture of the higher civilisation that they had entered; some of them like the great Theodoric ('Dietrich of Bern' [Verona] regarded themselves as the heirs and protectors rather than the destroyers of the Empire. And the Church was co-extensive with that Empire. Neither was conceivable without the other. As the Church was still there, the Empire could not have perished. Thus it was, wrote Bryce, that 'the men of the 5th century, clinging to preconceived ideas, refused to believe in the dissolution of the Empire which they saw with their own eyes. Because it could not die, it lived.'[2] But it was to live in a very different form, and but for the Church it could not have survived at all.

---

[1] 'If there is a subtle Platonism in much Christian piety which fails to appreciate the Incarnation and what follows from it, there is also, of course, the opposite worldliness which so rejoices in this world as to fail to see the sin in it.' Munby, *God and the Rich Society*, p. 179. Cf. my *Questioning Faith*, pp. 170 ff. See also the Epilogue, p. 275.

[2] Bryce, *The Holy Roman Empire*, pp. 23, 24.

Few historical episodes are more exciting than the way in which Christianity proved its power to bring order out of chaos, to supplant the dark gods of the northern forests, to deliver men from their fears and superstitions, their savage rites and predatory impulses, to bring them the lamps of truth and beauty, to teach them something of the gentleness and moral purity of Jesus Christ, to give them new visions of human life in its length and breadth and depth and height, and gradually step by step to fashion a new Christian civilisation out of stubbornly resistant materials. Western civilisation is Christian civilisation; it is unintelligible on other terms and unworkable on any other basis. Just that is now its spiritual crisis.

The institutional structure was the bridge over which the Roman religion passed into the legacy of the successor States. As the Church had been an empire within an Empire, the ecclesiastical organisation had become very largely the counterpart of the civil. Like that, it was based upon the *civitas*, so that the clergy were thought of as the *ordo* and the laity, their subjects, as the *plebs* – incidentally, the first, fatal step towards the disaster of clericalisation. The dioceses, provinces and patriarchiates were based on the larger administrative units, with which as a rule their boundaries were coterminous. Thus in a disordered society the Christian hierarchy in possession were the natural leaders of the bewildered people and the conservators of the ancient culture. As both the Roman provincial organisation and the Germanic tribal systems broke down, the Church, with its proven organising genius and its inheritance of Roman law, remained as the centre of ordered government.

The inexperienced Teutonic kingdoms, attempting to establish some kind of order, some islands of legitimate authority, in a wild sea of anarchy and violence, had no recourse but to call in the bishops and clergy, the only educated men available and trained in traditions of administration, to do what they could not do for themselves. The clergy became, what they were to remain for centuries, the 'clerks' in a largely illiterate population, the educators, the experts in law and the personnel of the royal civil service – the situation familiar in our own history.

In Rome itself it was almost inevitable that the Pope should step into the vacant place of Caesar. There might be an imperial Exarch in Ravenna, impotent either for government or defence, a mere shadow of far-away Byzantium. But the mystique of the eternal city, now left, as it were, ghostlike and disembodied, came to be incarnated and personified in the one man who represented its traditions, the one man with Roman authority in his voice and who was still administering Roman law (not only to Christians) from his episcopal chair. Gregory the Great well illustrates the process.

Meanwhile, the acceptance of Catholic Christianity by the powerful, emergent Frankish kingdom was preparing the way for a changed balance of power which involved a new 'axis' for the Christian world. Leo III took the final step when, regardless of his allegiance to Byzantium, he solemnly crowned Charles the Great as Emperor (Christmas Day, A.D. 800). 'From that moment modern history begins.' The Roman empire was to come alive again in Christian form as the Holy Roman Empire, which was at once united and distracted, so long as it lived, by the love-hate relationship between the Germanic Empire and the Papacy.

There could not be, in mediaeval theory, any rivalry between the two systems. In the heyday of the Holy Roman Empire, there were indeed two names for the same system – one single body, the *Corpus Christianum*. 'A king could not be universal sovereign, for there were many kings. The emperor must be, for there had never been but one emperor; he had, in older and brighter days, been the actual lord of the civilised world; the seat of his power was placed beside that of the spiritual autocrat of Christendom. God reigns supreme over heaven and earth. The Vicar of Christ, raised above all Christians, rules over the souls of men in this world: the emperor, as his earthly vicar, rules over their temporal welfare. The spiritual and the temporal power are related to one another as soul to body.'[1]

III

Here, then, is the famous mediaeval synthesis, the universal Christian civilisation – a society dedicated to a proposition, in

[1] 'It was characteristic of the middle ages that, demanding the existence of an emperor, they were careless who he was or how he was chosen, so he had been duly inaugurated; and that they were not shocked by the contrast between unbounded rights and actual helplessness. At no time in the world's history has theory, pretending all the time to control practice, been so utterly divorced from it. Ferocious and sensual, that age worshipped humility and asceticism: there has never been a purer ideal of love nor a grosser profligacy of life.' Bryce, op. cit., p. 121.

which all thought and all forms of human activity and the very idea of what constitutes a society were directly inspired and directed by religion and a uniform creed which all held in common, and which was imposed both by the temporal and by the spiritual authority (for it was in its very nature a 'closed' society) – an essentially 'sacral' or religious culture in which life was a whole and its own acknowledged centre was man's true end in God and eternity. That gave that profoundly religious age a greatness, a depth, a sense of meaning and mystery which makes the culture of our rationalistic and sceptical age seem cheap and tawdry. It unified knowledge; and there were no 'two cultures', no 'crisis in the university'. It nurtured Dante and Giotto, it built the cathedrals, it produced saints, it created great works of art, it united mankind in the worship of the true God. Or so we think or so it did in theory. Yet it must be remembered that its superb achievements were erected over an abyss of squalor, disease, violence, cruelty and oppression, while the feudal lords went their own way regardless, and the masses were largely despised and left out of account. Christians today look back on that age nostalgically. But how far was this really a Christian society? And is this what a Christian society must mean or ought to mean? There are few things about which it is easier to talk nonsense or to be hypnotised by a legend than about the so-called ages of faith.

The intellectual basis for Christendom was laid by the philosophy of the Scholastics and pre-eminently by St. Thomas Aquinas. It was his magnificent intellectual structure which provided the philosophical support for a universal Christian civilisation; and although, as we shall see, the Thomist notion of what constitutes a Christian society has tended in practice to become fixated in the circumstances and conditions of its own time, the general thought of St. Thomas had within it the dynamic principle which could reach beyond that. The system was built not on Plato but on Aristotle – as *par excellence* 'the philosopher'. This carried with it the Aristotelian interest in particulars, in actual things, and especially in natural phenomena. Philosophy, as they both understand it, is the study of nature in its totality. Here were the seeds of Christian renaissance in a new concern for experimental as opposed to a merely deductive science, led by Franciscans such as Roger Bacon, who was contemporary with Aquinas. This, it has been remarked, was the same spirit as prompted the protests of

Galileo against the traditionalism of 'Greek' science (supposedly Aristotelian) in the seventeenth century.[1] Thus the breakdown of the intellectual structure by which mediaeval Christendom was sustained was partly, at any rate, brought about by influences within Christianity itself, and not simply by a 'revolt against religion'.

Our concern here, however, is with his *moral* philosophy. This too depended, as we have seen already (Chapter Two), on a substructure of Aristotelian ethics. The authority to which St. Thomas appeals for his moral judgements is not, for the most part, the New Testament or the Christian revelation but 'the philosopher' and the law of nature. His great strength is that he founds morality not on any specifically Christian doctrine but squarely and massively on Reason; as such it has universal validity. For him, as Gerald Vann put it, Christian ethics 'comprises principles of conduct which are not confined to Christianity or Judaeo-Christianity but are in effect universal: these are called the "natural law" as being consonant with and determined by the nature of man . . . thus far Christian and Humanist march together; and love of the law rightly understood *is* love of life'.[2] You do not, in other words, have to be a Christian to recognise the moral obligation of truth, honesty, chastity or respect for life. It belongs to the nature of man as a rational creature: as I put it above (see p. 48), it is part of the way the world is made. The fundamental or basic moral principles men can, accordingly, find out for themselves – or moralists any-

---

[1] Galileo did not contradict the Bible; his offence was to have contradicted Aristotle (or at least the current interpretations of Aristotle), and that was too much for Jesuit inquisitors – even though at that moment Jesuit missionaries were teaching the 'new' astronomy in the far East. 'Unlike his later followers,' wrote Miss Deanesley, 'St. Thomas would have remained undisturbed by the discoveries of Galileo'. *History of the Mediaeval Church*, p. 175. But on a less 'popular' level, see the remarks on the 'myth of Galileo' in C. F. Von Weizsacher's Gifford lectures. The myth runs that the 'dark ages' were dominated by Aristotelian speculation, unfounded on observation, but that Galileo blazed the path for science by describing the world as we really experience it. The facts, says Weizsacher are almost exactly the opposite. Galileo did not appeal directly to experience and observation. 'The main weakness of Aristotle was that he was too empirical. Therefore he could not achieve a mathematical theory of nature. Galileo took his great step in daring to describe the world as we do not experience it. He stated laws which in the form in which he stated them never hold in actual experience and which therefore cannot be verified by any single observation, but are mathematically simple.' *The Relevance of Science*, Collins, 1964, p. 104.

[2] Gerald Vann, *Moral Dilemmas* (posthumous), Collins, 1965, p. 17.

I

how can find out for them – without recourse to divine revelation or acceptance of Christian theology. Though they inhere in God's ordering of the world, they can be discerned by reason apart from faith. The 'cardinal virtues' of classical tradition – Prudence (Wisdom), Temperance, Fortitude and Justice – are thus permanent elements in the human legacy and are taken for granted by Christianity. They are the indispensable foundation of the Christian life and a Christian society.[1]

On this foundation, common to the whole building, St. Thomas then plans the Christian superstructure. Christianity rests on revelation and can only be apprehended by faith, not simply by 'unaided' reason, though faith is not in opposition to reason and can indeed be rationally vindicated. Faith, however, presupposes the grace of God – a gift 'super-added' to his gift of reason, in which all men share as rational human beings. This gift is given to Christians through Christ and the endowments of the Holy Spirit. But grace complements, it does not destroy nature. Thus above and in addition to the ordinary social virtues which respond to the common requirements of society, but in no way either cancelling or transforming them, are the three so-called 'theological' virtues, the famous triad Faith, Hope and Charity – infused by grace and responding to the Gospel. Christians, therefore, are called to live on two levels – their obligations to God and one another implicit in the revealed law of Christ, as taught by the Church and sustained by the sacraments, and the common demands of human association – the family, business, civic life and so forth. The latter are the foundation of the former; justice is the foundation for Christian love to build upon. The social virtues, and indeed the whole task of preserving an ordered society at all, are 'ministerial' to the development of specifically Christian living, elements in the pursuit of man's true end, and so come within the circumference of God's will.

In the perfect society of God's creation, that is to say, apart from the Fall, St. Thomas holds as Augustine held, there would be no property, no law, no forces; the natural law which binds us is

---

[1] Whatever view may be taken about Thomist ethics as a system, it seems to me that this reminder is permanently important. It is fatally easy to be more religious than other people but less moral. Despite St. Paul there is a real sense in which the Gospel can never dispense with the Law. Protestantism can take its protests against legalism much too far. (cf. pp. 233). See Dodd, *Gospel and Law*, pp. 12 ff.

therefore relative; not the expression of God's absolute law but the law for society in this sinful world, that is, in the only world we know.

Yet above and beyond and transcending all this, even transcending Faith, Hope and Charity, is the will of God for man's ultimate end and perfection, the vision of God himself and eternal life.

Here, then, is the total articulated scheme, embracing the whole range of human life in a unitary Christian society, family, work, money, education, government, laity and clergy, every man in his own station, every man discharging his own proper function, all subserving the true end of man, within the embrace of the Christian moral law. There was nothing to which that law was not applicable, no aspect of life to which it was irrelevant. The Christian society is all-embracing: there are no alien enclaves within it, no department of human experience left outside it. The Church and the world are identical and coterminous. There is the complete and fascinating synthesis which still lives in subconscious Christian memory. It seems to us in our fragmentated culture in which religion is merely one department – in the popular mind a very unimportant one – among all the other functional specialisations, a picture of Christian society at its best, even, perhaps, in its archetypal form. What has the modern Christian to say about it? For before the ink was dry on the manuscript it was ceasing to correspond with the realities.

The concept of natural law in itself has already been discussed in a previous chapter (see Ch. II) and there is no need to repeat that discussion. We must here, however, examine certain weaknesses which seem to appear, both in the theory as stated, and in the constitution of that society which it both assumed and helped to keep in being.

(1) It presupposes a two-tier morality, operating, or so it appears, in parallel planes; and if what has been said in Chapter Four about the nature of Christian ethics is true, we shall probably find it impossible to accept that. Justice, for example, is surely not just *there*, independently of Christian love, a foundation on which love can proceed to build? Justice is one expression of Christian love, but Christian love penetrates and transforms it, finds far richer meanings in what is just – what is due to a man depends on what you think a man is – and may perhaps end in transcending it altogether. And the same would apply all along the

scale. Surely, once Christianity has come in it will, or should, transform a man's whole outlook and leave no moral positions quite as it found them.

(2) Given the belief in some uncorrupted society existing somewhere before a historical Fall – though the Bible in fact says nothing to encourage it – anyone can understand the intention behind the idea of 'relative' natural law. Yet it certainly seems to be vulnerable to criticism. For it really involves, as Niebuhr pointed out, that the Church has got to say in the same breath both that things like inequalities of wealth, slavery, litigation and the use of force are contrary to the will of God and that nevertheless they are willed by him because of or as a punishment for sin. And that takes all the moral dynamic out of any attempt to redeem the social order. Moreover it lends itself much too easily to the moral dualism which is so crippling if not in Luther himself, at least in Lutheranism.

(3) The great thing about the Thomist ethic is that it brings the ordinary man with his traditional 'bourgeois morality', the morality of 'my station and duties', and even a standard of common or garden decency under the aegis of Christianity. The 'merely moral' life is an achievement which is only made possible by the grace of God, little though the average sensual man may recognise that. (It is indeed rather a weakness in St. Thomas that he did not emphasise that himself.) But all the same, the two-tier morality does seem to suggest a two-tier design in the structure of the Christian society. As a monk and an Aristotelian, St. Thomas was bound to believe that the contemplative life is in some way 'higher' or more Christian than the life of practical affairs, the 'religious' life holier than the secular – an idea which is fundamentally inconsistent with the Christian theology of the Incarnation. Few Christians will doubt, and many will wish to emphasise, that some men and women in every generation are specially called to the 'religious' life. But time devoted to religious exercises is not time given to God in any sense more than time devoted to getting on with one's job or meeting the Christian claims of family life. Contemplation is not in itself 'more spiritual' than recording a vote or managing a business.[1] But because he thought as he did St. Thomas is led to a quite illegitimate *grading* of Christians into more perfect and less perfect – that is, in effect, into religious and

[1] See the criticism of Jeremy Taylor on this score in Waddams' *A New Introduction to Moral Theology*, S.C.M., 1964, pp. 87, 88.

secular, and that served to justify the disastrous clericalism which stifled the life of the mediaeval Church and almost left it, as Yves Congar said, like a priesthood without a church at all.

Troeltsch remarked that St. Thomas had introduced an idea which is not yet found in the New Testament – 'the incorporation of the existing situation into the cosmos of life-values'.[1] But the whole notion of secular vocation was something that had still to be worked out and this could not be till changed economic circumstances opened up professional careers outside the sphere of the Church and the Law.

(4) The synthesis achieved by St. Thomas reflects the actual social situation at the beginning of the thirteenth century and could only have been achieved in that form at that particular moment in history. (Troeltsch showed, for example, how deeply it is coloured by the mediaeval small-town economy.) It reflects an essentially static, hierarchical and paternalistic social order, supported by a deductive philosophy in which everything follows from logical necessity, so that there is no real room for change or redistribution of the social balances. Everyone must stay in that state of life into which it had pleased the syllogism to call him. (Even Luther was to say that an attempt to move up into a higher class was sinful, a violation of God's appointed order.) Thomism, with its Aristotelian background, had no real historical understanding, and therefore its idea of the 'natural' order is inevitably conditioned by history and fixated in mediaeval conditions. Once again, the relative is absolutised. As Troeltsch complains, 'Nothing ever happens. All that is essential is already in existence, has been already "given" . . . no room at all is left for any idea of a great social transformation which the state, by means of new legislation, might introduce for the moulding of new conditions.'[2]

Justice was for the mediaeval mind the supreme good, and in those wild times it is easy to understand that. But if Justice was interpreted as *ordo* and *ordo* envisaged in terms of rational concepts, the ideal of society that emerges is bound to be static rather than dynamic. The result has been that the Church, all through the centuries, has tended to think of the Christian social ethic rather in terms of Justice than Love, as the preservation of an appointed order rather than a redemptive transformation of it. This is part of

---

[1] Troeltsch, *Social Teaching I*, p. 294.
[2] Op. cit., p. 1308.

the price of a rightful reliance on Reason – till Reason itself, in the age of the enlightenment, becomes radicalism and acts as a social solvent (p. 44). Perhaps what Christian theology really says, what is involved in saying that God is Love, is that Order, whether in nature or history, is not something that is just 'there', but something that is to be and is being achieved – is, indeed, what the creative process means – and is achieved by sacrificial Love. (The Logos is the Redeemer of the world. Creation and 'Atonement' meet together.)

The mediaeval synthesis could not be permanent. Like the Roman Empire it had to make way. The question is, did the inevitable transition from mediaeval to modern carry with it the necessity that the new kind of society should be less Christian than what it had supplanted? In other words, does a 'Christian' society *mean* what it seemed to mean to the Middle Ages?

Quite apart from the rising forces of nationalism which were to destroy the original pattern of 'Christendom', the realities of the *Corpus Christianum* were dropping out at least by the fifteenth century. But the idea lived on and is not quite dead yet. It was certainly not destroyed by the Reformation. Both Lutheranism and Calvinism accepted it. Neither Luther nor Calvin supposed that they were founding new sectarian 'churches': they thought they were reforming the Catholic system, reforming a Church which embraced the entire community.[1] Lutheranism tended towards a State-church, Calvinism towards a Church-state; but both believed in a unitary society. (This appears even in the cynicism of *cuius regio, eius religio*.) Neither could have conceived a neutral State or one in which heresy was tolerated or real freedom of opinion safeguarded. And the notion that both a Christian society and the maintenance of political cohesion required uniformity of belief, so that nonconformists of any colour, even if tolerated at all, must be kept in their place by civic disabilities, dominated the English Restoration government and persisted well into the nineteenth century. It was not finally disavowed here until the Catholic Emancipation Act.

The Restoration parliament was still thinking of politics in theological terms. By the middle of the eighteenth century men were

[1] On this see John Baillie, op. cit., pp. 22 ff.

talking the very different language of secular, rationalistic common sense. Under the Enlightenment both Reason and Natural Law take on new connotations (see pp. 36, 44). Reason now becomes the critical instrument, probing all traditional institutions, and natural law is employed as a fulcrum to assist the rising demand for emancipation from political or religious authoritarianism. The American Declaration of Independence and the Constitution of the United States are (in the eighteenth century sense of the words) 'Natural Law' rather than 'Christian' documents. The secular, neutral State came into being. But it would have been extremely, and rightly, angry to be told that it had ceased to be Christian. Just what will a Christian society mean now? Can there still be a theology of politics?

Chapter Seven

THE SECULAR SOCIETY

RELIGION becomes relevant to the multitude in so far as it is expressed not only in doctrine and liturgy but in a culture. That was the mediaeval situation. Life was unified round a common centre and the whole culture was pervaded by the imagery of the Christian faith. 'At a time when actual living was still often brutal, harsh, foolish and cruel, the Church embodied rationality and ideal purpose: it gave collective dignity to human life at large as no other institution had ever done for so large a part of the Western world before. The mediaeval Christian was no follower of the intuitions of Jesus: nor was he, like the Romanesque Christian, one who turned away from the corruptions of a dying society: he was rather a person living according to the usages of the Christian Church, accepting its moral precepts, its laws, its ritual, its art, its language of symbols, its cosmology, as the medium of his own personal existence. The Christian Church now presided over life and death and all the momentous crises between. For each of these occasions it had a form and ceremony: to each of them it gave a rational meaning within the larger pattern of being.'[1]

Even the strange impulse to the Crusades 'was interwoven in men's thoughts with the insistent allegory which made the holy city inseparable from the heavenly Sion, the goal of life's pilgrimage and the object of daily aspiration.'[2]

In the modern, departmentalised society religion itself has become departmentalised, one specialised activity among others and seemingly only marginal to the culture. And that, rather than any overt difficulties of idiom, thought-forms and 'communications', is why it is commonly written off as irrelevant. Christians become despondent about this and tend to react to it like the Jews in exile, by apocalyptic dreams and power-fantasies, while they talk about 'recovering the lost provinces'. Or, like the Jews in mediaeval Europe, they acquiesce in a ghetto-mentality and think

[1] Mumford, *The Condition of Man*, Secker and Warburg, 1944, p. 150.
[2] Powicke, *The Thirteenth Century*, O.U.P., 1953, p. 81.

of the Church as a self-contained minority, a remnant in an alien society, while they talk about 'going back to the catacombs'. But neither meets the real situation, and both, perhaps, fail in Christian understanding. It must surely be recognised that what is happening is the ongoing movement of history and, however testing to Christian faith, we must not fail to see God at work in it nor fatally over-simplify the issue by thinking of it as merely anti-Christian. For indeed Christianity had a great deal to do with it. There are inherent in it creative forces which, because they cannot be confined within any one temporary social pattern, broke the bonds of the mediaeval synthesis and opened up for humanity new adventures. The acute academic thinking of the school-men stimulated the spirit of intellectual criticism which was bound to out-run the confines of their system, which 'broke down when theology became circumscribed, partly by authority, partly by its own logic, and so unable to admit other aspects of knowledge and truth'. But the further the pursuit of knowledge goes, the greater the specialisation it will require, until today one department of research can hardly communicate with another (see p. 148). And the same is true of all the technical processes by which modern society is maintained. So it has come about that the very forces which, during the high Middle Ages, were making for cohesion and unity have been making for division and functionalism, to produce our own fragmented society, a civilisation which is not a culture, which instils into sensitive and thoughtful men a profound experience of 'alienation'.

The break-up was partly due to external forces, political, economic and technical, But it was also partly due to internal causes, at some of which we have already hinted, and to the interior logic of Christianity. 'A Christian civilisation', says Butterfield, 'precisely because it must embrace so high a conception of personality, must move towards what Christians themselves may regard as its own undoing – towards freedom of conscience instead of greater solidarity in the faith. A world in which personality and conscience are respected, so that men may choose the god they will worship and the moral end they will serve – this and this only is a Christian civilisation when human development has reached a certain point.'[1]

If the Christian religion now seems to be left out, that is partly

[1] *History and Human Relations*, Collins, 1951, p. 132.

at any rate due to the mistake into which previous generations fell of supposing that their Rome was eternal; in other words, that a Christian society must always mean that particular form of society with which they, in their own period, were familiar. We must not fall into that mistake again. We must not talk as though what we now call 'secular' were in itself non-Christian or anti-God. The real question to be asked is this: Can the Church today 'create in a technological age what its fathers built of old, a Christendom, a culture in which men and women can affirm their work and their family and social life to be their Christian life and can offer its fruits in worship'?[1]

The State in England is not professedly secular. Disestablishment would make it so for the first time and it would break the back of English history. (Anglicans ought to think very carefully before they agitate for a step so drastic, even if they fervently believe that it would leave the Church in a stronger position. For the question that ought always to be asked is not What good will this do the Church? but How can the Church best serve the people?)

In a famous broadcast, Sir Winston Churchill said that on the issue of the Battle of Britain hung the future of Christian civilisation. Just how much did those burning words imply? Is the idea of a Christian civilisation compatible with the idea of a secular State or with a deeply secularised society? In constitutional theory at any rate, and in fact far more deeply and widely than that, Britain is still in some sense a Christian country, as our forefathers would have understood that, though just in what sense it is difficult to define. Blackstone could lay down in the eighteenth century that Christianity is part of the law of England. Even as lately as 1867 the House of Lords invalidated a will making bequests for what the high court of Parliament regarded as anti-Christian purposes, on the ground that this was illegal by English law. No court could conceivably take that line today.[2] In practice today the courts must be neutral – and from the Christian standpoint they ought to be – towards all religions, Christian or non-Christian. But as a distinguished lawyer has said, religious and political toleration 'rest on certain beliefs about man and society – the principle that the purpose of society and all its institutions is to nourish and en-

---

[1] *The Family in Contemporary Society*, S.P.C.K., 1958, pp. 22, 157.
[2] It was repudiated by the House of Lords (Bowman v. the Secular Society) in 1917.

rich the growth of every individual human spirit'.[1] This is a recognisably Christian principle. Toleration may have come to Europe partly in disgust with the Thirty Years' War, partly in a mood of political cynicism as though all religions were equally unimportant; but it rests on a fundamentally Christian basis. It is a vital Christian concern that men should be free to reject Christianity. Faith and coercion are incompatible terms. The secular State here stands on the Christian side as against the old-style Christian society.[2] It is notable that at its meeting in New Delhi the World Council of Churches passed a resolution laying on Christians the obligation to assist in building up the secular state – India was no doubt primarily in mind – with freedom and toleration for all religions, by contrast with monochrome regimes, whether anti-God or professedly religious. In this respect at least we may agree that 'the modern secular state is framed more nearly in accordance with the will of God as we see it in Scripture, in the incarnation, in the way God actually treats men, than in [sic] those societies which have attempted to impose on the mass of men what a small Christian group have believed to be in accordance with God's will'.[3]

Christians are part of the secular society. We live in it and we are dependent on it, and it is in a real sense part of us. Christians cannot live in a cultural vacuum. No man can exist or function as a Christian, any more than he can function as a human being, independently of the society which has moulded him. We think and act as twentieth-century men. We are bound up in one bundle of life with the whole twentieth-century social system, relying on the support of its institutions, making use of its technical expertise, and involved in the tensions and contradictions of movements still very imperfectly understood. We are part of the world 'out-

---

[1] Lord Radcliffe, *The Law and its Compass*, Faber, 1961, pp. 16–21, 65.

[2] 'Baxter supported Stuart sabbatarianism on the ground that "it will make men in some sort religious whether they will or not; though they cannot be truly religious against their will, it will make them visibly religious". In New England too, the uses of hypocrisy were discovered. "At least hypocrites give God part of his due, the outward part", wrote John Cotton . . . so hypocrites were "serviceable and useful in their callings" so long as they kept up their hypocrisy. As in so many other respects, the social husk of the Puritan discipline survived after it had lost its religious kernel'. Christopher Hill, *Puritanism and Society in Pre-revolutionary England*, Secker and Warburg, 1964, pp. 257, 258.

[3] Munby, *The Idea of a Secular Society*, O.U.P., 1963, p. 83.

side' the Church and the world 'outside' is within our hearts and minds. Thus, as Van Buren remarks, 'modern man is not "out there" to be spoken to, he is within the being of every Christian trying to understand'.

It is therefore entirely impossible for us to say what the early Church said to the Empire – What has Athens to do with Jerusalem? – and to try to hold aloof from the world around us. Even if it were possible, it would be blind and faithless. It was written that God so loved the *world* – not only 'good' and religiously-minded people – that he gave his only begotten Son. God's love embraces all mankind, and where men and women are, there the Church must be, trying to help them to make the most of life, to overcome their frustrations and despairs, seeking to understand their moral predicaments in the light of Christian insight and experience. The negative answer would mean abdication.

It would moreover be tantamount to saying, what is contradicted by the whole Bible, that God is concerned only with 'religion' and is not at work in the secular movements of history. God does not stop his work when men stop watching it nor withdraw his Presence when men are no longer aware of it. There is a great deal of wickedness in the world, but 'secular' does not in itself mean 'wicked'. And the Christian would be spiritually blind who failed to see what a vast amount of good there is in the secular civilisation of our time despite its apparent loss of belief in God. For example, the passion for social justice, 'the moral driving force of the twentieth century', is a very great deal stronger today than it was in the earlier Christian civilisation – and who will deny that God is at work in *that*? It is, no doubt, true to claim that Justice was the cardinal virtue of mediaeval ethics, but it was an almost entirely static concept (see p. 133). Secular civilisation has understood, as the *corpus Christianum* did not, the economic conditions of the good life; and, however unpalatable the admission, it has done far more for human welfare in this regard than Christendom ever did. The reason for that is, of course, partly technical. Only now have the material resources and social techniques become available. But it is also partly due to the fact that the Church, when it was in a dominant position, saw no real need to reform society. 'What for the early Church was too difficult, to the mediaeval Church seemed superfluous.'[1]

[1] Troeltsch, op. cit., I, p. 303.

Christians, who believe that the will of God is the fulfilment of human personality, are surely bound to trace the hand of Providence and the operation of the Holy Spirit in all these movements of social amelioration. The new techniques are a gift and trust from God.

If God is what the Bible says he is, then the welfare of human society is a concern to him. All who are honestly working for that end – whether or not they call themselves believers – may therefore be truly said to be serving God, and indeed to be on the side of Christ – he that is not against us is for us (Luke ix: 49, 50).

God's redemptive activity in the world is clearly not confined to 'religious' channels. How much has been done for the enhancement of human dignity and self-respect, and so for the moral enrichment of God's children, by such elementary inventions as nylon stockings and cheap washable cottons, by domestic plumbing and bathrooms and such-like; and still more by the application of new knowledge to physical health, to maternity, to old age. And God has yet greater things in store for us. It is now within man's power to abolish poverty and virtually to eliminate disease. What is not within his power is to control the hatreds and fears and lusts within his own heart. All God's gifts may be and are misused. Sin is an all-pervading corruption and no new techniques can deliver mankind from that. But there is no *necessary* connexion between the new control over nature and the growth of wickedness – if it is indeed growing – for lack of moral training and education and the modern defiance of the law of God. Secular achievements are real achievements, gifts of God and revelations of God, summoning man to wider opportunities; and the Church, as Bonhoeffer insisted, must meet religionless man in his strength, not simply waiting to cash in on his failures. Yet his very strength and skill may betray him; for it is as a rule what is strongest in a man, not his weakness, which is the point of moral danger, and that seems from the story of the Temptation to have been true about the Lord himself. Accordingly, the secular man of our time, who assumes that belief in God is merely irrelevant, needs to be reminded of two things at once; first, that he has in fact some real experience of God, some actual contact with him, already, through the 'secular' gifts which he takes for granted, and secondly, that he is in the gravest danger of destroying himself and his world together if he ignores or defies the law of God and God's transforming grace through the gift of Christ.

When we talk about Christianising the secular world, how do we envisage a Christian social order? 'A Christian social order', says D. L. Munby, 'will be a society in which men can live as God created them to live; and Christians are not a special kind of men. It will therefore be compounded of the ordinary tissue of social life; the ordinary ideas and institutions of the so-called secular world.'[1] It is probably true that there are no activities which are in themselves specifically Christian. Teaching, for example, or being a priest or a doctor, is not in itself more Christian or more religious than keeping a shop or working in a factory. The religion is in the spirit in which we meet it and the sense of responsibility to God in which we accept both its opportunities and its inevitable limitations.

But Christians have their own understanding of the nature and destiny of man and of how God created men to live. It will therefore be their perpetual concern to secure by all means within their power the realisation of those conditions, whether economic or legal or cultural, which will move any obstacles that may be removable and will make it more possible for men freely to grow to the full height of their stature as moral and spiritual personalities. In our complex, interlocking society, this involves the institutional structures, the social and political machinery, on which human well-being now depends. And the paradox is that the secular society, by transforming itself into a welfare-state, has become inextricably involved in ethics and cannot evade moral considerations, however much neutrality it professes. There is therefore pressing need for consultation, both at the centre and in the local parishes, between representatives of the Christian churches and experts in the various technical and scientific fields of human well-being – Christians and non-Christians alike, so long as they have the necessary knowledge – either to plan some immediate practical steps, or to produce an authoritative statement for the influencing of public opinion. By such methods the Church can count for a great deal, earning respect and the right to be listened to. On the other hand much harm can be done by amateurish pronouncements on social questions from pulpits or even *ex cathedra*. Stongest of all, perhaps, will be the influence wielded by Christian Members of Parliament or representatives in local government in the course of normal political debate without any direct ecclesiastical reference.

[1] Munby, *God and the Rich Society*, p. 7; cf. also p. 179.

It is in such ways that under the changed conditions the Church can function as leaven in society, helping to create a Christian social order. But it is important to understand that its work will now often have to be done, and in fact can often be done far more effectively, through organisations other than its own, not directly under its own aegis nor solely by agents in its own employment.

When the Welfare State first came into being some Christians tended to sit around lamenting that the State had now taken the Church's work away and deprived the clergy of their social mission; and certainly the popular reaction was that there was nothing now left for the Church to do; what it once did, Government now does and does better. But that approach was deplorably superficial. What in earlier times Christians alone did for the love of Christ, with their limited resources, they have now taught the whole world to undertake, whether through national and local government, or the manifold international agencies, with developed techniques and public finance behind them – and that is a veritable Christian triumph. The welfare services of the modern State now provide new and better equipped instruments through which the Church can discharge its pastoral mission.

These services urgently need Christians, with their knowledge of God's strength and man's frailty, to help with the personal elements in case-work. And, as Beveridge always predicted, the greater the volume of statutory service, the greater the need for voluntary work. (Incidentally, the new situation seems to require of the Church some reassessment of its pastoral ministry – and of 'pastoralia'; but that is rather beyond the scope of this book.) But Christians have their own distinctive approach to the whole concept of the Welfare State. Christians will always be asking What is welfare? And that is an essentially theological question.

Thus the death of the sacral society in its Christian form – for it still survives in other forms – does not or should not mean that any hope of a Christian social order is now ruled out. We tend to become obsessed with the evils which corrupt contemporary society and to blame them all on 'secularisation'; this is the too-familiar theme of the pulpits – and no doubt I have often succumbed to that myself. We should be wrong if we minimised the evils. But the whole picture will surely be out of focus if we are not able to see the hand of God in the world of our time, and not only the tail of the Devil. And what I have been trying to suggest is that much in the post-war secular society seems to be full of vitality and promise, offering Christians wider opportunities and unexpected alliance and support, despite its repudiation of Christianity; and in all that God is evidently at work. He has not left himself without witness. We cannot reserve some particular area in the total situation for God and ascribe the rest to historical or natural causes. He must be at work in it everywhere or nowhere.

That, needless to say, must not be taken to mean that whatever happens in it is God's will or that the purpose of God can be equated with the actual dialectic of history. After all, we are trinitarians, not pantheists. We shall need deep and disciplined Christian insight to discern what in secular civilisation is on Christ's side and what is his enemy, what are, so to speak, the moral growing-points and what are the symptoms and warnings of decay, what is of God and what is of the Devil: and true Christian judgements will not always tally with the stock ecclesiastical reactions. There will always be false Christs and false prophets and people crying Lo here, Lo there. We shall have to be extremely reserved and critical in claiming anything as 'the Christian answer'. My own generation was constantly in danger of identifying the cause of the Kingdom of God with the latest social or international cure-all, the League of Nations or some leftist policy; and when that broke down we felt that the cause was lost. On the other hand, we must be extremely careful lest we fail to see God at work in movements which may ostensibly deny him. When we have labelled Communism 'Godless', we have not thereby made a valid Christian judgement on it. That judgement would have to be based on quite different grounds – the end which it is attempting to realise, the legitimacy of the means employed to that end, the value attributed to personality, and in general the quality of human life which it seeks to create or is actually creating. The Christian must deal with realities rather than labels, and conventionally 'religious' valuations can sometimes fail to discern the real issue. When I still had a seat in the House of Lords, I felt more than once that Lady Wootton, starting out from avowedly non-Christian premises, ended in a more radical Christian judgement than some of us who sat on the Bishops' Bench.

More than one writer lately has spoken of Christ 'incognito' in secular society. That is sound Biblical and Christian doctrine;

'he was in the world and the world was made by him and the world knew him not'. And there are many movements in our world which do not call themselves by his name, and may even indeed in so many words repudiate him, in which surely we can see reflexions of the Logos, the True Light that lighteth every man. (We may recall St. Augustine's argument that no society could exist at all without some participation in the divine order, see p. 124.) The Church of Christ, as F. D. Maurice taught, is wider than its institutional frontiers; and the Church, in speaking to secular society, is not making claims for an Intruder from some foreign ecclesiastical country, but pointing to One who is in a real sense there already though still unacknowledged. And we must not even rule out the possibility that movements which were originally started in the Christian name and by Christian initiative have, in becoming 'secularised', been brought nearer to serving a recognisably Christian purpose.

The point I am trying to make may be illustrated and, I hope, sustained by referring to modern developments in education, particularly in the universities. The university as we have received it is a characteristic institution of Christendom. (In view of the current debate it may be remarked that the mediaeval universities like Oxford, Paris, Bologna or Salerno, were frankly and avowedly 'vocational'. Their purpose was to secure a supply of fit persons to serve God truly whether in Church or State, that is, roughly speaking as 'clerks' or lawyers, though Salerno was primarily medical. 'Vocational training or liberal education?' is indeed to a large extent a false antithesis which has been allowed to obscure the real issue.) Of course they were places of Christian education and the common lament in Christian circles nowadays is that they have ceased to be that and become secular. But the question is, How was that interpreted? Is it the fact that in becoming 'secular' they are thereby *necessarily* less Christian? We may note, incidentally, that the Church of England has made few mistakes more disastrous than its patronising and even hostile attitude to the first foundation of 'modern' universities, and the full price has not been paid for it yet.

Mediaeval Oxford symbolised in its layout what Christendom understood by a university and indeed by a Christian society. Within the city, bounded by its walls, houses, shops, colleges and churches were grouped round the centre of St. Mary's, the great

K

spire dominating the whole scene, interpreting, as it were, and giving meaning to everything that went on inside the walls. As the Christian faith made it a community, so it was what made the ancient university. That was what it was *for*, what the university meant – *Dominus Illuminatio mea*. Theology, as the queen of sciences, controlled the whole academic orientation. But theology was formal and deductive, consisting largely in analysing concepts and 'disputations' out of received texts. Everything, it was assumed, was already known; there was no need for the discovery of new truths, it was mainly a matter of indoctrination. (The Royal Commission in the eighteen-fifties complained that theology as then taught did not provide an adequate preparation for Anglican candidates for Ordination – Nonconformists were still not admitted – who were still the undergraduate majority.) Theology was too much like the wall. What was very imperfectly understood was that the genius of Christianity is essentially rather creative than constraining.

Right down to the middle of the nineteenth century it was assumed that the primary business of Oxford, and indeed of a university as such, was to guard and hand on a tradition. There was no need to find out anything new and new ideas would be dangerous and subversive. The minds of the young men must not be 'unsettled'. As for the notion that they might be taught Greek grammar or history or mathematics by men who were not Christian believers, that would be the end of 'religion and good learning' and destroy the whole 'idea of a university', the purpose of which was generally agreed to be 'to transmit a body of assured knowlege to their pupils rather than to foster speculative or original research. Men were to be trained in orthodoxy to follow moral virtue.' It could not have occurred to the clerical dons of that time – and it was the time of the Great Exhibition! – that a university might be a place in which the search for new truth was paramount, in which men might be deliberately exposed to all manner of strange ideas and conflicting theories, among which they must make up their own minds and re-examine the faith that they brought with them. That would have seemed to them nothing but apostasy. Thus when the University Commissioners (1852) proposed to relieve – they could not entirely abolish – religious tests and throw open the university, to provide for Professorships in new subjects and at least to encourage some advance in knowledge, that seemed to be the defeat of all they stood for and all that they thought Oxbridge ought to stand for. (The controversy about Research or teaching? and the clash between Jowett and Mark Pattison – and T. H. Green – was one skirmish in the bigger battle.) It was taking a Christian university and handing it over to something else – to Atheism. Dr. Pusey wrote, 'All things must speak of God, refer to God, or they are atheistic. History without God is a chaos without design or end or aim. Political economy without God would be a selfish teaching about the acquisition of wealth . . . Physics without God would be but a dull enquiry into certain meaningless phenomena; Ethics without God would be a varying rule, without principle or substance or centre or regulating hand. Metaphysics without God would make man his own temporary God, to be resolved after his brief hour here into the nothingness out of which he proceeded.'[1]

But the revolution, once started, gathered momentum, in spite of many attempts at clerical sabotage; the idea that the duty of a university is to seek for truth rather than edification and that everybody must be free to think unfettered by preconceived conclusions, unembarrassed by what J. S. Mill called 'the dead slumber of a decided (i.e. already fixed) opinion', gradually becomes axiomatic; and today the ancient Christian universities are in effect, no less than the new foundations, pluralist and secular institutions, in which Christianity, though officially recognised and even generously State-supported, is not protected and has to make its own case. Can it be doubted which of the two systems comes nearer to conformity with God's will? Christians ought surely to welcome the developments. And that not only because Christian faith is most healthy in a climate of free criticism but also, more objectively, because dedicated commitment to search for truth however disconcerting it may prove to be, is a fundamental Christian obligation.[2] It does not seem to me in the least to follow that the secularising of the universities necessarily means de-Christianising them. Indeed, the open-ended society may well be *poten-*

[1] This and the other quotations are from the extremely well documented and perceptive chapters XII and XIII in V. H. H. Green, *Religion at Oxford and Cambridge*, S.C.M., 1964.

[2] The State, through the University Grants Committee, supports Christian faculties of Theology in many if not all of the new universities, but of course any State-assisted institution must be neutral, pluralist and secular.

tially more Christian than the closed shop of the earlier Christian pattern. The Kingdom of God was compared to yeast, not bromide.[1]

As Plato said, that a civil constitution is the constitution of the soul 'writ large', so the twentieth century university is a microcosm of twentieth century culture, centrifugal, fragmentated and departmentalised with no acknowledged public philosophy, hardly any language of communication between the various specialised departments and hardly a common universe of discourse. Here is Moberly's *Crisis in the University*. How can a university hold together, how can it be conscious of a common purpose or be in any real sense a university, not merely an aggregation of students, without some commonly accepted world-view? The place that used to be held by Christian theology as the bond of cohesion being left vacant, what if anything is there to take its place? It is the current problem of the two cultures.

But it is far more than that – the problem of the whole future of the human race. As the Duke of Edinburgh lately remarked at Sydney, 'The outlook for humanity is very bleak indeed unless the engineers of humanity and the engineers of technology get together to design the sort of world in which mankind and all God's creatures can exist together . . . Unless these two cultures can grow together and work together, the development of the human community all over the world will degenerate into an aimless wandering like that of a driverless bulldozer. Science and technology are barren unless they form part of humanity's aspirations . . . Scientific and technological progress is not only valueless, it is actively harmful unless it is modified or directed by a social and humanitarian outlook.'[2] In the present, transitional situation in education and in the world at large, what can Christianity say or do to help?

---

[1] 'We do not deplore the anarchy and variety of ideas and systems but ask only that the sparks shall be kept flying – and indeed that there shall be more scepticism in both Christians and non-Christians over much of the spacious realm of thought – hoping that if the non-Christian is not converted even he may be induced to greater elasticity of mind. In particular, our educational institutions ought not to be quiet pools where intellect can comfortably settle down, but a seething cauldron of ideas, a fair arena for the clash and collision of intellectual systems.' Butterfield, op. cit., pp. 133, 134.
[2] *The Times*, February 24th, 1965.

Absolutely considered, Pusey was perfectly right. As nothing can exist without God, so nothing makes sense apart from its relation to him, and people today are only too bleakly aware of that. It may therefore truly be said that the knowledge of God is the presupposition of all knowledge and all understanding – the beginning of wisdom. With that, no Christian is going to disagree (it is really Augustine's *Credo ut intellegam*). But relatively to an educational programme and a Christian educational programme, and in the actual language which he used (in print), Pusey was making a catastrophic mistake – the old mistake about 'the queen of sciences'. All things, he said, must speak of God and *refer to God*, or they are atheistic. But physics, to take one of his own examples, has no right whatever to refer to God in the course of its physical investigations. The physicist may be a believing Christian and he will approach his study as a believer, well assured that all tested knowledge tells us something about the ways of God and may be offered to God's greater glory, but if he is thinking about final causes and theological presuppositions when he ought to be watching his experiment and entirely concerned with secondary causation, he will fail in his Christian vocation as a physicist. Moreover, if the experiment works out rightly, i.e. if the hypothesis was valid, then if he had been a professed atheist he would have reached precisely the same conclusions. There can be no 'Christian' scientific findings. There are no specifically 'Christian' physics or mathematics or history. Christianity, as we have already noted, has stimulated scientific enquiry; but the findings of science are what they are, and the Christian must respect them as such. Pusey, in other words, was presupposing that theology can in some way control or dictate the results of academic enquiry: and that comes very near to the lie in the soul. If theology wants to be the queen of the sciences in the sense of trying to regulate or rule them – it has plenty of ceremonial precedence – or as claiming a right to censor their conclusions, then it has not learnt its own lesson. For surely what follows from belief in God is that no intellectual structures – and that, of course, must include its own – are final; all are under the judgement of truth itself; just as no human authority is absolute, academic, civil or ecclesiastical; all are under the sovereignty of God.[1] Thus there is no 'Christian' kind of knowledge; what there is,

---

[1] Cf. the essay on Theology in the University in Richard Niebuhr, *Radical Monotheism and Western Culture*, Faber, 1961, pp. 93 sq.

is a Christian attitude to all knowledge – openness of mind, reverence and humility, within the total Christian world-view – and a
Christian purpose in the pursuit of knowledge which provides a
centre of intellectual reference and can thus furnish a true sense
of direction through all the mazes of specialisation and unify
seemingly unrelated disciplines. Christians, though they may be
in a minority, can do a great deal towards making this apparent.
That is their vocation in the university. About this I shall have
more to say in a moment.

What the Tractarian lacked was what the mediaevals lacked, a
true Christian theology of the secular. Von Hugel wrote somewhere
about Pusey himself that he seemed to be incapable of being interested in anything not technically 'religious', and that, as Von
Hugel so frequently insisted, tends to starve and narrow the
Christian life. Christianity is far more than 'religion'. Christianity
is an attitude to life. Taking Christianity into the whole of life
does not mean trying to make all life 'religious', for religion is just
not the whole of life; it means taking Christian obedience into all
of it and seeing it all in relation to God's will. Actions, in other
words, are not made Christian by injecting religious emotions
into them or using the language of piety about them.[1]

An industrial plant will not be made 'Christian' by hanging
religious texts on the machinery; it may be that the proper Christian approach to it will be the replanning of the structure or the
modernisation of the canteen kitchen. We do not need to 'refer to
God' directly in order to be obedient to his will or before we can be
faithful to his truth. The whole idea of the secular as something
existing, under God, in its own right, is due to the Christian doc-

---

[1] This can easily breed a strained and anxious pietism, or degenerate
into a shallow sentimentality. Cf. the following comment about mediaeval
religion, or religiosity. 'The strong need of giving a concrete form to all
the emotions accompanying religious thought (led to) an irresistible
tendency to reduce the infinite to the finite, to degrade all mystery. The
highest mysteries of the creed became covered with a crust of superficial
piety. Even the professed belief in the Eucharist expands into childish
beliefs . . . This familiarity with sacred things is on the one hand a sign
of deep and ingenuous faith, on the other, it entails irreverence whenever mental contact with the Infinite fails.' Huizinga, *The Waning of the
Middle Ages*, Arnold, 1924, p. 139. This is not quite the same point, but it
is a valuable warning against allowing the statement 'Christianity covers
the whole of life' to be equated with a different statement 'Religion covers
the whole of life', which is dangerous and, as I have argued in the text,
simply not true.

trine of Creation, which the Church has been for too long for-
getting. The created order is under the rule of God; but he has
endowed the creation with at least a relative measure of autonomy.
Life is comprised of manifold activities all of which are governed
by their own laws, all of which have their relative independence;
if we are truly to serve the will of God in them all require their
appropriate response – a response which will not be technically
'religious' – and if we are not to fall short of the claim they make
upon us we ought to be thinking about the matter in hand, not
specifically about God or religion. We cannot suppose that there
are two classes of things, one called religious or sacred and the
other secular or profane; that is surely ruled out by the Incarnation. There are not two classes of activity, there are different
qualities of mind and spirit, different attitudes or responses to life.
The opposite of Christian is not secular, it is rather what we commonly call worldliness – impure motive, an eye for the main chance,
godlessness or irreverence before life. A true Christian spirit will
'hallow all it finds' in its response to the manifold tasks and interests and claims and opportunities of life. The worldly temper
will make profanation of anything and not least of religion itself.

A good deal of confusion has been imported into Christian
thought and perhaps into preaching by the rather vague and unde-
fined meaning of words like secular, secularised and secularist.
They are too often used indiscriminately to suggest an apostasy
from the Christian faith. All our moral confusions are ascribed
to the fact that our society is now secular. But secular does not in
itself mean godless. What is meant by a secular State is a neutral
State by contrast with a sacral society organised and controlled by
religion – Christendom, or the Islamic State, or, in reverse, by
totalitarian Communism.[1] It need not be committed to secularism.[2]
According to the Shorter Oxford Dictionary secular connotes in
Christian language 'the world' as contrasted with the Church.
Thus secular clergy, as opposed to regular, as ministering in the
world and its affairs. In general it means 'civil, lay, temporal' and is

[1] There are non-Christian sacral societies – Pakistan, for example, or
Algiers – which are as it were national successor States to the ancient
Islamic counterpart to Christendom. See some striking articles on Religion
and Politics in *The Times Literary Supplement*, March 3rd, 1965.
[2] On the difference, see three good pages in Harvey Cox, *The Secular
City*, S.C.M., 1965, pp. 18–21.

chiefly used 'as a negative term meaning non-ecclesiastical, non-religious, non-sacred', as of buildings not dedicated to religious uses (1450) or of education (1526). Secularism, on the other hand, is defined as 'the doctrine that morality should be based solely with regard to the well being of mankind in this present life, to the exclusion of all considerations drawn from belief in God or in a future State'. It is in this sense that we speak of a 'secularised' as distinct from a 'secular' society. A secularist is one who believes in Secularism.

The Christian attitude to life as a whole and so to the various fields of thought and enquiry, however remote they may seem from religious concerns, is what can bring unity and coherence into the apparently unrelated and even disparate departmental interests of the new-style, pluralist university, – unity in freedom in an open world. It is unity, moreover, in a common purpose which bridges the gulf between 'technical' and 'humane': it is dedication to God's will for *persons*.

Christians are likely to be in a minority: the Humanist organisations at Oxbridge are said to outnumber the Christian societies in proportions of something like four to one. And though they will be given generous opportunities, Christians will have and should expect no privileged status. But in my own observation it is remarkable how penetrating an influence they can exercise. They will meet together regularly for worship, and the worshipping community of Christians provides a stable, unifying centre which fosters a real and genuine sense of community – in Christian language, a reconciliation – in the academic society around them.[1] Meaning for oneself and membership in community are, it seems, intricately interwoven, and both with the sense of 'belonging' in the scheme of things – that is, in the end, with faith in God and worship. The Christian interpretation of the world thus gives cohesion both to thought and to life. And the Christian world-view is through and through personalist.

In school education, on the other hand, we encounter a rather anomalous situation. All schools were formerly under Church con-

[1] This is also true in the wider society. The Provost of Coventry said in a broadcast that he thought the Cathedral would provide a focus, a 'means for this city to discover reconciliation within itself', for people to find out that they *belonged* to Coventry and to one another and were not merely unrelated units in con-location of stratified Departments. The full text is given in my *Mervyn Haigh*, S.P.C.K., 1964, pp. 208 ff.

trol. It was from the Church's pioneer work that at length the whole community has learnt that it must accept the responsibility of providing universal education. Christians, of course, are thankful that it has done so; and though the result has been to secularise, it is in itself a Christian achievement. Clearly, State-provided education must be religiously neutral and 'secular'. That, however, has not been interpreted, as it has been in the United States, to mean that religious teaching is ruled out. On the contrary, the Butler Education Act laid down that the whole national system was to rest on the foundation of Christianity. Religious teaching is given in school-time as a regular part of the prescribed curriculum. There is no other country in the world, so far as I know, in which State-provided schools are under this statutory obligation – at any rate at the post-primary level. It is now being urged from the secularist side that this violates the neutrality which the State ought to assume towards religion, and a lobby is pressing for the abolition of R.I. and the daily act of worship. The Church may reply that when you are dealing with children there can be no neutrality in education; if they are not being positively taught religion they will be absorbing a secularist world-view. A recent opinion poll seems to indicate that some ninety per cent of parents interviewed want religious instruction to continue and the rising generation to be brought up in fundamental Christian faith and principles. If, with whatever changes in syllabuses and in interdenominational arrangements, the present system is to be continued, the Church's duty is to provide the State with a sufficient 'supply of fit persons' adequately trained and qualified for a task which is of almost superhuman difficulty, to give the religious teaching in the provided schools. How long the dual system will continue in this country, nobody can predict. But so long as the Church does retain its own schools and its own teacher training colleges, it has its chance to display an exhibition piece, to present education at its best and to show what it thinks Christian education means. (Whether it knows how to use it is another matter.) But it goes without saying that this will not be limited to the technically religious instruction but will include the entire educational field.

All education will be bogus if it does not help to restore that 'structure of meaning' which has collapsed in contemporary society. We must not forget the warning of what happened when Roman education became 'rhetoric', teaching people how to be

clever, and how to 'get on' in a careerist society while it gave up
trying to teach them how to be good.

If we want to see a revival of religion, Christians ought to be very
much concerned with the content of statutory education – to press
for the inclusion of 'subjects' which inculcate a sense of depth and
mystery and stimulate and foster imagination.

But religious and moral values in education are communicated
not only and perhaps not even mainly through religious channels –
the Divinity periods or the Chapel Services. They are given and
almost unconsciously received through the ethos, tone and tradition of the society – the aims and standards found to be accepted
in it, what it approves and what it disapproves, what qualities
it holds most in honour, how its members treat one another.
And what will be distinctively Christian here, surely, is respect
and reverence for personality, the conviction that people matter
more than things, that the system was made for man, not man for
the system, that all that is taught and learnt has a 'human' purpose
– is a preparation for serving human needs, not only a certificate
for a good job – and that the object of the entire exercise is the
nurture and fulfilment of persons. (The word education, after all,
means nourishment.) That would be the hallmark of a Christian
school, however 'secular' might be the timetable. And indeed the
'note' of any society which can rightly be thought of or described
as Christian will be that it recognises, and is trying in all its operations to give effect to, the primacy of personal values.

Christianity is the religion of personality. It brings men the
offer of salvation, that is, of fulfilment and liberation as persons in
fellowship with God and one another. Salvation is primarily a
religious hope. But it is a promise for *people*, not for 'souls', and
therefore includes much more than religion. And indeed the
Church will best discharge its mission in the religionless culture
of this age if it will think about it in 'secular' terms, on more
elementary, non-religious levels.

'The mission is concerned with nothing less than man's full
salvation, but the meaning of salvation does not have to be un-
folded in religious categories. Indeed, it may be necessary to
lift it clear of every technical vocabulary, whether sociological,
theological or psychological, and spell it out in terms of inter-
human needs and relationships before its meaning can be brought
home with any force at all. A man can get mildly interested in

the idea of himself as a soul just as he does in the idea of himself as a case; but most of the time he thinks of himself as a person, and needs to be regarded as a human being. For it is precisely his human-ness which is threatened with destruction, it is the personal in him which needs to be saved. Behind all that de-humanises lurks the Enemy of souls, and the eternal issue is joined wherever the value of the person is threatened in the urban situation, wherever the freedom of the mind is subverted by propaganda. We wrestle against principalities and powers to maintain truly human relationships when, in the midst of tensions, cynicism and despair tempt us to abandon relationship. We are struggling for a rediscovery of meaning after the breakdown of every traditional interpretation of life. It is in these terms that today we have to spell out the great eternal doctrines and find them fresh and relevant.'[1]

Christians, therefore, will always be engaged in every enterprise which tends towards the enrichment and liberation of personal life, in some humble local effort or on the world scale. They will join in the fight against all conditions, material or physical, social, educational, which make for its deprivation or maiming – bad housing, physical and mental illness, ignorance, ugliness, the tyrannies of commercial exploitation, the inordinate powers of mass-advertising, and maybe against some of the axioms of the Law, for which property counts for more than people. (A thirty-year sentence for a train robbery; how much for raping, or murdering, a child?) With all this the Church will identify itself, bringing to bear its own Christian insights. But it will come into every situation not to dictate or to 'stand up for its rights' but in the form of a servant in Christ's name. In effect and in practice a secular society means one that is lay rather than Church dominated. But no society ought to be Church dominated. The Church ought not to want to dominate anything. Like its Master, the Church is in the world not to be ministered unto but to minister.

Yet, in the end, this cannot be the last word. The Church can never cease to be in protest. It may never silence its prophetic ministry. As Munby says, there is no society, however good, but, from the Christian standpoint, it cannot and ought not to be made better. The world is not, or is not yet, the Church. However far it

[1] J. V. Taylor in *C.M.S. Newsletter*, February, 1965.

goes, and by the principle of the Incarnation that must mean the whole way, in identifying itself with the world, the Church must yet remain in some measure detached from it. A Church that was perfectly 'conformed to this world' would have nothing important left to offer it, no authoritative word to utter, no redemptive savour to bring into it. An urgent need of the secular society is a theological critique of its still largely unexamined axioms. The Church knows that human personality can never be completed or fulfilled in any form of temporal civilisation – it is on pilgrimage to the Eternal City. Thus Christians here will always be 'resident aliens'. There will always be something 'strange' about Christianity. There will always seem to be something incommensurable with any standard of rational common sense about a faith with a public execution and an empty grave at the centre of its world-view. A Church concerned with man's eternal destiny will always be challenging to our society which, by and large, has accepted short-term pleasure as the only valid criterion of conduct, and it must expect to be branded as inhuman, puritanical and 'undemocratic'. But 'the only way of making Christianity seem important again is not to obscure its rough edges but to emphasise them'.[1]

Nor, however wide its compassion, however skilled its pastoral understanding, in ministering to hard-pressed men and women – and about that something has been said already (see pp. 24, 72) – may the Church lower the Christian moral standards in order to make them palatable or popular. If it did that it would break faith with God and deservedly forfeit the respect of men. If the salt has lost its savour, as the Lord said, it is good for nothing and people throw it out.

[1] From a review of the German edition of *Honest to God* in Gollwitzer, *The Existence of God*, S.C.M., 1965, p. 253.

The theme secular - secularised - secularist has been admirably presented by Alan Richardson in Ch. II of *Religion in Contemporary Debate* (S.C.M. paperback). But it was not published until this book was already in proof.

Chapter Eight

CHARITY AND CHASTITY

I

IT did not need a Reith lecture to remind us that Charity is the First and Great Commandment. That is what Christian ethics are about. What was surprising was the lecturer's notion that Charity might be in conflict with Chastity. Charity means, at the least, respect for persons, and accordingly never to use them as means to my own satisfaction, physical or emotional. Charity therefore clearly includes Chastity. But to say this carries with it that Chastity must be seen in the context of personal relationships and not merely of physical acts or abstentions, and in creative not merely formal terms (see p. 177). In the past it has been interpreted far too negatively – and still is in some Christian circles – and even equated with physical virginity, so that people have come to think of the Christian ethic as 'inhuman', cold-blooded and repressive.

Glad though I should be to avoid mention of a topic which is now becoming obsessional, no treatment of Christian ethics can evade some attempt at discussing the place of the natural instincts (including 'sex') in the fulfilment of persons. That, it may be urged, is the right way of putting the question. For what we ought to be thinking and talking about, if we are to be thinking as Christians or indeed as rational beings at all, is not about something called sex, but about people, moral personalities, about the Christian understanding and interpretation of human life and the place of biological instincts in it. And it is only within that frame of reference that we can be talking in Christian or ethical terms.

We must first disavow the fallacy of origins, as expressed in the popular phrase 'it is human nature to be' pugnacious, acquisitive or sensual. It is fatally easy to think that because man is a product of biological evolution, biology can determine our moral judgements.[1]

[1] For the fallacy of evolutionist ethics, even Sir Julian Huxley's, as involving a circular argument, see Owen, *The Moral Argument for Chris-*

Man inherits the pre-human instincts. But in man the inherited instincts are no longer simply biological facts. He is able to reflect upon them, work upon them in thought and imagination, to bring them under rational control, to choose the objects of their satisfaction, to direct them as means to his own ends and purposes; and in all these ways they are profoundly modified. Of course we can never ignore them or try to eradicate them. It is not merely a false spirituality, it is mentally and spiritually dangerous to starve the irrational and subconscious factors in us. (This does not mean the same as 'repressing' or controlling them; pp. 161, 177.) We have our roots in pre-human nature and it is at our peril that we forget it. But, as was emphasised in an earlier chapter, part of what it is to be a man is to transcend nature (including his own nature) although he remains all the time involved in it – to stand over against it and to work upon it.

In everyday language we frequently distinguish what is 'natural' from what is 'artificial' – organic from synthetic fertilisers, the growing crops from the processed food in a packet, the raw material from the finished product, the primitive instincts from conventional behaviour-patterns. And it is important to recognise that if we use the word 'natural' in that sense, nothing that man

---

tian Theism, George Allen and Unwin, 1965, pp. 15, 16. 'Morality can be derived from evolution only if evolution is first read in the light of pre-conceived moral terms. Morality is first equated with what is "more evolved" . . . but what is "more evolved" – the direction which the evolutionary process takes – turns out to be what is in accordance with those moral standards that we independently possess.' Huxley says that evolutionary direction requires that we should cultivate the fulfilment of human potentialities, but then goes on to add: 'Of course, not all fulfilment or enjoyment is good or right, any more than all biological development is progressive. It is the business of moral systems to make such valuations.' Thus on his own admission the evolutionary process does not provide us with moral criteria. And in any case it is surely quite illegitimate to import ethical overtones into what is simply a biological theory. That is one very widespread example of the naturalistic fallacy, i.e. defining Goodness in terms of something else. (We can say Pleasure is good, but we can't say (and mean anything) Good is pleasure.) Evolution is not another name for improvement or progress. Whether and how far it ever does involve improvement has to be decided on other grounds; as, for example, if we were discussing the evolution of parliamentary government or of the small car. But evolution is used there only by analogy and ought not to be used about natural phenomena (the evolution of species) where the criteria are biological, fitness meaning fitness to survive, not *deserving* to survive or 'better'. (See further on this p. 55.)

does is ever simply natural; it is always artificial, a work of art deliberately *contrived* to fulfil his aims and provide satisfaction for his desires. (In that sense and at that level Hume was right: reason acts as the servant of 'passion'.) This implies that in man the instinctive drives and hungers are just not the same as they are in his dogs and cats. Because they are elements in the life of a person and are thus the potential stuff of character, they can be humanised, civilised, moralised. (We do not just feed, we have meals, which are normally framed in a certain amount of ritual, and may in themselves become religious rituals.) They can be directed in one way or in another to fulfil a personal life or to wreck it. So the question is: How is a man fulfilled; what is he? Therefore a Christian theology of sex will be a theology of personality and the rightful place of the biological impulses in man's psychophysical constitution. Thus the ground-plan for any further discussion of sexual ethics and conduct today has already been laid down in Chapter Three.

But it is only within a setting of this kind and by some such order of procedure that we can deal with the so-called 'facts of life' as in human experience they really are, to say nothing of Christian initiation into them. We do not try to teach children not to be greedy by showing them pictures of the digestive organs, or to train them in controlling their tempers by giving them lectures on endocrine secretions: we tell them how human beings ought to behave. We try to supply them with some moral principles – or at lowest with some standard of etiquette – in the light of which they can learn to control and harmonise their still un-coordinated impulses and so to grow up, to become mature and adult. But when it comes to trying to forearm them for the onset of puberty and adolescence, too many educational authorities and even Church-sponsored organisations have supposed that the proper way to set about it was to show them films of the reproductive processes in the pond, in the fishes and in rabbits, and at last, rather shyly, in human beings, and that the knowledge of such facts, *in vacuo*, unrelated to *personal* life or (for Christian children) to God and the means of grace will enable them to cope with their clamouring impulses. But surely this is getting it upside down. The most important fact for them to know is how men and women are *different* from rabbits, what is meant by moral personality. For a Christian child the first and the most important thing is to learn that though he is cousin to the apes – which he knows in experience pretty well already – what he is essentially is a child of God and an heir of everlasting life, and that through faith and worship, prayer and sacraments, he may hope to grow up into Christian maturity, 'glorifying God in his mortal body'. Then 'sex' will fall into its due proportion and the 'facts of life' can be given him as he needs them. The isolation of 'sex' can do positive harm.

It is needless to say, I hope, that I am not arguing against the provision of frank sex-instruction to help boys and girls to 'know themselves' and to prepare them for marriage and parenthood. Of course such information must be given and it is primarily the parents' job. Indeed they ought to be told far more than they are. Young people do not know nearly as much as they think they know or as older people tend to assume that they know, and too many marriages break down for that reason. For sheer lack of physiological knowledge love may turn to hate on the honeymoon (and perhaps more often than we like to think) even after a Christian marriage in church and with the highest possible intentions. I am not asking for a prudish reticence, only that all our thinking on the whole subject should be in its proper framework and setting, personalist and not merely biological.

The world around us is haunted with sexuality. Aphrodite is resuming her ancient throne – for, as we have noted, the old gods 'never die' – stepping back into that dangerous vacuum to which I drew attention in Chapter One. This is partly due to the psychological consequences of modern social and economic pressures – the de-humanisation which seems to be inherent in a rationalised, technical society – and the need to compensate for them or escape from them, as well as to that moral fragmentation which tends to regard short-term gratification as the one valid criterion of conduct, and the general spiritual insecurity which leads people to think that in sexual relations they may find some kind of emotional anchorage. Some of these deeper underlying causes I shall try to examine in a later paragraph. But it has to be said that it is also partly due to shameless commercial exploitation. Sex is news and there's money to be made from it; much subtlety and high-power organisation is devoted to finding new ways of making it.[1] The whole atmosphere we breathe is vitiated with sexual stimulations and

---

[1] There is a perceptive discussion of the Girl (Miss America and her opposite numbers) as symbols of contemporary culture in Ch. IX (Sex and Secularisation) of Harvey Cox, *The Secular City*, S.C.M., 1965.

suggestions. And the Church seems to have got it on the brain too, ignoring far more important moral questions and going far to confirm the popular notion that Christian ethics means just this and no more. It would be far better if Christians talked much less about it. At the same time it is true that for young people, left in a transitional society without authoritative moral standards, this is the point of gravest confusion and, for some, of most painful personal perplexity, as well as the point at which Christian teaching can be most easily misrepresented and equated with negativity and repression. Any presentation of the Christian case which can hope for serious considerations must rest not on *a priori* propositions but on a study of human nature itself and the light which Christianity has to throw on it.

The inherited biological impulses are the driving power of the human psyche. It is not only physical survival but all mental and spiritual health too which are bound up with harnessing them in the right way. If they are starved altogether, that is suicide. If we run away from them or try to dodge them by driving them down below the level of consciousness, we are likely to be compulsively at their mercy. If they are uncontrolled or misdirected, we shall be like powerful cars with faulty steering wheels. Most if not all the personal disorders which are submitted for psychiatric treatment have situations of such kinds at their base. Moral breakdown is in the main bound up with failure to control, direct or sublimate. The instincts, as they are called in the older text-books, 'vitalities' and 'drives' as Niebuhr calls them, are the fundamental dynamic forces of man's psychophysical make-up. In themselves, they are neither moral nor immoral; they are just facts, the condition of our existence and the raw material of character. They are certainly not 'sinful' or shameful. They are the gifts of God the Creator, without which life on the earth could not continue, and as God's endowments they are essentially good. It is therefore not a religious or Christian attitude to be ashamed of them or of enjoying their exercise. We do not feel ashamed of wanting our dinner, nor is an under-sexed man or woman for that reason holier than another. But as often it is a man's strength rather than his weaknesses that betrays him, so obviously very powerful and urgent impulses are going to need strong control and discipline if they are to be offered to the glory of God.

A man so powered may indeed do well to remember that what

L

we call sexual desire is the strongest force in the whole organic world – the urgent march of ongoing life itself, which will batter down every opposing obstacle and accept no denial or defeat, caring not how prodigal is the wastage, how much death and suffering to individuals, to secure the continuation of the species. (Millions of eggs and sperms are squandered so that one new life may be brought about. Everything born must be removed by death in order that new life may succeed to it.) It will be his wisdom not to *provoke* a conflict, by exposing himself to erotic titillations which lead irrevocably to tumescence, with a giant whom he may not be able to master. For here if anywhere Coué's law is operative: in a head-on fight between will and imagination, imagination always wins.

In themselves the animal instincts are not sinful. But there is a (probably primitive) sense of shame attendant upon sexual activity.[1]

Freud, of course, attributed all guilt-feelings, which he regarded as always pathological, to the conflict caused by social convention repressing the primitive *libido*. But, as Niebuhr has aptly pointed out, the sense of shame antedates the social convention. While the control which all societies known to us have always tried to impose shows that the 'inordinacy' of sexual passion, both 'sacred' and potentially destructive, is the cause not the result of the conventions.[2] Mankind has never been willing to accept the idea that this, any more than marriage (see Chapter Nine), is simply a man's own private affair.

The primitive sense of shame still persists. Many people today are oppressed by guilt-feelings in all this sphere of emotional experience and need to be told that they are not guilty at all. It is not a sign of sin to have strong desires. It is not, or anyhow need not be, a sign that a man or woman is not in a state of grace if they have recurrent sex-dreams or fantasies. These belong to their

[1] This may be due in part to association between the genitalia and excretion. It is also probably due to some 'mystical' feeling about the 'sacredness' of the semen. (Compare the Hebrew feeling about blood; 'The blood is the life'.) In primitive thought the idea of the sacred merges easily with that of the shameful or unclean. Before what is 'numinous' or uncanny you stand in awe and you feel ashamed. The Old Testament regards menstruation as at once shameful (or 'dirty') and semi-religious. The aprons which Adam and Eve made themselves symbolise the primitive feeling of sex-guilt.

[2] Niebuhr, *The Nature and Destiny of Man*, pp. 247 ff.

nature as embodied spirits. What *is* wrong, or at the least extremely foolish, is to court stimulation of such fantasies on the wrong occasion or towards the wrong objects. For once tension has reached a certain point what follows is automatic and uncontrollable.

It can, of course, be objected that the use of the word 'wrong' is begging the major question. There are those who would insist that the gratification of the appetites is just a 'natural' function to which ethical judgements are inapplicable – that *coitus* is simply a physical act like having a drink or smoking a cigarette, and that there is nothing more in it.[1] But once again we must ask, What does 'natural' mean? For that argument is not merely shocking to clergymen, it simply ignores the facts of human nature – the facts, quite apart from any Christian judgement on them. Because man is man and not an ape or a goat, in him these impulses exist and function within a potentially moral situation. A dog feels a mighty urge and satisfies it and there is nothing more than that to it. He fulfils the law of his nature that way, and in following the way God has made him may be said to be obeying the law of God. But man as a personal and moral being requires more than physical satisfactions, and if he stays on the purely physical level he is behaving as something less than man. Moreover man, as self-conscious spirit, can make his desires the object of his own thought, and can therefore direct or misdirect them and can be deeply injured psychologically – and often, of course, physically as well – by the misdirection of appetite. Then he is violating his own nature, and in acting against the way God has made him may be said to be disobeying the law of God. A dog cannot 'lust', a man can. What are commonly called the sins of the flesh are essentially sins of thought and imagination. If a man 'sins in his sex', or becomes a glutton or a drunkard, that is not because sex or hunger or thirst are sinful but because *he* is sinful and perverts them. Human beings alone, because they are human beings, are capable of 'inordinate' desire.

This is more or less what St. Augustine meant when he spoke of Concupiscence as the primal sin. For, though it has been disastrously true that Christian ethics in some of its traditions – and in some moods Augustine himself too – has been prone to regard sexual desire as almost the definition of sin, Concupiscence is not

[1] Cp. I Corinthians vi, 13 – 'meats for the belly and the belly for meats'.

'lust' but the cause of it. For it is the absolutising of the relative – closely connected with Pride or the will-to-power or prostituting the whole to the part. As a man can identify himself with drinking, not as a means but for its own sake, so he can identify himself with insatiable sexual gratification. (One form of this can be seen in the propensity of 'romantic' lovers to fall in love with love. See p. 171.)

Thus there is a right way for man and a wrong way. Here as elsewhere the right way will be that which does justice to all the facts of human nature and leads to human fulfilment and maturity. The question is whether the Christian attitude to the whole problem satisfies that requirement. But we must not isolate this particular problem from the total context of human moral experience in which alone moral judgements can make sense.

'The sum of our ethical problem is our need for wholeness. We shall never make progress in that direction if we treat our sex as a detachable entity which can be dealt with on its own. And here again, of course, the Christian is bound to make an assumption which is not universally received. For he is bound to acknowledge that his own wholeness, his own salvation, is only achieved in concert with the identical needs of others, not least of his sexual partner. The deepest personal relationships do not come into being overnight. They do not just happen. Neither does sexual union, of itself, create them. Indeed, in the case of casual sexual adventure, it frequently destroys them, and it can leave indelible scars on those who looked for an easy way and found the easiness an illusion . . . Whether we like it or not, elements in our whole personality are involved in every exercise of our sexual powers. We are not sexual machines but persons. If we degrade our sexuality we degrade the whole of ourselves. Trivial sex is the de-humanising of personality.'[1]

Coition penetrates more deeply into personality and, for good or evil, affects it more profoundly than anything else. Even in its most irresponsible and casual form, in encounter with a prostitute, it cannot remain, as St. Paul points out, on the same level as keeping the belly quiet by giving it food (I Corinthians vi: 13 ff.). For such an encounter is one between two persons not merely between one body and another and the two parties are personally involved. (This is what he means by 'one flesh': *Sarx* in St. Paul does not normally mean 'body'.) And each of these two is exploiting the

[1] H. E. Root, *God, Sex and War*, Fontana, 1964, pp. 48, 49, 58.

other person, treating him/her not as a person but as a thing. The prostitute is exploiting her customer as merely a means to her fee or to mink and jewelry, the man has no personal interest in the prostitute, who is merely a means to indulging his passions. This is complete irresponsibility and each is really dehumanising the other.

Thus sex can never be merely a 'private affair', for another is always equally involved; and while it can integrate and fulfil two persons, it can also injure and even destroy both. Moreover its normal issue is a birth, which affects an entire social situation. And therefore, although there appear to be some primitives who have never yet got round to understanding the connexion between intercourse and pregnancy, almost every society we know of has tried to control it and make regulations for it. The rules, the 'sexual *mores*', differ widely as between one society and another, as anthropological research has demonstrated. The important fact to emphasise is that there *are* rules and that they are rigorously enforced, violation often involving a death-sentence. They awaken a feeling of absolute obligation, and the 'horror' of incest has religious overtones (see p. 50). This is the point that theology has to notice, for it gives the whole question an anchorage in an absolute. 'The concrete systems are admittedly relative. No theologian should deny the relativity of the moral contents, no ethnologist should deny the absolute character of the ethical demand.'[1]

The early missionaries and explorers did not understand what they saw. They sent back highly-coloured reports about 'beastly' and merely degraded promiscuity and said that the tribesmen were living 'like animals'. They did not realise – and indeed how could they? – that practices which appeared to them promiscuous were in fact probably under strict control as part of the formal pattern of clan-marriage (see pp. 188 ff.) or some other approved social institution; any more than they realised that polygamy, as it prevailed and still prevails in Africa, was an arrangement inextricably bound up with the whole social and economic life of the tribe. The 'free love' which causes such delight to some writers about Polynesian society is in fact, in all probability, rigidly controlled by elaborate protocol, sanctioned by mysterious tabus, of which the onlooker from the west has not been, or been allowed to be, aware.

[1] Tillich: *Theology of Culture*, Galaxy Books, O.U.P. New York, 1964, p. 137.

The claim that sex is a matter of 'private morality', simply 'our own affair', with which society – or even University regulations – has no right to interfere, is a claim which has nearly all history against it. Whether or not, in the modern situation, private sexual acts between consenting adults are proper subjects for *legal* regulation is a question for further investigation later (see pp. 232 ff.). The point is now that sexual activity has always been seen in a social context, as involving more than those directly concerned, and that society has from the first beginnings attempted to regulate, socialise and moralise it.

The root fallacy of current attitudes is not only to tear sex out of its social context but also to isolate 'love' from the totality of the personal relationships involved in it and from the human make-up as a whole. 'Love' means simply sexual attraction. The story of 'my love-life' by a film star means in effect a list of the men she has slept with. Such love, we are told, is supreme and absolute and nothing can be allowed to stand in the way of it, no consideration for other people, no regard for vows solemnly undertaken, no 'outworn conventions of religion'. Alternatively that nothing *can* stand in the way of it, for it is a power that simply takes possession of men and women, sweeping them to their destiny. Here are two people 'meant' for one another and it is both futile and immoral to attempt to put any obstacles between them. ('Adultery is not wrong if you love.') What is called Free Love is not free, it is dictated; it is a passive surrender to an impulse which there is no attempt to control, which indeed is often alleged to be uncontrollable and overwhelms all rational calculations. This 'romantic' notion of love is examined more closely in later paragraphs (see pp. 171 ff.). But, as Dr. Sherwin Bailey has pointed out, the notion is 'essentially fatalistic – an irresistible compulsion in the grip of which men and women are the impotent playthings of destiny'.[1]

But what then *is* love in this particular context? For the strange fact is that hardly before our own time has Christian thought had very much to say about this. The Christian tradition has carried along with it ideas inherited from various sources: Jewish, Roman, Hellenistic and oriental, which have never been really welded into a whole. And the tradition, it must be remembered, first began to be formed against a background of eroticism, laxity and corruption to which it could hardly avoid reacting with a rather puritanic and

[1] S. Bailey, *Common-Sense About Sexual Ethics*, Gollancz, 1962, p. 114.

negative emphasis. The New Testament, of course, does recognise certain truths about sexual relations as being inherent in the new way (see p. 85). But it would not be unfair to say that on the whole traditional Christian thinking has regarded sex with fear and with some distaste. It is only recently, perhaps indeed only within my own life-time, that theology has 'discovered' sexual love and begun to explore its implications in depth, with results which are already far-reaching in the theological understanding of marriage (see pp. 176 note, 202).

The fundamental biological basis of love right up to its highest possible levels is clearly the fact of bi-sexuality. 'Male and female created he them.' This is a 'given' fact to be accepted as one of the conditions of human life, as part of God's order of creation. Our Lord quotes that as what was 'in the beginning' – or as it may perhaps mean, 'in principle', as something inherent in the divine purpose – as the ultimate ground of lifelong marriage, implying full equality of the sexes. Man and woman are correlative terms. Man and woman are made for one another. Men and women alone are incomplete, they need one another, reach out for one another. There was indeed a widespread primitive myth – brilliantly set forth by Aristophanes in his speech in Plato's *Symposium*, and implied, at least according to some of the commentators, in the story of the creation of Eve – that the first, original man was androgynous and then divided into male and female. Ever since, the two separated segments of the total whole are seeking to come together again, each to find completion in the other. (A modern version of this myth can be seen in Jung's mythology of the unconscious.) That is a vivid statement of actual fact. Human life needs for its fulfilment this mutuality between man and woman, complementary to one another, and each supplying what the other lacks: neither man nor woman alone is self-sufficient. This is far more than a reproductive mechanism. (Eve was created to be Adam's 'helpmeet', not merely the mother of his children.) Far more is implied than physical attraction – though probably all human relationships have their roots in physical attraction, however much that may be refined, sublimated, Christianised and sanctified. Modern life tends to assume that men and women are concerned only with one another's bodies; but their essential need is for one another, not simply as bodies but as persons. 'Sexual partnership means nothing less than the free and equal association of man and woman in all the manifold interests and enterprises of social, political and ecclesiastical life, thus liberating the creative dynamic of sex for the furtherance of the common good and the enrichment and elevation of human life as a whole.'[1]

II

This is no doubt a comparatively new thing and can only occur in highly developed societies. It can rightly be called 'sexual' in the sense that it is a later historical expression of that need of men and women for one another which is implicit in man's bi-sexual nature. It is a kind of extension or sublimation of the fundamental biological impulse which drives the sexes to seek for one another; indeed it is more like friendship than 'love' in its ordinary, sexual connotation. If Briffault is right, even the mating instinct is a comparatively late development. Among primitive peoples, he remarks, there is little or no conjugal affection but there is a strong and even in some cases an extravagant maternal affection. He goes on to say that love between the sexes is an extension of the maternal instinct and a kind of transference from the female to the predatory and sex-hungry male. 'Maternal affection, not sexual attraction, is the original source of love.'[2] If this is true it provides an illustration of the way in which, once man has arrived, the original instincts are recombined and modified, and of the way in which man and woman, in their incompleteness and fragmentation, are mutually affecting one another. But, though this may have happened very early, there can never have been a time when male and female were not hungrily seeking for one another – as witness, the primitive 'venuses' of the cave-paintings. This is the physical basis of love in the sense in which we are now discussing it, even though, as I have been labouring to insist, something more than physical is inherent in it, jut because it is essentially a relationship not between two bodies but between two people. How is this attraction, physical at its roots, related to Christian Charity or *Agape*?

The 'reformed' tradition in Christian theology, always too ready to throw out from the legacy whatever has come from Graeco-

---

[1] Bailey, op. cit., pp. 89, 90.
[2] Briffault, *The Mothers*, Vol. I, p. 151.

Roman sources, has probably gone a great deal too far in reaction against the Platonic idea of love. Nygren's book, *Eros and Agape*, seems now to be treated as almost canonical, and under its influence many Protestant writers now tend to assume an absolute distinction between Plato's Eros and Christian love. It ought, no doubt, in fairness to be recognised that the Christian reaction here is partly due to the pederasty which Plato takes for granted. That, however, reflects the prevailing customs and conventions of Hellenic society. It is a local and temporary element and is not really essential to his thought. And in fact the theological rejection of Eros has rested on quite different grounds. Eros, it is urged, is essentially possessive, *Agape* is essentially self-giving. Eros seeks the object of its desire, that towards which it experiences attraction, as its 'end', its 'good', its 'happiness' and fulfilment, Eros is love for what is conceived as lovable. *Agape* is, as it were, the overflow of God's perfect and unconditioned Goodness towards the unlovable and the undeserving, the unattractive and even the enemy. They are, it is urged, two entirely different things and Christians must be on their guard against confusing them.

When one is intoxicated by Plato, as I was myself in my undergraduate days, the Symposium seems very near to Christianity. But it is important to have the distinction made. What is meant by Christian love in the New Testament *is* something that is specifically Christian. Yet this distinction cannot be made absolute. For one thing, it can hardly be supposed that Christian love is born entirely *in vacuo*. Grace refines nature but does not supplant it; and we must not forget that the Lord himself appealed to 'natural' parental affection as the ground of an *a fortiori* argument for the love of God towards the children of men (Matthew vii: 9–11). Moreover, as Professor Gould of Amherst, in a valuable study published last year, has pertinently asked, can this distinction be rightly applied to man's love for God? There is, he reminds us, a strongly Platonic element in the thought of Augustine, Dante and St. Thomas. The love that moves the sun and the other stars is not the love of God for the world – Aristotle's God, so far from loving the world, could not be even aware of its existence – it is the outreach of the world towards its true 'end'. (God 'moves as the Object of desire': it is in that teleological sense that he is conceived as the First Mover.) In like manner, the love of man for God is certainly not the 'production of the overflow of his own goodness' but the expression of his need. It is his outreach towards fulfilment, his attraction towards his end and final good (cf. Philippians iv: 8). And this love, says Gould, is what Plato is really talking about. 'Plato believes that Reality is lovable, so that in loving it, the Good, man finds his true happiness and fulfilment.'[1]

Theologians have objected that this 'Eudaemonism' – happiness or self-fulfilment as the end of life – is in final analysis selfish and possessive, incompatible with 'disinterested' *Agape*. It is, however, a pretty big assumption that love can be completely disinterested or entirely devoid of emotional content without forfeiting its right to the name. Charity surely must be the crown, not the negation, of everything we know about human love even apart from the Gospel. In the Bible, at any rate, God's 'loving-kindness' is the motive of his impartial generosity, sending rain on the evil and on the good. And our Lord did say things which have shocked the rigorists about our reward being great in heaven.

I do not want to labour this point too much. But that there is an element of Eros, however much transcended and transfigured, in Christian love for God and the neighbour seems to be not only what we should expect but, more than that, something that we ought to emphasise, if we are to claim that Christianity is the fulfilment of human possibility.

Eros means more than Venus or Aphrodite. It is the desire for the desired object – for that which, as we commonly say, 'appeals' to us, and in which we expect to find self-fulfilment. Quite obviously it is not 'disinterested'. (If a boy told a girl that his love for her was 'disinterested', that would probably be the last word he spoke to her.) It is the desire for the Beloved – 'who means more than anything in the world to me', in whom I expect to find satisfaction, the completion of a yet unsatisfied need. But that does not make it 'selfish' or merely possessive; at its best it is the desire for the beloved as the person that he or she is, as a person and for his/her sake, with all the claims and loyalties implied in that. The two lovers' mutual self-giving is one aspect of their mutual receiving and self-completion each in the other.

Something like that, it would seem, is the material out of which Charity is fashioned. But Christian theology, strange as it may appear, has been so obsessed with Venus and Aphrodite – the physical expressions of mutuality – that for centuries it seems never

[1] Gould, *Platonic Love*, Routledge and Kegan Paul, 1964, pp. 5, 13.

to have asked itself what sexual love really is and implies. The idea that people should marry 'for love' was thought to be rather shocking and revolutionary right into the reign of Queen Victoria (see p. 188). When the romantic notion of Courtly love spread from Provence all through the courts of Europe and permeated the orders of Chivalry, the Church felt suspicious about the whole movement. Nor is that surprising when it is remembered that, with all its high-flown and Christian-sounding language, Courtly Love was founded upon adultery. 'Marriage was a sin not a sacrament: it turns "love" cold-bloodedly to the uses of worldly society.' The love of the troubadours and the knights-errant was 'slave-like adoration for the lady, who was ideally the wife of her lover's lord' and should be herself both pure and disdainful – *La Belle Dame Sans Merci*! It was thus doomed to be never fulfilled or realised. Making impossible demands of life, asking for the sun and the moon and the stars, jealous and resentful of all rivalry, contemptuous of 'conventional morality', it was really a kind of being in love with love and generated a self-consuming passion. And thus, as Professor Gould points out, it tended towards oblivion and death. As Persephone was the bride of Death, Dido is destroyed by her passion for Aeneas, and the motif persists in the great Shakespearian dramas, notably in *Antony and Cleopatra*.

This Courtly Love was in the background of the nineteenth-century Romantic Movement. ('If two people love one another nothing else matters.') And perhaps one direct cause of the latter was the rise and growth of the new mechanical sciences with the bleak and chilling world-view implicit in them. 'The romantic was the man who was disillusioned with reality. The scientific explanations for human motives and the origins of human institutions were as depressing as they were convincing . . . the romantic was searching restlessly for the lost key.' The romantics tended to idealise the 'mediaeval', the far-way and the long-ago, 'not because they liked the world as it is but because they hated it'. And accordingly, Professor Gould goes on, in what seems to me an important piece of analysis, the attempt to be honest about the world as it is would mean a recognition and description of the mean, the sordid, the petty and the stupid. This is the connexion between romantic love and the 'realistic' (and frequently revolting) fiction and drama of twentieth-century fashion.[1]

[1] For the two paragraphs above see Gould, op. cit., pp. 8–11.

The compulsive eroticism of our own time, with its threat to the whole moral basis of civilisation, can probably be best understood as the reaction, on the part of people with no faith in God to give personal life significance, against the tyrannical impersonality of a rationalised, technical society – the attempt to find personal 'salvation' through intense and recurrent sexual experience, as others seek it through drink and addictive drugs. Niebuhr has shown that what he calls 'sensuality' (in which he includes gluttony and drunkenness as specialised forms of 'conspicuous waste') may have, consciously or unconsciously, two aims. Either it may aim at displaying power by enhancing status and prestige, that is, at asserting a self which is insecure – and this almost certainly goes a long way to explaining the promiscuity of 'teenagers'. Or it may be a frantic attempt to escape from the self altogether – not merely the shortest way out of Manchester but the quickest relief from the burden of conscious self-hood. And sexuality can arise in like manner either from the desire to assert the self by the domination of one life over another, or from the self-abnegation of the same life through the 'deification' of the Other: or it may be 'taken' like dope as an anodyne – a way of escaping the tension of life through being completely merged in the other or the total abandonment to sensation, into oblivion and, as it were, to death – sexuality, as Freud insisted, being closely related to the death-wish.[1]

---

[1] *The Nature and Destiny of Man*, Vol. I, pp. 248–53. I add here a very relevant quotation from Professor H. D. Lewis. (The human mind cannot ever enter fully into another mind, only the mind of God can do that.) 'Not apprehending the final character of this limitation we strive obstinately to overcome it or in some other way rebel against it. We expect to know one another as we are known by God. This leads to frustrations and distortions of aim which are most evident in intimate personal relationships such as those of sex and the family; and about this we have much to learn, I believe, from the obscure and unsystematic but often discerning writers like recent existentialists. Sartre in particular had much to say about sex in this vein. A judicious view of sex must encounter the tendency for it to become an outstanding form of the desire of human beings to surpass their own limitations respecting their coming to know one-another, and thus to appear as a kind of appetite which, instead of taking its place in happy and healthy relationships, tends to become maddeningly insatiable. This is one of the ways in which religion impinges very closely on problems of sex and the family. On the one hand, it should induce the humility by which we accept our finite, created status and do not attempt to set ourselves up as God; and, on the other, when distorted and idolatrous forms of religion encourage men to aspire to some divine or quasi-divine status, this will inflame perverted forms of sexual aspiration and

Most of the current talk about sex-relation is of this pseudo-romantic type. 'If two people love one another, nothing else matters.' Here love implies little more than 'Venus' and it is, as we saw, essentially fatalistic, and, as popularly conceived, irrational, overwhelming all reasonable calculations. (Love, says Gould, as Plato understands it, is the essence not of irrationality but of rationality.[1]) To leave Venus out will falsify all our thinking. But thinking will be even more deeply falsified if we are content to identify human love with its physical roots in our pre-human ancestry. True love, as Sherwin Bailey puts it, 'involves a free decision by two people who understand one another, who give themselves unreservedly to one another, and who accept one another as real persons, not as symbols or channels of an erotic experience which is sought for its own sake'.[2] If it stops short of that and is no more than relief of a physical emotional tension, then it may easily leave the two parties – one or other or both – frustrated, maimed and injured, and it fails to achieve its true 'end' or fulfilment. (The male orgasm, it should be remembered, is a single act, bringing instant relief. For the woman it is the beginning of a cycle, ending in birth, lactation and motherhood, which she is precluded from fulfilling.) Because it does not satisfy man's real needs or fulfil the demands of his nature as man – Christians would add, man as God has created him – therefore fornication is always morally wrong.

It follows from this that the so-called trial-trip, casual, furtive, temporary and often guilt-laden, is so completely unlike the real thing that it might be described as 'a trip on a different course'.[3] And figures do indicate, for what they are worth, that a high proportion of marriages that break down are those in which one or both parties have indulged in pre-marital adventures.

Christians too easily indulge in wild talk about the sexual morals of so-called teenagers. The situation is serious enough when girls of fourteen are unmarried mothers and one bride in every eight is pregnant; but it serves no useful purpose to overcolour it. The first thing to remember and thank God for is the large number of

---

be inflamed by it.' The passage goes on to refer to the orgiastic worships of antiquity. *Prospect for Metaphysics*, pp. 212, 213.

[1] Op. cit., p. 37.
[2] Op. cit., p. 115.
[3] Montefiore in *God, Sex and War*, p. 94.

boys and girls who go straight, often under almost intolerable difficulties, and triumph over the world, the flesh and the devil. Nevertheless, among substantial groups of them it appears to be the case that promiscuity is universal and virtually obligatory.[1] The conventions of their sub-culture demand it as the condition of social acceptance, which is their deepest psychological need.[2] Time was when 'war, moral ties and temptation threatening the immortal soul were tests of manhood; now the supreme test is ability to satisfy a woman'.[3] The worst thing that could happen to a man, it tends to be thought, is to fail in masculinity. It becomes a kind of inverted moral duty for a boy to 'prove his manhood' as soon as possible; and this seems to provide a compensation for that self-distrust and insecurity which is probably what has made him a social deviant. It may at times be the girls who make the running. But the girls too are apparently under compulsion – the fear of losing their boys if they refuse and being despised by the gang in consequence. (To be twenty and not engaged is to be a failure.)

These young people, physically mature – the age of puberty seems to be steadily falling – but mentally and emotionally unstable, find themselves in possession of this high-power engine while character is still too unformed to manage it. They are in urgent need of support and guidance. But adult society offers them little help and certainly sets no standard that they can respect. Nowhere is the cynical irresponsibility of the affluent society more lamentable than in its unconcern for such groups as these. And meanwhile they are constantly exposed to relentless and cunningly devised pressures by the Press and mass-media and hidden persuaders, playing on all that is worst and weakest in them, encouraging them to live up to their reputation, stimulating them with low-grade scenes of violence (notoriously akin to the sex impulse) and by dwelling on the private scandals of the entertainers who are (so oddly!) their heroes, instilling into them the whole time the suggestion that to be chaste is to be chicken. (It is hardly too much

[1] This statement may perhaps need some qualification in the light of Schofield's researches for the Central Council for Health Education (see *The Sunday Times*, May 28th, 1965) now published in *The Sexual Behaviour of Young People*. Yet according to the latest figures V.D. is increasing among the younger age groups.

[2] These scowling, resentful boys and girls are the rejects of the new meritocracy. See the terribly revealing cover photograph of the recent study, *The Unattached*, Penguin, 1965.

[3] Gould, op. cit., p. 12.

to say that the teenagers, as a self-conscious group, were deliberately *invented* – through the subtle organisations of publicity – by business interests seeking to create a new market by exploiting some of the most highly paid and most vulnerable because least responsible elements in the whole population.)

Apart from the effort of rebuilding home-life and 'pure religion breathing household laws', which clearly matters more than anything else, it would seem that the most constructive approach to these problems would be to conduct an informed and critical scrutiny of the ethics, and the existing laws, of advertising, the general quality of the mass-media, with the arguments for and against public control of them, and beyond that into secondary education and the present workings of the apprentice system. We are really faced here with questions of social structure rather than, directly, of personal behaviour.

Teenagers find a kind of obligation to promiscuity in their in-group *mores*. So too, paradoxically enough, advocates of the so-called New Morality are seeking for some new kind of moral authority, to replace the traditional and Christian standard, for what is in effect moral anarchy. There are, however, probably few people who have given any serious thought to its long-term social implications who would be prepared to argue for promiscuity as a valid principle for sexual ethics. The most live question in this field today, and that about which the younger generation most urgently needs a guidance that it can accept, is the question about pre-marital intercourse. Here Christian thinking needs to be realistic. Quite clearly Christianity cannot approve of it. But it is surely quite unrealistic if we try to insist that pre-marital intercourse is, so to speak, on the same level of sinfulness as promiscuous fornication or adultery. We are dealing here with a different situation. This is not a matter of lust but of love. Here are two young people 'going steady', knowing, loving and trusting one another, fully intending to marry in due course, and, as often, already formally engaged. 'I am willing, she is willing, why not?' What have hitherto normally acted as deterrents – on the one hand social disapproval, to say nothing of religious scruple, fear of pregnancy on the other – are now nearly but not quite eliminated. Not quite, for pregnancy does still frequently happen and there are alarmingly many shot-gun marriages. But the shot-gun marriage is marriage under duress, into which the parties have by their own act introduced complicating strains and tensions – and maybe a child whom neither of them wanted. To bring an unwanted child into the world must in all circumstances be morally wrong. How much delinquency may be the result of this?

But apart from any such unintentional consequences, how far and why is anticipation of marriage on the part of betrothed couples morally wrong? Can Christians rightly regard it as mortal sin? For we cannot take the line that the sexual act is in itself something wrong and sinful and only made morally tolerable by marriage (see pp. 177, 202). If, however, we argue, as Christians must, that its 'end', its fulfilment, is the 'one-flesh' union, that is to say the union of two persons totally committed to one another, living and sharing the whole of life together, then it is clear that sex before marriage is debarred from the realisation of its true end and can in that sense rightly be called 'un-natural'.[1] What exactly is meant by the wedding if it is simply an *ex post facto* ceremony, not an initiation into a new life? What new revelations has the marriage night if it has already been furtively anticipated? 'Betrothal is not the same as marriage. Until they are actually married it is unlikely that they will be able to share their lives without reserve' or to be living permanently together. 'Until that happens the sexual act cannot fully symbolise their union.'[2] Therefore so far from preparing themselves for their marriage they may be in fact putting obstacles in its way. The chief need of two people who are in love 'is not merely to assist each other's immediate wants but to establish a foundation for future growth and creativity. This demands control.'[3]

Once intercourse has been indulged the question arises, Is it just for this one occasion or shall it be continued? But it virtually answers itself. For sexual desire is progressive and is not at all likely to cease with a single act. If the young couple resolve to stand fast and not to drift into impossible situations, they will have to exercise a deliberate discipline over the depth to which they carry their 'petting'. Otherwise they may find themselves involved

[1] For an excellent theological investigation of *coitus* and its implications, see *The Family in Contemporary Society* S.P.C.K. 1958, pp. 137 ff; and see below p. 202.

[2] Montefiore in *God, Sex and War*, pp. 95–98. The case can hardly be better stated than it is there.

[3] Bailey, op. cit., p. 132.

either in a traumatic frustration or humiliating loss of self-control which will not enhance their mutual respect. But such discipline, such agreed self-control, can be a positive preparation for married life. 'Control successfully exerted can be a source of mutual trust and confidence in marriage, conveying the assurance that when abstention is enforced by illness or separation, each can depend absolutely on the other's fidelity.'[1]

Thus here too Charity will bear fruit in Chastity. But Christians must take a closer look at Chastity. It appears that some American student circles take for granted 'petting up to the point of orgasm'.[2] By this means they can get immediate gratification and yet claim to have kept on the right side of 'morality'. The girl in the case is still technically virgin and has retained her virtue and her chastity, whereas she would have 'sinned' and lost both if she had allowed the boy to 'go the whole way'. But is this more than a merely conventional judgement? Can it possibly be squared with the Christian outlook? Neither party has been chaste in soul. Each has really been lusting after the other. They got what they wanted, but they saved appearances. Each can formally claim to remain virgin though they have in effect committed fornication. Fornication without offending Mrs. Grundy cannot be, surely, what Christians mean by Chastity. That lovely virtue is not be equated with mere abstention from extra-marital intercourse. Chastity is a spiritual attitude and it is concerned with personal relationships. Christian judgement is almost bound to go wrong if it thinks of Chastity solely and exclusively in its relation to physical coition and primarily in negative terms at that.

Christianity here is too easily misrepresented and indeed too easily misrepresents itself. It can give the impression of saying no more than this, that outside marriage all sex is wrong, inside marriage sex is all right because, however regrettable in itself, the human race cannot go on without it. That in effect makes marriage a kind of frontier, and the moral valuations of sex different on the two sides of the line. Here I should myself agree with the Bishop of Woolwich and others who have lately discussed the same subject, that this fails badly in Christian discernment. Sex-relations be-

[1] Bailey, p. 135.
[2] See a searching article by Harvey Cox reprinted in *Prism*, December, 1964.

M

tween a man and his wife may be selfish, cruel and generally immoral, and the fact that the two parties are married does not make them chaste or moral or Christian. So again the two may be formally faithful, in the sense of having no affairs outside, and yet remain cold, self-centred and unloving; and such a relation is neither chaste nor Christian. In other words, Chastity means something far more than formal abstention from illicit intercourse. What Chastity ought to mean, in Christian language, is the joyful consummation of sexual love in complete, exclusive mutual self-giving between two persons who keep nothing back and share life together till death them do part.

Such a bond, sanctified by the Spirit of Christ and sustained by Christian faith, prayer and sacrament, can be and is a symbol, however imperfect, of the love of God 'all human thought transcending'. From that standpoint we can begin to understand the tremendous language, quoted in the marriage service, that it 'signifies the mystical union that is betwixt Christ and his Church'. But of course the mere fact of being married in Church does not in itself make a marriage Christian.

INVERSION AND PERVERSION

This chapter would be incomplete without some brief consideration of what is commonly called homosexuality – a subject long regarded as unmentionable. but now very much a matter of public debate. This is another case where new knowledge requires a new approach to the whole problem and a responsible re-examination of certain inherited Christian moral judgements, which is in fact actively going on – and the Church, which is always wrong whatever it does, is now getting blamed for that too!

Sex may be always to some extent ambivalent, as it certainly seems to be in some of the animals. (Cows, for example, appear to have 'lesbian' tendencies.) There are some normally heterosexual people who from time to time feel attracted towards their own sex, just as others with homosexual tendencies may respond to heterosexual stimulation and may finally settle down in successful marriage. There are infinite variations and degrees. At the end of the scale, however, there are notoriously a considerable number of both men and women who are constitutionally incapable of any attraction towards the opposite sex and whose whole sexual development is fixated and inverted within their own. Any 'normal' sex-life, any real experience of the love between man and woman, is out of the question for them. (To advise them to 'get married' may be ruinous – should a colour-blind man be advised to take up painting? That is just their problem – they *can't*; they are physically or mentally precluded from the fullest satisfactions of human life.) These are the inverts, the homosexuals proper, and they are indeed a class of 'deprived' people, cut off from a full share in the common life, and for whom society ought to feel responsible, as it does for its blind or otherwise handicapped members, meeting them with compassion rather than indignation.

This condition was not known to, or recognised by, the Bible or earlier Christian generations, and the tendency was in the past – and indeed still is – to equate 'homosexual' with 'sodomite' and include all forms of sexual abnormality under a common moral condemnation, as though all homosexuals were perverts or guilty of sordid, 'un-natural' vice. Far too little is known even now. Much more research and study are still needed. But at least the condition is now recognised; and that means that the fact of inversion must be approached as being in itself a clinical rather than a moral question. It has far-reaching moral implications. People with this predisposition or psycho-somatic disability may be led to all manner of morally evil acts and perpetrate sexual perversions. But in itself it is no more wicked or morally culpable to be an invert than it is to be blind or to lack a limb. It is just the way the unfortunate man is. That is his handicap, his deprivation, and, as with any other disability, he has to learn to accept it and live with it and make the best that he can of life in spite of it.

If they are to be helped to lead useful and happy lives, inverts must be released from the guilt-complex which will drive them into yet deeper introversion. They must first be able to accept themselves; and the most effective means to that end is to feel that they are accepted by society and not shut out as a pariah caste of 'queers'. (Christians of course will wish to go further than that and say that the surest hope for these people is to know themselves accepted by God and, in Tillich's phrase, to accept their acceptance – the ultimate secret of psychiatric healing.) The more they are cold-shouldered and left out, the more they are treated as a class apart, the more likely are they to be driven into overt acts of sexual perversion, and the greater will be their danger to society as pockets of moral infection in its midst. What they need is what the mentally ill need – association with those who are sound and healthy. That is recognised now in the treatment of mental illness. Inverts however are still too often treated like the lepers in mediaeval society. The result has been the creation of an underworld – an unhealthy, conspiratorial moral ghetto – bound together by secret signs and guilty loyalties, preyed upon by spies and blackmailers, and a septic breeding-ground of corruption. (The Press alleges that there are sodomy clubs. Whether or not these actually exist, enough facts come to the surface from time to time to reveal how much rottenness there is below.) And it must be said that the criminal law as it stands serves to drive homosexuality underground and is merely sweeping the dirt under the carpet. (The legal situation and the Wolfenden report are discussed on pp. 233 ff.).

The constructive moral approach to the whole problem involves a radical change of public opinion in its attitude towards 'homosexuals' – understanding and readiness to help rather than condemnation, contempt and ostracism. It is in the re-education of opinion with a more positive and forgiving attitude that Christians can probably make their most fruitful and most distinctively Christian contribution.

Thus the mere fact of being, whether congenitally or from whatever cause, a sex-invert – the aetiology of this condition is still very imperfectly understood – is not in itself a matter for moral judgement. Though it calls for a great deal of moral help from others, it is simply raw material, morally neutral. Moral judgement (and criminal procedure) can apply only to homosexual *actions* – that is, roughly speaking, to sexual perversion in its various forms and degrees of guilt and harmfulness. Here we are dealing with something morally evil, which no Christian is likely, or ought, to minimise. If we love righteousness we must hate iniquity, and there is a place for righteous indignation. But it is important in thinking about these crimes, which arouse such intensely heated feelings, to retain some true sense of moral proportion and not to allow our emotional reactions or the traditional and ingrained attitudes of past generations to overwhelm our judgement. If we want to achieve a sound moral judgement we must take the heat out of homosexuality and invoke dispassionate, objective reason. Mere denunciation will get us nowhere.

On what grounds do not only Christians but nearly all ordinarily 'decent' people feel such profound repugnance as they do to 'un-natural vice' and sexual perversion? For it might be maintained – though St. Thomas will have none of it – that adultery, which breaks up a home, or even fornication (which our society has almost ceased to regard as immoral at all), are more injurious in their social consequences and are therefore even more heinously sinful. Why are these latter judged so much more lightly? Why is it that this peculiar reprobation is reserved for homosexual deviations? The answer, no doubt, lies in the word un-natural. Violating the order of creation, they seem to be overturning the law of God and to be making a kind of indecent assault on all that makes humanity human. But the ancients, apparently, did not feel like that. The feeling seems to have come into the West from the Judaic strain in our inheritance; and, so far as the Christian tradition is con-cerned, it has been indubitably bound up with the Biblical story of Sodom and Gomorrah.

Some modern writers like to make merry about the belief of the Emperor Justininian that sodomy was the cause of earthquakes. Yet with the evidence at his disposal, as the data were at that time interpreted, it was a perfectly rational conclusion and there were solid grounds for his apprehensions. If God had destroyed the cities of the plain for precisely that reason, why not Byzantium? Here, almost certainly, is the reason why governments have re-acted so violently against 'the abominable crime of buggery', as it is described in the English statute-book. It endangered the existence of the State, for it might provoke the divine retribu-tion which had fallen on Sodom and Gomorrah. Theodosius made it a capital offence – it had always been so by the Mosaic law – and it continued to be so in this country, at least in theory, till 1861, when penal servitude for life was substituted.

This reference back to Biblical precedent has dominated the Western tradition.[1] The more modern, critical attitude to the Bible may incline us now to regard the story in Genesis rather in the light

[1] Blackstone wrote of 'the crime against nature, one which the voice of nature and reason and the express law of God determine to be capital. Of which we have a signal instance, long before the Jewish dispensation, in the destruction of the cities by fire from heaven; so that this is a universal not merely a provincial precept.'

of an aetiological myth, although it is thought to rest on some factual basis. But even taking the story as it stands, some scholars now think it at least highly doubtful whether the sin of Sodom *was* 'sodomy'. ('Know' in Genesis xix: 5 does not *necessarily* mean carnal knowledge and may in fact simply mean what it says.) The law and the prophets, no less than the Christian writers, are of course uncompromising in condemnation of sexual acts which 'changed the natural use into that which is against nature' (Romans i: 27). But it is significant that nowhere, either in the Old Testament or the New, does the Bible make the express identification of homosexual vice with the sin of Sodom earlier than the Epistle of Jude (cf. 'strange flesh' in verse 7) and that is commonly held to be dependent on the late-Jewish Testaments of the Patriarchs. Indeed, as Sherwin Bailey suggests, the projection of perversion on to the Cities, as the specially monstrous sin which caused their overthrow, may reflect the revulsion of Jews in the Diaspora against the septic sexual corruption in decadent Hellenistic society. For the Jews of the Dispersion and the early Christians Sodom and Gomorrah were 'types' of Rome, Alexandria and Corinth.[1]

If that tale can be moved from upstage to the wings we shall no longer be thinking under coercion of any alleged divine disapproval of this one sin as distinguished from all the others. We can therefore attempt to form a moral judgement in the light both of accepted Christian principles and of general considerations of social welfare.

The intense disgust and horror which is aroused in men, especially men of the public school type, by the male forms of perversion, whereas the female appears to excite no such indignation, is one more reminder that our sexual ethic is almost exclusively masculine in origin – and too much celibate-masculine at

[1] The story in Genesis *may* be related to another myth of 'un-natural' intercourse – that of the sons of God with the daughters of men (Genesis vi: 1–4, ? cp. Jude 6). For full discussion see Sherwin Bailey, *Homosexuality and the Western Christian Tradition*, Longmans, 1955, Ch. I. On the general subject the whole book should be consulted. See also *Sexual Offenders and Social Punishment*, Church Information Office, 1956, being the evidence submitted to the Departmental Committee on homosexual offences and prostitution by the Church of England Moral Welfare Council, with some valuable additional matter. Readers of either or both these books will realise how much I owe to them in this note.

I make no attempt here to discuss Lesbianism, with which I have never had any pastoral contact. An analytical discussion will be found in Simone de Beauvoir, *The Second Sex*, Jonathan Cape, 1953, Part IV, Ch. IV.

that. (Lesbianism seems to be regarded in the popular mind as a social curiosity rather than as a 'sink' of moral corruption.) There seems to be something particularly revolting in 'making a man into a woman' – an outrage crying out to heaven and defiling the whole moral atmosphere. Provided that both sexes are included, Christians will of course judge that perversion, deflecting the laws of creation from their course and submitting human beings to degradation, is grievously sinful in the sight of God. Will they, however, necessarily judge that it is in itself more morally evil or that it demands more condign social punishment than other forms of sexual exploitation which, though not exposed to the criminal law and incurring far less rigorous moral judgement in the popular mind, and often indeed condoned, may be more injurious in their social consequences?

It is often said that imperial Roman society collapsed because it was rotted to the core by pederasty and shameless perversion. That it was morally rotten is certain enough (see p. 71). But the probability is that perversion on a widespread scale ought to be regarded rather as a symptom than as a cause. 'In any society, the extent of homosexual practices and perversion is always one of the most striking indications of a general corruption or defect in its sexual life.'[1] Attempts to extirpate it by savage penalties are inevitably self-defeating. They merely succeed in driving it underground, where it acts like a septic sewer beneath the surface, and by increasing snooping and blackmail may defeat the ends of justice in other spheres and make for wider social demoralisation. (There have been cases recently in which men have been sentenced on charges raked up for offences committed five or even ten years ago. There are always homosexual suicides caused by persecution or fear of exposure. A boy of eighteen killed himself *in prison*.) Moreover, it encourages people to moral escapism in the subterfuge of compounding the sins they're most inclined to by damning those they have no mind to. The real causes will never be touched at all.

The constructive approach starts nearer home. 'Homosexuality', writes Dr. Bailey, 'is not in itself a fount of corrupting influence but only the ineluctable consequence of a corrosion which has already left its mark on family life and marriage and if not checked may ultimately undermine the whole social order and lead to

[1] Bailey, *op. cit.*, p. 168.

sexual anarchy.'[1] The morally realistic approach, therefore, is to tackle the evil at its source in the wider context of sex-life as a whole, through all the agencies making for sound homes and the re-education of opinion to recovery of a sane sexual discipline.

There is also need for much more research into the causes underlying inversion. At the moment there appears to be no agreement whether this condition has any physiological or biological or genetic basis. There is a good deal of evidence to suggest that parental inadequacy, or deprivation, or broken homes may be factors in producing it. But the social emphasis must be on curing it rather than on the punishment of offenders. Minors must be protected from corruption and standards of public decency defended. Some subjects are dangerous and may have to be segregated. But to send homosexuals to prison, as a Member remarked in the House of Commons, is like sending alcoholics to a brewery. They can never be rehabilitated that way.

In general, far greater efforts are needed for the rehabilitation of homosexuals through personal friendship and non-condescending counsel, and here there is scope for rewarding social service. There may be room for a salvaging operation, undertaken by normally-sexed citizens, to whom Christians might well give the lead, on the lines of Alcoholics Anonymous. And whatever happens to 'Wolfenden' recommendations, Christians must press for reform of the present laws, which, both in their tenor and in the capriciousness with which they are still too often administered, are irreconcilable with Christian principle or with Justice, Charity or Common Sense.

[1] Op. cit., p. 166.

Chapter Nine

THE FAMILY AND SOCIETY

IT is almost a cliché in Christian circles nowadays to assert that family life is breaking down and that the decline of religion is the cause of it. Look, we say, at the mounting number of divorces, the alarming statistics of illegitimacy, the broken homes, the juvenile delinquency, the irresponsibility of parents, the flight from the Christian obligations of marriage. All this is undermining the life of the nation and the very foundations of Christian morality. And the root of it all is forgetfulness of God. Therefore the first beginning of recovery must be the revival of family religion.

That sermon is being preached in a thousand pulpits, for indeed this offers the preacher a sitting target, and too often without much exploration of facts. But before they indulge in these sweeping condemnations Christians ought to examine the facts more closely, to find out what actually is happening, and what forces are operative in what is happening, and then to attempt to appraise the situation in the light of contemporary social movements and to bring Christian moral judgements to bear on it. Here if anywhere we must be on guard against 'stock reactions and conventional judgements'. Christian tradition alone is not enough, and as must be frankly admitted, Christian tradition in regard to marriage is not in itself by any means invulnerable. Christian ethics are always in the making. What we call contemporary social movements are in fact history unfolding; but here as always new situations bring with them not only new moral problems but also the need for critical reassessment of traditional or inherited moral judgements. Family life is changing rapidly, whether for better or worse, before our eyes. If we are to assess the changes realistically we need theological interpretation and not merely attitudes that we have inherited. Unless we expect that Christian family life can remain static and as it were insulated in the midst of a rapidly changing society – and that means, in the end, to put it in a museum – we must not try to equate the Christian family with the social patterns of earlier generations.

The greatness of a nation is in its homes. The social and moral health of any community is bound up with the quality of its family life. Communists of all kinds from Plato onwards have suspected and wished to disintegrate the family. Partly, no doubt, because by its very nature it is the mediator of tradition and therefore resistant to radical social planning; partly also because it stands, as a society within a society, between individuals and the totalitarian State. Nothing matters more to a free people, nothing matters more to the Church, than this nursery of faith and character, sanctified by the life of the home at Nazareth. Indeed to be admitted to share in the common life of a truly Christian family is the nearest approach to the Kingdom of God on earth that any of us is likely to find in this world. But that, and the Holy Family itself, is the sanctification of the natural family, not something that can or should try to supersede it. Its roots are in nature, Grace perfects the blossom.

But when they say that its roots are in nature, Christian spokesmen need to be rather careful not to claim more than is warranted by the facts. The family is the basic human unit. Its historical and biological origin is the helplessness of the human baby. But it is not simply a biological fact – marriage, after all, is not necessary for the mere continuation of the species – it is from the beginning a social and therefore potentially moral institution. As far back as our knowledge goes, the terms of marriage have always been regulated by society. It has never been a purely private affair but always tightly controlled by social *mores*. Lord Devlin accordingly goes the length of saying that 'the institution of marriage is the creation of morality'.[1] The changing patterns of marriage are inseparable from changing social and economic structures, which in turn are related to technical developments.[2] The family in the shape that we know today, and as it has been through most of recorded history, is a comparatively late arrival in the long story of social evolution.

The pre-human and earliest human type of family appears to be

---

[1] Devlin, *The Enforcement of Morals*, O.U.P., 1965, p. 60.

[2] As we have noticed already (see p. 185). African polygamy is bound up with the tribal economic structure. For the disastrous consequences of its sudden termination see *The Family in Contemporary Society*, S.P.C.K., 1958, p. 300. The Roman law of marriage was bound up with the law of property – a fact which by its influence on the Canonists, has given a dubiously Christian slant to some of the traditional Christian thinking.

that of mother with offspring. The two parents do not normally co-habitate and the male need be no more than a seasonal visitor. Few animal species are monogamous. Mother-with-child is the primitive human family. But it could not hope to survive in isolation, and there is no trace of *homo sapiens* in any such tiny, isolated families. The earliest form of human society seems to have been the clan or the group of families. But the female parents are the dominant figures in it. 'That the human social group should be much larger than the animal family is a condition of human progress (and survival) no less indispensable than the permanency of its character.'[1] This group of associated families 'has no precedent in biological history'. But the families would have lost their identity unless some means were found for retaining their original feminine constitution while at the same time constantly expanding; and that was that the sons should leave the group while the daughters remained and paired with males from another group. This was the probable origin of the rule known to anthropologists as Exogamy. Very generally, if not universally, the matriarchal (and normally polyandrous) form of social organisation was established long before the patriarchal, which we now tend to regard as archetypal. Traces of matriarchal organisation are to be found not only among primitives but in comparatively advanced societies in historical or near-historical times.[2]

The transition to patriarchal organisation was closely related to economic changes.[3] The social organisation of the Hebrews is

[1] Briffault, *The Mothers*, I, 199.

[2] For example, the Roman kingship passed in the female line. The Roman nobles 'knew their mothers but not their fathers'. (This does not refer to promiscuity.) The Roman Jurists regarded the maternal relation as 'natural', belonging to the law of nature, the paternal, and the paternal name, as juridical. Briffault op. cit., I, p. 522.

[3] 'The ultimate basis of the respective status of the sexes in advanced patriarchal societies is the fact that women, not being economically productive, are economically dependent, whereas the men exercise economic power both as producers and owners of private property . . . The matriarchal constitution of the primitive group resolves itself, like all functional adjustments, into economic relations; functional sexual differences leading to social differences must necessarily translate themselves into economic relations. In the earliest phases economic power does not depend on property, for there exists in such phases no durable wealth . . . The sole form of wealth and economic power consists, at those primitive social stages, in power to produce. The economic advantages which such power bestows is wholly in favour of women; for women in primitive society are . . . the chief producers.' Briffault, op. cit., I, pp. 433, 435.

reflected in early strata of the Old Testament. These describe a patriarchal society which still remains to a certain extent polygamous, though the prophets were always working for monogamy. But in these refreshing stories of the Patriarchs we are often able to see revealing traces of the original idea of marriage as a contract, not between a man and a woman but between the groups to which they belong (cp. Genesis xxxiv: 16). There were manifold and bewildering varieties in the forms and sanctions of group or clan marriage. The stories of Isaac and Jacob point to one. Another may survive in the Levirate (see Mark xii: 18 ff.), called in the books 'Fraternal Polyandry'(!), which was held to be a binding obligation. But the same conclusion emerges from all of them. The idea that a man and woman should be married as a matter of private arrangement between themselves, of their free choice and because they wanted to, because they were in love with one another, without reference to their tribe or kin, would have seemed immoral to early society and would probably have shocked Queen Victoria.

The arranged marriage, dynastic or otherwise, often between children of tender age, persisted all through the mediaeval period and seems to have been taken for granted till the seventeenth or even the eighteenth century. The whole idea of marriage for love, which the West now regards as axiomatic, is a very recent arrival on the scene and has only about three hundred years behind it. The monogamous patriarchal family gradually became accepted as standard in the West – Luther condoned bigamy on occasion – and seems to be one of the few institutions which the new nations want to take over from it. But the family pattern which we now take for granted – father, mother and children in one household in a marriage based on personal choice or 'love' – is still a very young and delicate plant; and there is much in the twentieth century climate uncongenial and even dangerous to its growth. Any Christian judgement on family life today must proceed from a deeply compassionate understanding of the strains to which it is now being subjected, and admiring respect for those many husbands and wives who are building up sound homes and happy marriages in spite of all the forces pitted against them.

It is common form to speak about Christian marriage, but the phrase is on the whole better avoided. There are not two different kinds of marriage, there is just marriage, as there is birth and death, and there is a Christian approach to and interpretation of all of them. The middle ages did try to make a distinction between 'natural' and 'Christian' marriage, the latter being reserved for the baptised, and, since it was effected by Grace, regarded as being 'in some sense invested with the permanent and indestructible character of the supernatural marriage of Christ with the Church'. Christian marriage was thus *per se* indissoluble. 'The teaching of St. Augustine and the early Church that the marriage bond is one of moral obligation was superseded by a novel concept according to which the marriage of Christians no longer *ought* not to be broken but *could* not be broken.'[1] This has passed into the law of the modern Church and is now the point of collision between the marriage laws of the Church and the State.

But marriage as it has now become established in this country and in Western society is 'Christian' marriage: it has grown up under the aegis of the Church and is now accepted as part of the moral tradition of Christianised Western civilisation. There are probably few who would wish to have it otherwise. The Humanist demand for 'liberalising' means in effect easier grounds for dissolving it. The State can of course only enforce standards which represent agreed moral principles, apart from specifically Christian doctrine. Neither Church nor State can make – or unmake – a marriage; only the two parties can do that. What Church and State do is to prescribe the terms on which they will recognise and protect it. 'Being married' bestows that recognition, and the Church blesses the union in Christ's name. But in both cases the terms are the same. Church and State mean the same thing – that is, permanent and exclusive union between one man and one woman for life. (A solemn declaration to that effect is made by the Registrar at a civil marriage.) Marriage as recognised by the law of England is essentially what Christians mean by it. And there is a pretty general agreement that it best corresponds with human needs. 'The freethinker in Western civilisation would, I believe, accept monogamy as good in itself', both for the parties, the children and society. 'He would also accept as inherently sound the Christian idea of the spouses' duty to one another. It is essential that they should live together, that they should cherish and support one another, sharing each other's fortunes and providing the foundation for a family. It is also essential to monogamy that there should be sexual fidelity.'[2] And it can, surely, be taken as self-

[1] Bailey, op. cit., p. 41.   [2] Devlin, *The Enforcement of Morals*, p. 63.

evident that nothing short of monogamy can consist either with the recorded teaching of Christ himself or with the dignity of the human person and the mutuality of man and woman which are inherent in Christian valuations.

We have seen that marriage as men now understand it has behind it a long history of development, and that the changing patterns of family life have been closely related to economic changes. The family as we have received it, in the form in which it had become consolidated in the stable nineteenth-century society, is now once again in a changing social environment. The technical and economic forces which are changing the structures of our society are bound to have their impact on the family and subject it to severe strains and tensions. Its shape and pattern are bound to be readjusted, indeed that is happening before our eyes; and though some of these changes ought, in the long run, to prove to be liberating and enriching, yet some, at the first experience of their impact, seem now to be threatening if not disruptive. Christians need to examine them more closely.[1]

The Welfare State with its network of social services sustains and upholds the family by protecting it against the worst economic threats to which in the past it has too often succumbed, and by easing some of its internal stresses through health visiting, child-care, home-help and so forth. But the Welfare State, whose right and avowed purpose is to foster and reinforce responsibility, is still in an early, experimental stage, and not everyone has yet learnt how to co-operate. There are still some individuals and families who look on it as a kind of earthly providence, a universal provider of 'free' benefits to which everyone has a right to come to be supplied with whatever they happen to want, without cost or effort on their own part. The result cannot be anything but demoralising. It is undeniably true that from time to time the aid of what ought to be its powerful ally does tend to weaken the life of the family, in so far as parents may make of it a pretext for unloading their own responsibility for the moral and physical welfare of the children. Notoriously, there are too many parents passively content

[1] For what follows see G. R. Dunstan, *The Family is not Broken*, S.C.M., 1962, which is invaluable, and *The Family in Contemporary Society*, S.P.C.K., 1958, which, by common consent, is one of the best reports yet produced on behalf of the Church of England.

to leave it to the schools to do what they ought to be doing at home themselves. And if, as often happens, there is a clash between standards inculcated in the schools and standards taught or accepted in the home, the strain on the children is more than they can absorb. (But the lower standards will nearly always win. It is only the very exceptional boy or girl who is likely to be able to live consistently much above the level prevailing in his own home.)

So too the enormous improvement and extension of the statutory educational services, with all the new opportunities implied in that, ought in the long run to bring wider interests and mental enrichment into every home; whether it will, depends on the competition between education and popular entertainment, which would be ruined if people began to think.[1] Yet at the moment, for this generation, it is not by any means an unmixed blessing. In many homes today the young people are far better educated than their elders. Not only do they possess more information, they have often also strongly contrasted values and seem to live almost in a different world of experience and ideas from that of their parents, whom they tend to regard as stuffy and out of date. This gap between the two generations, which of course is even more marked in Africa, can produce a fatal disruption in the family. No doubt the complaint that all this education is 'putting ideas' into young people's heads and jeopardising the good old-fashioned virtues is one of the stock complaints of all history – the Athenians put Socrates to death for it. If there were not a gap between the generations there could be little hope of social progress. But it is dangerously wide today, so that instead of learning from one another in the normal give and take of family life, the two generations tend to live apart, with the highly undesirable result that the population is stratified by age-groups – and tha thelps to create the problems of deviant youth.

The same tendency can be seen from another angle. The breathless rapidity of change in the technical processes of industry means that the skill a tradesman has acquired may be out of date in perhaps twenty years. So to the streamlined son as he grows up the father may seem to be hopelessly inefficient, semi-skilled if not almost unemployable; and that does not increase the son's respect for him. This situation is likely to become worse. In many such ways

[1] See *Discrimination and Popular Culture*, Penguin, 1965, a stimulating symposium with some valuable facts and figures.

the impact of change is shaking the stable balance of family life.

Again, the need for mobility of labour in a highly industrialised society has uprooted the family from its ancestral dwelling-place. Till recently, people as they grew up and married normally made their home and settled down more or less where they had been born. The result was that the new family was supported by an 'extended', three-generation family, more like a survival of the primitive clan, of grandparents, parents and growing children, with all the collateral sisters and cousins and aunts, with Mum the presiding genius of the whole group. In a time of crisis help was always available and the group sustained all its constituent elements. But today, when the new home has to be made elsewhere, normally in a council estate, and is constantly moving from one place to another, the extended family tends to be broken up; the newly-married parents and their children are left alone and have to fend for themselves. On the housing estates there is no supply of aunts. And all this puts a new strain on the home.[1] Moreover, the lack of any community life or social amenity on these estates means that while the man is away at work the wife is exposed to frustrating loneliness which brings its own tensions and temptations with it, while the young have no adequate leisure-time facilities and therefore are prone to succumb to that boredom which lies behind much juvenile delinquency.

There is, too, an increasing demand for female labour, and as there are so few unmarried women – males predominate in the younger age-group – more and more married women go out to work. Some few do this from financial necessity, but more by way of increasing the family income and providing better equipment for the house, better clothes for themselves and more expensive holidays. (Holidays abroad have now become a status-symbol.) But still more, probably, simply because they like it. They enjoy the social contacts in the factory and escape from unmitigated domesticity. Moreover, it gives them a feeling of independence, which ministers to their self-respect. If Christians accept the present social set-up they must accept the fact that increasingly married women are likely to be at work. And today, with earlier

[1] For a study of some of the traumatic effects of this see Young and Wilmott, *Family and Kinship in East London* (Bethnal Green), Routledge, 1957. Analysing the figures of children taken into care, Dunstan (p. 32) points out that a high proportion of cases are just those in which the extended family would have taken over.

marriage, fewer pregnancies and longer expectation of life, the pattern of feminine life is being reshaped. Instead of being exhausted at fifty, a woman may now look forward to twenty years of active life after the children have grown up. It may well be that in future the normal thing will be for a woman at that point to resume work on which she had started before marriage or even to undergo training for new skills in teaching, nursing, social service or industry. But what about this while there are still young children, and indeed what about women's work at all? Ought the Christian attitude to it to be negative?

It is, of course, only a wealthy society which can afford to set women free from all other labour simply to 'run the home'. The Virtuous Woman engaged in trade and agriculture in addition to non-stop domestic assignments (Proverbs xxxi); and before the factories all women would be employed in domestic industries as 'spinsters', stocking-frame knitters and so forth. But the woman's place was still the home. What is new is that an opulent society should now again be asking women to work, whether in the professions or in industry, and that such work should be extra-domiciliary. Is this necessarily a bad thing or a retrograde step behind the factory acts? On which side ought the Christian judgement to come down?

The question must first be seen in the wider setting of the fact which dominates the whole scene – the changed position of women in modern society, their legal and social emancipation, the opening of all careers and professions (everywhere except in the Church of God which claims that in Christ there is neither man nor woman) and the growing if still incomplete recognition of equality between the two sexes. This is clearly something for Christians to rejoice in and, so far as it goes, a signal Christian achievement. It follows that wives must now be regarded as persons with lives of their own to live within the total partnership of the marriage, and not simply as Hausfrauen or married housekeepers. And this, though it must involve some strains and readjustments, cannot but lead to fuller and richer personal relationship between man and wife, and therefore in the long run to the deepening and strengthening of marriage. But it must be recognised that one aspect of it is going to be the demand on the wife's part for a job or profession in her own right and, by consequence, to an earned income in her own right. That will entail financial

N

independence, and this in its turn is creating a situation for which there is no precedent in history – marriage held together by 'love' alone and without the traditional economic nexus by which hitherto it has been sustained and buttressed. If the total weight is to fall on the personal bond, then the personal bond will have to be all the stronger. This is not going to make marriage easier, but it will in the end make it something still better.

At the same time adolescent children are frequently now financially independent and with more spending-money than the parents and this may tend, at any rate for the time being, to the weakening of parental authority, not least to the down-grading of the father. Here too the family seems to be in transition towards a changed pattern of relationships, more intimate, personal and mutual, and far less patriarchal in character. Few will doubt that this will be all to the good; but meanwhile there are temporary strains and tensions and not every home is strong enough to stand up to them.

'Women at work' is thus part of a much wider movement. Now the axiom of Christian social ethics is that personal values have absolute priority, and the family is the nursery of personal values. Therefore anything that may tend to weaken the family, whatever the plea of economic necessity, Christians must regard as a menace to social welfare. The Church will therefore rightly remind industry that production is not the sole duty of man, that, indeed, it was made for man not man for production, and that personal and human well-being is the purpose of the creation of wealth.[1] Accordingly it will ask that in framing its policies for recruitment and deployment of labour, industry should be careful to take no steps to attract married women away from their homes while there are still young children to be cared for.[2] No Christian and no responsible citizen can possibly approve of latch-key kids.

But apart from that, when the children are off her hands, or if proper arrangements can be made for them, then – contrary to

---

[1] For general Christian critique of the affluent society see pp. 263 ff.
[2] I understand that in fact firms are increasingly unwilling to do this on the ground that conscientious mothers are prone to be too frequently absent owing to children's illness or other domestic crises. The provision of factory creches has not, apparently, proved satisfactory and is now being generally given up. The only satisfactory solution would be the provision of internal schools for all grades, and only mammoth plants could afford that even if authority could be got.

much Christian opinion – I should say that on the whole it is a good thing for the woman herself, for her husband and for her family, that she should have some private life of her own outside the home, some friends and interests and some pride in her professional skill or status, to enrich the life of the home when she is in it. She is likely to be a considerably more interesting and more vivifying wife and mother than the little woman dressed in a frilly apron who has spent ten hours in preparing her husband's tea. Behind many marriages that have broken down sheer boredom has probably been a destructive force.

The higher market value of labour is also affecting the shape of the modern family. Whereas in the past the young saved to get married, they now get married first and save after. And they marry at a much earlier age, often while they are still in their teens and indeed before they are really adult. Some of these boy-and-girl marriages are feckless, and a high proportion of marriages that founder appear to be those of this youngest age-group. These adolescent ventures in marriage must obviously be always at risk. But early marriage is in itself a good thing on biological grounds if no others, and Christian opinion ought not to frown on them, not even in the case of prospective curates! In any case, nothing is now going to stop them, and the real question for Christians is what needs doing to give them the best chance of being successful. These marriages tend now to be planned in two tiers. In the first stage there can be no thought of children. Both parties are earning and saving for their deposit and probably sharing a house with in-laws. (This is in some ways a strange reversion to the primitive practice of 'matrilocal' marriage, traces of which may still be found in the story of Jacob's long residence in Laban's household, Genesis xxix–xxxi.) In the second stage they settle down in their own home – if they can find anywhere to do it – and often make a magnificent success of it. But the main question here concerns housing, for the odds against a marriage are cruelly heavy – in modern life, though it may not have been so anciently – if it has not got privacy to enclose it.

Meanwhile, amid all these changes without and within, much more is now being expected from the family and far more exacting demands are being made on it. For one thing, the rising standard of life means that the old style working-class home is accepting the ethos and habits of the middle class. Home-ownership is becoming normal and a man's home is increasingly his castle. The impersonal processes of mass-production, in which 'hands' are interchangeable spare parts, mean that a man can be far more a person when he is at home than when he is at work. He spends far more time in it than he used to, it is not now merely the place where he sleeps. He takes great pride in his home, and spends his leisure in redecoration or in doing the garden. He is likely to be at home in the evenings rather than at the local or the club and is therefore far more accessible to his family. He shares the domestic chores with his wife. And all this is civilising, enriching, humanising for the man himself and the quality of the home-life. But it does, at the same time, mean that he is asking from it almost more than the average home can give, to do, indeed, what only the Church can do for him. Unless he is a believer, the home is the one place left where he can hope to find anything approaching 'salvation'.

The reverse side of these hopeful and promising tendencies is that they can too easily result in making the home into a closed system, too nearly self-contained and self-sufficient. And a self-centred home can be resistant alike to the claims of social obligation and to penetration by any religious influences, content to 'keep itself to itself'. Christians must be careful not to suggest that the family is an end in itself. It is part of a larger social and moral structure and only fulfils itself in that larger whole. It *can* defeat more important ends. We must not forget that our Lord himself was 'difficult' when his family circle made inordinate claims upon him. There are claims, he said, which must take precedence, even to the length of 'hating' father and mother.

Thus the pattern of family life is now changing, as it always has been since the beginning, in response to changing environmental facts. Meanwhile, at the moment, there are far-reaching changes in the way in which people are thinking about marriage; and not all of them are necessarily hostile to the Christian ideals and principles of marriage, however much they may, on the surface, seem to be. It may be that some of the reaction against what are thought to be Christian principles may in fact be a reaction against elements in the tradition which are still sub-Christian. And indeed within the Church itself there are marked developments in Christian thinking. New facts in the social situation, new medical and psychological knowledge and a deeper theological awareness, are leading to critical reconsideration of at least some attitudes hitherto taken for granted. The Church is criticising its own ethic, as it always continually ought to be, and this is something full of creative promise. There is perhaps no point in the tradition at which there is more need for rethinking and at which more rethinking is going on, than in the whole vexed question of family planning; and to this we must now devote some attention.

God has permitted man, through procreation, to share in his own divine work as Creator – that is part of the meaning of being made in God's image. There can be no greater responsibility than that of bringing a new soul into the world, though strangely enough, the traditional Christian ethic, obsessed as it has been either with the legalities or with the sexual act in itself, has laid too little emphasis on that. From the Christian standpoint it must be morally wrong to bring an unwanted child into the world, or, at the least, to do this deliberately. And responsibility does not cease at birth; there must be at least reasonable prospect of providing for the child's proper upbringing. Thus the number of children, and their spacing, becomes a matter of major moral decision. Christian parenthood must be responsible parenthood. That is now generally recognised, and family planning – which, in its very nature, may imply family limitation – is now widely accepted as a Christian duty. But we have now, as our predecessors had not, knowledge of means by which to control conception which are not incompatible with continuing intercourse. All this creates a new moral situation with which Christian ethics must come to terms – 'not lightly, wantonly or unadvisedly but soberly, discreetly and in the fear of God'.

It is obvious that knowledge of contraceptives has made for the increase of promiscuity, and it is no less clear that within marriage they can be used for immoral and selfish ends – to avoid giving up luxuries or even the trouble of having a family at all; and that, as defeating the primary end of marriage, is unnatural and a sin against God. But all new discoveries bring new moral problems in so far as they widen the area of choice. And it can be only in the context of Christian responsibility before God that this question can be raised as a Christian question. If we try to ask it from that standpoint, it will mean an attempt to evaluate the signs of positive good in the new situation and how it can be used for the glory of God, as well as being on guard against its dangers. That requires both a sociological and a theological 'appreciation'; neither will be sufficient without the other.

The traditional Christian attitude to the whole matter, which seems to us now on so many grounds inadequate, took shape, it must be remembered, at times and places where the need was for an increased population, and no question arose of wanting to keep it down. And it was not needed only for this world; it was needed also to populate heaven and repair the wastage caused by the Fall, the hope being that it would please God shortly 'to accomplish the number of his elect and to finish his kingdom'. (That strange idea survives, perhaps appropriately, in the burial office of the Church of England.) So far as concerns this sub-lunar world, the need in the past has normally been for growth, and that not only for military reasons by which our pre-war governments were motivated; it was only thus that wealth could be increased and the general level of civilisation raised. In poor, pre-industrial societies, children are economic assets and indeed are economic necessities. In the early days of industrial revolution in this country, before the Factory Acts, little children toiled in the dark satanic mills to eke out the sweated wages of their parents. Happy the man that had his quiver full of them. When, with higher standards of living (built on the wealth which that generation created) and the education of the social conscience, child-labour is legally prohibited, children become economic liabilities. Moreover, until the late nineteenth century the death-rate per thousand was still very high and the infantile mortality rate was appalling. Thus the natural increase in population was checked by these terrible external forces – apart from the fact which Malthus left out, that as the standard of living goes up the size of the family nearly always comes down – and never threatened to overwhelm society. But today in this country and throughout the world medical and nutritional advance has changed the whole demographic situation by which social ethics are, in the end, dictated.

In a pre-scientific age the Christian approach, like any other approach to such questions, was inevitably too fatalistic. Few seem to have given any thought to the physical and hygienic conditions under which children would have to be born and grow up – what chance they would have of healthy and happy development, even whether there would be food for them to eat. After all, there was nothing that anyone could do about it. The Lord will provide; or mortality will eliminate. We recognise now that man's God-given 'dominion' covers not only beasts, fowls and fishes but also his own natural environment and the procreation of his own species. Moreover the techniques are now available for controlling the outward conditions of human life, and man betrays his trust if he does not use them. (Epidemics and infantile mortality are due not to what God has done but to what men and women have left undone.)

Further, in none of the classical Christian documents is it easy to find any trace of consideration for the health of the wife who has to bear the children or for the conditions of her confinements. Early Christian thinking was blanketed by the Fall story. Woman was the temptress and the beginning of sin and she still lured men to damnation by her wiles and the stimulation of their carnal appetites. The sufferings that she had to endure in childbirth were the punishment for the sin of Eve – and for that there seemed to be Scriptural authority (Genesis iii: 16). Horrible as all this sounds to us, it expresses a permanent strain in the tradition. Despite the clear implications of the Gospel and the teaching of St. Paul at his best – the two partners are under a mutual obligation (I Corinthians vii: 3, 4) – there has always been a proneness to forget that the wife had any claim to consideration. The man is the head of the woman and she must 'obey', dutifully submitting to what was coming to her. Dr. Bailey has pointed out that one reason for the long subordination of woman, even within the Christian community, is that the ancients did not understand the physiological facts of reproduction. It was not, apparently, till the eighteenth century that the process of ovulation was discovered. Till then it was thought that semen was literal 'seed', in which the child or 'homunculus' was contained, much as the oak is contained within the acorn. The woman's part was thus thought to be purely passive; she was little more than a human incubator.[1]

For centuries, too, it was taken as axiomatic that procreation was the sole end and moral justification of intercourse. Any attempt to 'interfere' with that end was, said St. Thomas, a 'sin against

[1] Bailey, op. cit., p. 67, and Glanville Williams, *The Sanctity of Life and the Criminal Law* (Faber, 1958), pp. 206 ff. For further results of this on the ethical judgements of the theologians, see p. 162.

nature'. In other words nature must always 'take its course'. No
amount of theological ferocity has been able, thank God, to prevent
husbands and wives from loving and compassionate understanding.
But something like this has been the *official* attitude throughout
the course of Christian civilisation. The result, so far as this country is concerned, can be judged from the monuments in our ancient
churches, vast families produced by annual pregnancies, a large
proportion of children dying in infancy, duly represented below
their parents, and the wife, if she survived, an old lady when today
she would still be in the prime of life. The Victorian family has
become proverbial. By that time, medical and hygienic measures
had begun substantially to reduce the death-rate. But what has
been distinctive about Britain is that industrialisation was well
developed, in an expanding economy, before these measures began
to take effect. Nearly everywhere else it has been the other way
round, and most notably in the 'undeveloped' countries in Africa,
Asia and the Far East. Everywhere today the whole human race
is threatened by an 'explosion' of population which is the dominant fact of this twentieth century – a cyclonic force which, unless
it can be arrested, is likely to sweep mankind to destruction. Beside
it, our little churchy preoccupations often seem to be strangely
irrelevant. If nature is left to take its course, if the size of the
family is not reduced, then in India, to take but one example,
millions of children are going to be born only to die of starvation
and disease, and eventually the world's food-resources will fail
to meet the pressure of population. Here are new facts and Christian moral judgements cannot possibly fail to take account of them.

Some economists, it is true, protest against these neo-Mal-
thusian predictions on the ground that they are based on the
assumption that food-resources are a fixed constant. In fact, it is
urged, they can be increased indefinitely. Long ago the Dutch
discovered how to make *land*. The Sahara might even yet be reclaimed. Irrigation, terracing, control of grazing, can increase the
productivity of the soil. Artificial lakes can be made and stocked
with fish. The wealth of the oceans can be harvested. Now of
course it is being proved today in Africa how much can be achieved
by such methods. Nevertheless, it must be said, there *are* limits,
and meanwhile the supplies of coal, oil and so forth are being used
recklessly and may become exhausted. In any case, what real hope
is there that the results of any such inventiveness can keep ahead

of the growth of population in a geometrical ratio of progression? Normally, no doubt, a rising standard of living acts to reduce the size of the family – as happened here in the late nineteenth century – but always provided that it proceeds faster than the natural increase of population. In Asia today there is no foreseeable chance of that. Industrialisation is inevitable but industrialisation alone is no answer. And, as we know from experience in this country, it brings other evils in its train with it and breaks up the traditional patterns of community, thus creating further social and moral problems.[1]

All in all, there is no real alternative. World-wide measures of family limitation must be recognised as not only indispensable but as now morally imperative. The question remaining is, how is this to be done? In Western society contraceptive methods are now almost universally practised. That does not in itself make them morally right and the Church has hitherto strongly disapproved of them. Ought this condemnation to be maintained or is it possible that Christian ethics is now called upon to revise its moral judgements and take a more positive and creative line? Christian thought in this matter is moving rapidly. The reports of the successive Lambeth conferences from 1920 (which was strongly conservative) to 1948 and 1958 make an interesting record of its development. At this present moment the Roman Catholic Church is committed to startlingly new approaches in which rational and moral criticism looks like supplanting what had hitherto been assumed to be the rulings of Natural Law. Indeed we are now within sight of a reversal of a Christian judgement which has remained unquestioned and unquestionable for nearly two thousand years.

No Christian will underrate the moral value and importance of voluntarily accepted discipline within married life as much as everywhere else. But to say, as the Church has hitherto said, that abstention is 'the Christian answer' to this particular problem of family planning is no real solution. Not just because it makes such heavy demands on the frailty of man's mortal nature – Christianity need not shrink from that – but because its moral validity is dubious. Abstention prolonged, as it might be, over years, can put an almost intolerable strain on a marriage, if it does not entirely

[1] For valuable and informed surveys of Asia, Africa and the Caribbean from this point of view see *The Family in Contemporary Society*, pp. 35–94. Some of the figures no doubt now need revision.

wreck it, and at best can have damaging psychological consequences. And unless it is by mutual agreement prolonged abstention may be morally wrong. (After all, wilful refusal is a recognised
ground for legal nullification.) It is arguable that objections of
the same kind can be brought against recourse to the 'rhythmic'
method of reliance on the so-called safe period. Even if we assume
that it does work reliably, even so, all those elaborate calculations
and looking up of dates in the diary introduce an anxiety and hesitation into what should be joyful spontaneity and can drive a wedge
between man and wife in their most intimate relationships. Moreover it means that the wife must accept intercourse only at those
times when she least desires it – and if that is not 'un-natural'
what is? For anyone not trained in Roman casuistry it is very hard
to grasp the moral distinction between rhythm so planned as to
avoid conception and contraception employed to exclude it. Are
they not both equally 'against nature'? (For the doctrine of 'double
effect' see pp. 250, 254.)

St. Augustine and many mediaeval writers regard Venus with
horror and disgust, as defiling and unworthy of a Christian. It
must, by a regrettable necessity, be indulged for the propagation
of the species but only so was it tolerable at all; and even so, the
less it was enjoyed, the less unspiritual and 'unChristian'. It was
even suggested that 'Platonic' marriages would be holier than
gross, carnal unions, and some groups tried the perilous experiment of virginal or 'spiritual' marriages. (See I Corinthians vii:
25 ff., if this *is* what St. Paul is referring to.) Sexual intercourse
for any purpose other than procreation was mortal sin. (Expedients
such as *coitus interruptus* would all be classed as 'sins against
nature'.) Any suggestion that the sexual act might have any positive moral value in itself as a bond of marriage would have been
utterly unthinkable.[1] Recent theological exploration of coition has
found much deeper meanings in it. The sex-act, quite apart from
procreation, may have, it is now held, positive moral value for the
deepening of the love between the spouses and as a sacramental

---

[1] Some of this morbidity was no doubt traceable to early infiltration
from oriental sources. There seems also to have been a kind of pathological fixation on the semen. Even nocturnal emission in sleep was regarded as pollution requiring penance. Perhaps this helps to explain
the hysterical reaction of our predecessors to masturbation and the
savage treatment of male homosexuality while Lesbianism was not regarded as criminal.

expression of the 'one flesh' husband-and-wife relationship. It may therefore rightly continue and, indeed, ought normally to continue, even at such times and occasions as the partners, by mutual consent, do not intend the birth of another child. Christian ethics must now draw the corollary.[1]

The objections to the use of contraceptives have probably been at bottom aesthetic. That is understandable enough but it does not make them strictly moral judgements. They are really objections not to the thing itself but to the kinds of apparatus employed. New and better techniques will help to modify them. Debate goes on, with headlines in the Press, whether this or that particular method (or 'pill') will be or should be authorised by the Church. But surely this is essentially an area where the Church cannot and must not attempt to dictate. This is a choice for the two partners themselves after full consideration of all the circumstances and with the relevant medical advice, in complete mutual agreement, in their responsible freedom before God. Parental freedom must be respected. Christians ought firmly to resist any attempt made by any State to *impose* limitation on families or to prescribe any particular form of it – though it may perhaps be rightly encouraged, for example, by limiting family allowances to not more than a stated number of children.

If Christians accept the position as here defended, it must follow that they will not offer opposition to instruction in contraceptive methods being provided either at State clinics or by Marriage Guidance Councils and similar agencies. Should it be denied to unmarried young people? The instinctive Christian reaction to that is '*Of course*; it is not our job to make fornication easy'. But is this quite certainly the right answer? The result is only too likely to be an increase in the number of illegal abortions. It is arguable that this is one of the points at which Christian citizens in a sinful world have no choice but to opt for the lesser of two evils. In any case, you cannot compel people to avoid fornication by withholding knowledge from them. That policy brings inevitable nemesis.

[1] A dawning anticipation of this revised judgement may be seen in the second 'cause' of marriage in the introduction to the service in the 1928 Prayer Book, which also includes the significant addition, the increase of mankind *according to the will of God*, i.e. in a purposive and moral context.

DIVORCE

Marriage presupposes a life-long union and indeed the irrevocability of the vows is one of its strongest defences and supports. A marriage that starts with the back door left open will be in danger at every difficult turning, when, instead of helping one another round it, the couple decide that 'it doesn't work' and separate. If they know, and intend it, that they are committed to one another 'till death us do part', they will get round it and on to the main road again. Quite apart from the wider theological questions, this is the empirical justification for resisting demands for easier divorce or for divorce simply by consent. Not only would the latter reduce marriage to a contract terminable 'for any cause' (Matthew xix: 3), i.e. for any trivial reason; it would also ignore the far-reaching social consequences of a broken marriage – the disturbed children, the aftermath of delinquency, the sapping of the foundation of family life. (Some psychologists think that children suffer less even from a cat-and-dog home than from the traumatic emotional shock of divorce.) Society can have no greater interest than the preservation of permanent, stable marriages. Conversely, when the divorce rate is high, society cannot abjure responsibility. It must ask itself: Where is the social order failing? What have we left undone that we ought to have done, what have we done that we ought not to have done, that so many marriages are failing? For divorce is not merely a matter of statistics, it is a matter of poignant human suffering – as a rule, both parties are desperately hurt – and often of ruinous consequences in other lives, from one generation to another. When a marriage founders it is a major tragedy which calls for compassion rather than condemnation – however much the parties may be to blame for it – and a rebuke to the Christian social conscience.

It is commonly said that what is distinctively Christian in the Christian doctrine of marriage is the insistence that it is indissoluble whereas the State freely dissolves marriages. This is perhaps an exaggerated statement. For, as we have seen (see p. 189), it came into the Western Church only during the mediaeval period, and the Eastern Church still today, following the code of Justinian, is prepared to admit divorce on various grounds. But one of the unsolved problems of Christian ethics is, what is meant by indissolubility? Does it mean that it *cannot* be dissolved? For in that case no divorce ever happens, because it is something that *per se* cannot happen (just as, if the laws of nature cannot be broken and a miracle is an infringement of natural law, then a miracle is something that cannot happen). In that case, as Micklem remarks laconically, 'Divorce would be no more than the innocuous recognition of an event that had not occurred'.[1] Or does it mean that in its very nature marriage is something that ought not to be dissolved – that by 'what it is to be' marriage presupposes a lifelong and indissoluble union? There are in fact thousands of men and women, far outside professingly Christian circles, who would wholeheartedly agree with that and are trying heroically to preserve their marriage because marriage means so infinitely more to them than a terminable legal contract.

When it comes to saying what makes a marriage indissoluble, the West has, notoriously, been confused. 'There is no point,' wrote Creighton, 'upon which the Western Church has displayed such incompetence, for I can call it by no other name than that, than in dealing with the question of marriage. The Church found it exceedingly difficult and showed exceeding reluctance in defining what marriage was. Therefore, while it is perfectly true to say that a valid marriage properly contracted was indissoluble, yet during the greater part of the middle ages it was almost impossible to say what a valid marriage was and how a valid marriage could be contracted.'[2]

The only possible principle of marriage, which alone consists with its essential nature as Christians (and many others too) understand it, is that it should be approached as indissoluble. That is what our Lord said in the decisive *Logion*. In the beginning, in principle, in the mind of God and his purpose in creation, it cannot be broken. 'What therefore God has joined together let not man put asunder.' (It should be noted that 'what God has joined' is not the same as 'those whom God has joined', referring to this particular couple, whose motives no human judgement can penetrate, though the Church rightly assumes the best.) Jesus, as always, takes an absolute line, and goes far beyond the prevailing thought of his time. Asked to declare himself in the Rabbinic controversy between the more lax and the more rigorous view of the grounds on which divorce was permissible, he replied, On no

---

[1] Micklem, *The Theology of Politics*, p. 149.
[2] Quoted in W. G. Fallows, *Mandell Creighton and the English Church*, O.U.P., 1964, p. 84.

grounds at all. Marriage is in its nature interminable. No wife must ever be at her husband's mercy. Male and female are equal in God's sight.[1]

Jesus himself, as always, refused to legislate or to elaborate any rules of casuistry. Self-evidently, the principle which he laid down is mandatory for all Christian thinking. (One question that is seldom faced is, on what grounds has the Church taken this one saying out of all the recorded teaching of our Lord, as the basis of ecclesiastical legislation?) But he recognised that human sin and failing, 'the hardness of men's hearts', may lead to a breakdown. What is the Church to do then? He gave no directions.

Is the cause of marriage best served by holding together in a legal tie two people whose love has turned to hate, where the moral realities of marriage have altogether ceased to exist? Where the situation has become intolerable, through cruelty, sustained infidelity, total incompatibility and so forth, the Church has always recognised that divorce, in the sense of separation from bed and board, is allowable as the lesser of two evils. Contrary to popular belief, the fact of being divorced does not bring anybody under ecclesiastical censure. The question arises about the right to remarriage, that is, the cancellation of the *vinculum*. Has the marriage now ceased to exist, so that the parties are free to marry again, or are they to be judged to be still married, in some profound theological sense, in spite of a dissolution by the civil courts, and therefore debarred from making a new start, during the lifetime of both former partners? (Church thinking is strangely inconsistent at this point. If marriage really is a sacramental union of two immortal souls and *per se* indissoluble, why is it assumed to be terminated by death, so that death severs the bond? On the full

[1] It is now almost universally agreed that the original form of the saying is given in Mark. The excepting clause in Matthew xix: 9, peculiar to Matthew or its special source, is a later amplification of which St. Paul seems to be unaware (I Corinthians vii: 10) and is beginning to turn the absolute principle into legislation. It is included in both versions of the saying in Matthew v: 31, 32 and xix: 9: Mark's own additional clause in x, 12, is already a contextualisation (in Rome?) of the original saying. Under Jewish law the wife could not divorce the husband.

It may well be that the background of the Pharisees' question was the matrimonial adventures of Herod Antipas – a *cause célèbre* at the time like the King's matter under Henry VIII. He had put away his own wife and married his sister-in-law Herodias, who had herself been put away by his brother Philip. John Baptist's rebuke had cost his life (see Mark vi: 17 ff., Matthew xiv: 3–12).

Christian showing death does not 'part' and the words in the marriage service should be 'in this life and the next' or 'forever'. In that case, the marriage of a widow or widower is unlawful, and the Church does not take that line, though in earlier centuries it sometimes did, at any rate in the case of ecclesiastics.) This is where the Church collides with the civil law.

By the law of the land a clergyman is exempt from any obligation to take a wedding (or allow the use of the parish church for it) between persons who have been through the divorce court. The Convocations of the Church of England have laid it down that he *may* never do so although by law he is free to decide for himself – an extremely unsatisfactory situation. This Church indeed adopts a more rigorist attitude to the question than any other Church in Christendom. The Episcopal Church in U.S.A. has provided by Canon for a court of appeal. The diocesan bishop, advised by a council, is invested with a discretionary power and can, if the grounds are judged to be sufficient, authorise the remarriage by the Church of an innocent party to divorce proceedings. It is doubtful whether an absolute prohibition with no discretionary power anywhere is really serving its own declared ends. Creighton said, writing to Archbishop Benson, 'What people call "the law of the Church" became unworkable when dispensations were cut off'.[1] The time may well have come when the Church of England ought to take a fresh look at the whole position.

There are, of course, too, many remarriages, some of which attract notoriety, in which the divorce is merely a pretext, and obtained by committing adultery, or providing faked evidence of adultery. (Randall Davidson once asked a noble Lord, 'Do I understand that you claim the right to be married on grounds of adultery or on grounds of perjury?') The case is not that of a marriage breaking down – a marriage will not break down through one act of adultery if it is not already foundering on other grounds and the parties want it to break down altogether – but of being deliberately broken up in order to 'give him (or her) his freedom'. No conceivable Christian case can be made for this: the Church would be compromising its own witness and inflicting moral injury on society if it were 'more tolerant' of such escapades. There will be no serious argument about that.

The real question is about remarriages which are morally poles

[1] Quoted by Fallows, op. cit. p. 85.

apart from these. Once the original marriage has broken down there is set in motion a train of consequences in which no ideally right course is any longer within the reach of either party. What is morally right for them now is to do the best that *can* be done in the circumstances. To tell them that they must now live as celibates is either to invite fornication or to put a strain on human nature that can only be endured by heroic sanctity. These poor people have often been terribly wounded by the failure of the first, hopeful marriage and the subsequent ignominy of the divorce court. They often hate themselves and are deeply penitent (even the guilty party) for their share in it. If a new marriage now comes within their reach in which they can find true love and a fresh start, some new faith and growth in Christian character – and the second marriage often does bring these things – may not this be the way of healing and forgiveness? Is the Church doing right to say that all such marriages alike are sinful? You can 'uphold the standard of Christian marriage' and yet fail to strengthen and foster Christian marriages. Ecclesiastical discipline is important, but the Church's pastoral office is much more important. The Church's primary concern in these cases is surely to help people to make the most Christian thing they can of the second marriage. Can it be maintained, without moral unreality, that two people who were divorced forty years ago and have not even seen one another since are still tied in the bond of holy matrimony?

In any case, whether or not in the coming years there is any revision of the existing rule so that some remarriages do take place in church, one thing ought to be laid down by authority, namely that remarriage does not exclude people, as some of them suppose and as some clergy insist that it does, from Holy Communion. The sacraments of the Church are not good-conduct prizes but means of grace for the sinners that we all are.

Something needs to be added about the legal aspect of the present disagreement between Church and State in this matter of divorce and remarriage. As Lord Devlin points out in a notable chapter,[1] the whole existing confusion has arisen through the transference first to Parliament and then to the Divorce, Admiralty and Probate Division of the High Courts of a spiritual jurisdiction which had, prior to 1857, been exercised by ecclesiastical courts.

[1] *The Enforcement of Morals*, Ch. IV.

Then the State, which must command the moral assent of all citizens, Christian and otherwise, had to do what in fact the Church alone *can* do. It had to deal not only with 'separation' – that is, to dispense from the mutual obligations of the two spouses (*a mensa et thoro*) – it had to sever the spiritual *vinculum* – and that is something that no State can do.

Thus existing law is a conflation of secular-legal and spiritual functions. Because of its interest in the family the State must define the conditions on which it will recognise marriage and give it legal protection, and must try to defend and uphold that kind of marriage which is approved by the general moral sense of the secular society as a whole. So far Church and State are at one. Marriage in English law is 'Christian' marriage – monogamous (not merely 'one at a time') and dependent on mutual fidelity; and Lord Devlin holds that public opinion on the whole has no desire that it should be otherwise. The Church recognises 'civil' marriage as having full validity for the Christian. The State gives protection to the marriage vows by granting relief when they are violated.

But if the State defines the conditions on which the marriage is lawfully contracted, it must also lay down the conditions on which the contract can lawfully be terminated, and give legal effect to its termination. This is the decree of judicial separation 'That is the physical divorce, the winding up of the partnership and the absolution of one partner from the obligation of living with the other . . . By that decree the court relieves the parties completely from the temporal and physical obligations of marriage . . . When a temporal court has so decreed it has exhausted its powers . . . How, in a country in which no one is compelled to believe in any religion, can the State assume power to dissolve a spiritual bond as distinct from a temporal obligation? The State does not claim to make marriages, only to recognise and register them; and likewise it can register no more than their physical and temporal conclusion.'[1]

When it goes beyond legal separation and pronounces a decree of divorce, what is the State purporting to do? What it is really doing, says Devlin, is to issue licence for a second marriage. 'What the State is really doing is to say that it will recognise any other marriage that either party chooses to make. That is the practical effect – indeed it is the only effect, unless it is supposed that

[1] Op. cit., p. 65.

O

the court has spiritual powers – of the decree.' But because the application to marry again is granted in the form of a divorce decree, it is regarded as a form of relief *inter partes*. This has led to the doctrine of the matrimonial offence, with all its subterfuges and unrealities, as well as to the notion that the innocent party must always be given the right to remarry. But in fact – and the whole position would be clarified if this were given legal recognition – the two processes are quite different and distinct. There is, first, the private *lis* of the two parties, which is ended (or in a revised procedure should be ended) by the decree of separation – the legal and temporal termination of marriage. And there is, secondly, the public case – the application for licence to marry again – in which 'the State is the real respondent'. Such licence should not be given automatically, the determining factor now is the public interest. There is no room now for 'grounds of divorce', the question now is whether the new marriage will serve or injure the welfare of society. (In deciding that, part of the relevant evidence will no doubt be the applicant's matrimonial past.) If the State may rightly define the conditions of marriage, it has also a moral right to withhold the licence to remarry, where there are sufficient grounds.

'Whatever the theory may be, the Church of England does not in practice recognise the decree of divorce as a dissolution of the spiritual bond and it can now only be embarrassed by the thought that things of the spirit are being administered from the Strand . . . To my mind the time has come for a clean break [i.e. not between Church and State but between the two spheres of jurisdiction] and both the Church and the Law would be the stronger for it. The mingling of the spiritual and temporal jurisdictions has been good for neither.' (There is only space here for this inadequate summary of Lord Devlin's case. The whole chapter should be carefully studied.)

No society can feel complacent in face of the current statistics of Divorce. In the year 1963 – the latest year for which figures are available – the total number of decrees absolute is recorded as 31,052 – an increase of 2,676 on the previous year. Certainly this is serious enough – though even so, the increase in the number of marriages exceeded by 395 the increase in the number of divorces – but too much capital ought not to be made of it, nor ought the total position to be exaggerated. The increase, for one thing, is partly the reflexion both of the natural increase in population and of the increasing number of marriages. Not only are there more people in the country but more of those people are now being married and more of those who are married are married younger – and the expectation of life is longer. Actually, the figure for 1963 is less by 27,398 than that of the peak year 1947 – the aftermath of feckless war-weddings – since when, in ratio to the population, the figure has been, on the whole, tending to fall. In 1960 the Registrar General estimated the divorce-rate at two per thousand of existing marriages.[1] But what needs most to be emphasised is this – that the increase in the number of divorces does not in itself provide reliable evidence of an increase in the number of failed marriages. There can never be statistics for that. Before the present facilities were available people just had to suffer and stick it out. Separation was the only relief within the reach of any but the wealthy. Now that every citizen has access to divorce courts and free legal aid, more unhappy marriages find their way there; it does not follow that more are unhappy, and many observers believe that they are fewer. (It is noticeable that as divorces increase the number of legal separations is falling to almost negligible figures (124 in 1961, 114 in 1963). More of those whose marriages have foundered are seeking full relief with the right to remarry. Is it certain that more marriages are foundering?)

In an often-quoted remark of Professor Titmuss, 'It is probable that the proportion of broken marriages under the age of sixty, marriages broken by death, desertion and divorce is, in total, smaller today than at any time in this century, despite the rise in the number of divorces.'[2]

Note: This chapter was in print before the report of the Archbishop's Commission ('Putting Asunder') had been published.

[1] Figures are given and interpreted by Dunstan, op. cit., pp. 66–71. The 1963 figures are broken down by age-groups in *Marriage Guidance*, October, 1965, pp. 352, 353.
[2] Quoted in *The Family in Contemporary Society*, p. 108.

PART TWO

Chapter Ten

CHRISTIAN SOCIAL ETHICS

I. THE REALITIES OF POWER

IT has recently been remarked of Stanley Baldwin that 'too often he seemed to feel that if a thing had been well said there was no need to do anything more about it. He moved easiest among large generalities and found it pleasanter to enunciate ideals than to apply them in detail.'[1] How far that judgement is fair is not now the point. But it is sadly and undeniably true that too much Christian teaching has been like that – vague talk about Christian ideals or about 'applying the Sermon on the Mount' – as though it could be 'applied' in a society which does not know how to keep the Ten Commandments! – which too easily ends in moral sentimentalism. ('If only people were nicer than they are, how much nicer the world would be than it is.') On the whole, the pre-war 'social Gospel' was too prone to suggest that love (or 'goodwill') could by itself create a Christian society without involving a radical critique of its social and economic structures. But the social Gospel took no account of Karl Marx, and it needed a far more searching dialectic. As William Temple repeatedly insisted, goodwill alone is not enough. We are not loving our neighbours as ourselves simply by feeling well-disposed towards them.

There is no constructing a Christian social ethic simply by direct appeal to the New Testament.[2] It has to be worked out by critical reason informed by the ultimate principles implied in the Christian valuation of human life, analysis of the factual situation and the gathered moral experience of mankind. As we have seen (pp. 21 ff.) Western civilisation and the Christian morality which is built-in to it have been formed by the confluence of the ancient wisdom with the Judaeo-Christian tradition. By rejecting the whole notion of natural law – or at least (shall we say?) that classical inheritance from which the idea of natural law derives – and relying on the New

---

[1] Lord Francis Williams, *A Pattern of Rulers*, Longmans, 1965, p. 33.
[2] Cp. *Christ and Culture*, pp. 177, 191.

Testament exclusively, too much pre-war protestant Christianity had condemned itself to ineffective moralising and failed to offer contemporary society any realistic or workable social ethic. But in all the churches now, and not least the Anglican, with their boards of social responsibility and their new-found readiness to invite the aid of professional experts in the social field, we may thankfully see the beginning of better days.

Christian theology must now move out from its arcane, esoteric preoccupations[1] to offer a Christian philosophy of life that is meaningful for twentieth-century man, and a Christian 'appreciation' of twentieth-century man's social context. Christians are now beginning to understand that the Church must step forth from the sacristy to the market place and verify the Christian life in the secular. But have they fully realised what is implied in that? For as soon as they do move out into the public world of industry or of law and politics, Christians are going to find themselves involved in all manner of painful strains and tensions and will desperately need the skilled guidance which not all their pastors are yet equipped to offer them. They may also be exposed, quite illegitimately, to the charge of 'compromising' their ideals and trying to make the best of both worlds. That, of course, is exactly what they have got to do! Christians have to live in two worlds at once (see p. 84). They must live by the loyalties of the heavenly city, but must live them out in the cities of this world. They must therefore accept historical limitations and the actual circumstances of time and place. That is not, in the evil sense of the word, compromise. It could fairly be called a mark of Christian sanity. It is only lunatics who try to live in a private fantasy world that is not there, and Christianity lives in a real world – the world in which good men are crucified. That would be a sound enough defence for accepting the limiting conditions, but Christians will want to say much more than that. It is what God himself did in Jesus Christ.

The question is not how converted Christians ought to try to behave to one another in an ideally Christian community. We know that already, however little we act upon it; we know that

---

[1] 'There may be a theology which could be written to speak to the man of the twentieth century, but it does not seem that our theologians are equipped to write it. They have made their subject academically respectable at the expense of making it usable by the ordinary educated man, much less [sic] the man in the street'. Munby, *The Idea of a Secular Society*, p. 83.

from the Sermon on the Mount. The question is how they ought to behave in a mixed, sub-Christian social order, how the love-commandment can be obeyed in a society built on competition, and how – *things being what they are* – the earthly city can be brought nearer to the realisation of God's will for men. What it is right for the Christian to do will be what it is right for anyone else to do – the best that is possible in the actual circumstances. (He will have his own understanding of what is 'best'.)

But all this means that a Christian social ethic must face a jungle of seeming contradictions. The political expression of Love is Justice; but the only way in which justice can be vindicated – i.e. by arming it with force – appears to be the contradiction of love. For love by itself cannot create justice. It can and does find ever richer and deeper meanings in it by exposing it to the light of God's righteousness – for all human justice is at the best rough justice – and by its distinctive valuation of persons. The advance, and the Christianisation, of society may indeed be said to consist to a large extent in the wider and deeper understanding of what is really implied in social justice. (T. H. Green said that morality advances through the 'widening of the area of common good'.) But love by itself cannot create, nor can it defend and 'execute' justice. That, says the Litany, is for the magistrates – that is, for the legal sanctions of the State. And although, as I try to emphasise later (see pp. 222 ff.), reason not force is the basis of the State and 'the ultimate justification of law is that it serves moral ends', yet law without force behind it is impotent. Any State that abjured the use of force in the last resort would collapse in anarchy. (Any *literalist* interpretation of the saying about turning the other cheek, as a *rule* for secular society, would bring civilisation to an end.) Justice requires an organisation strong enough to secure the relative equalisation of power by control of the various conflicting interests, organised as they are in competing power-groups. All politics are power-politics. Power, indeed, is what politics are about; and political power implies, in the end, coercion. Any relevant Christian social ethic has, therefore, to be prepared to encounter without flinching the realities of the power-structures – industrial, financial, social (class, etc.), legal, technical – by which a modern society is stratified. In order to make effective some partial and imperfect obedience to the love-commandment, Christians may have

[1] Ginsberg, *On Justice in Society*, Pelican, 1965, p. 235.

to do or to consent to things which are apparently incompatible with it. They may have to approve the use of the criminal code, or, in the last dreadful resort, of armed forces, to defend the weak and deliver the oppressed. But are not love and force contradictories? Jesus said Resist not the evil. Jesus refused the twelve legions of angels (Matthew xxvi: 53). But in truth all these moral contradictions meet in the cross of Christ himself and are reconciled in that Reconciliation. The love-commandment comes out of the Christian Gospel. The Christian ethic would break Christian hearts were it not that we are able to take for granted an ultimate Forgiveness at the heart of things. There may be times when the only choice open to us is between the greater and the lesser evil and we have to say: This is my Christian duty – but may God forgive me for doing it.

The Radicals – the Tertullians and the Tolstoys – have attempted their own 'un-compromising' solution. 'Touch no unclean thing,' they have said. Politics is a dirty game, keep out of it. The Christian keeps his hands clean. (See pp. 110, 111.) But they were really answering the wrong question. The question is not: Is it possible for the Christian to take part in civic life without compromising or even renouncing his Christian principles, and if not, must he not refuse to take part? After all, the choice is not really open to him. He cannot help taking some part in civic life, if only walking on the municipal sidewalks. The real question is: What is a Christian citizen, as distinct from a man who is a citizen but happens to be a Christian in his private life? How is that vocation to be fulfilled? How is a man to keep faith with his Christian loyalties and allegiance to the Lordship of Christ, how is he to implement his Christian principles, in and through his activity as a citizen? For this, after all, is the sphere of his Christian calling. This defines the setting of Christian vocation in its widest and most general framework. Within that some are called to be Christian husbands, doctors or priests, bankers or lorry-drivers,[1] but all of us have got to be Christian citizens.

---

[1] 'What is the job of a Christian lorry-driver? The job of a Christian lorry-driver is to drive a lorry and to glorify God by driving it well.'
I vividly remember still how when a group of young chaplains on the Somme, led by Neville Talbot, were able to find that answer, it was one of the great illuminations in our thinking. Before that, we should probably have said something about 'giving part of his time to God' (what about the rest of his time?) by being a server or singing in the choir.

Now the central Christian aim in all these activities is 'the glory of God and the relief of man's estate' – obedience to the two Great Commandments. But every sphere of life, under God, has its own relative autonomy, its own rules and procedures, and these are based on its own inherent limits and possibilities – what can be done through it and what can't, and how anything can be done at all. But these are the ways in which God's world is made, what Brunner calls 'orders of creation'. We can only keep God's holy will and commandments by respecting these built-in conditions. Nobody can function as a Christian doctor by employing the techniques of an engineer. Nor can any man function as a Christian judge if he uses the techniques of a confessor. The State is not the same thing as the Church. Both are instruments of God's will. Both are under the lordship of Christ, even although not many States acknowledge it. Both of them are means, under God, for attaining the true ends of human life and the fulfilment of the law of love. But they must work each through their own methods. What the Christian citizen has to ask himself is how he can best do what can be done for the setting forward of Justice and Charity and the liberation of human personality, through the methods proper to politics. This will range from the elementary act of voting right up to being a Christian Prime Minister.

In saying this I am making an assumption that not all Christians have been prepared to make – that the State and its powers are not in themselves evil; and here we may recall what Augustine said, that if it had not something of God's justice in it no State could continue to exist at all (see p. 124). Not all Christian traditions have accepted that. (In Domitian's reign the New Testament did not. See p. 116.) In Lutheranism, perhaps most conspicuously, the State with its use of force has been regarded as something entirely alien from the Church. There cannot be such a thing as a Christian State, nor, strictly speaking, can there be Christian citizens, only citizens who in their private lives are Christians. And this has led, by an ironic paradox, to a virtual doctrine of passive obedience. For good or for evil the State must be obeyed. As to that, Calvin was equally emphatic; but for him the government was the servant of religious men.[1] 'For Luther the church of God was the ark

---

[1] 'No obligation rests upon the Christian to change the social structures so that they might conform more perfectly' with the requirements of brotherhood. In his attitude to the peasants' revolt Luther rigorously

tossed upon the waters of a wicked world; if the storms rage, so
much the worse, if the sea be calm, so much the better.' But in
either case there was nothing to be done about it. (The ark still
survives in the Anglican baptismal service.) The Church was to
save men out of the world and in spite of it. But 'for Calvin the
world was not like the sea but like a salt and treacherous marsh to
be reclaimed by the elect'.[1] The metaphor here was singularly well
chosen. For Calvinism, in that later form which Weber called
secular asceticism, became the religion of the American frontier.
There are few odder developments in history than that, as the
Freedom of the Christian Man was to lend support to Bismarckian
imperialism, so the end-product of the Genevan discipline should
have turned out to be Manchester economics, free enterprise and
the American way of life. (Whether Calvinism produced capitalism
or capitalism produced Calvinism will not be known till the day of
Judgement.[2])

---

applied this separation between the "spiritual kingdom" (the internal
realm of grace) and the "worldly" one and met the demands of the peasants for a greater degree of social justice with the charge that they were
confusing the two . . . Luther added an element of perversity to the social
ethic by enlarging upon this distinction between an "inner" and an
"outer" kingdom, so that it became, in effect, a distinction between public
and private morality . . . Luther had a morbid fear of anarchy and was
willing to permit the *Obrigkeit* any instrument to suppress it. The peasants,
on the other hand, as private citizens, were admonished to live in accordance with the ethic of the Sermon on the Mount. They were told that
their demand for justice violated the New Testament ethic of non-
resistance.' Niebuhr, *Nature and Destiny of Man*, Vol. II, p. 201. The
Calvinist policy, on the other hand, was a local re-incarnation of Christendom. Niebuhr on Brunner op. cit., p. 197.

[1] Micklem, *The Theology of Politics*, O.U.P., 1941, p. 46.

[2] The causal relation between Protestantism and Capitalism has become
a popular dogma since Tawney's book, however much criticised by
specialists. But capitalism was there first and was one of the causes making for moral corruption of the Catholic Church. See Mumford's section
on 'the role of the Musical Banks' (op. cit., p. 155 ff.). 'Capitalism was in
fact the great heresy of the middle ages; the chief challenge to the ideal
claims of Christianity.' 'Protestantism in religion came into being not as
an ally of capitalism but as its chief enemy; not as an attempt to swell the
energies of the *id* but to curb them before they became too powerful . . .
Instead of Protestantism being the new creed of the rising bourgeoisie,
Protestantism when it appeared in the twelfth century was an attempt to
prevent the rise of the bourgeoisie. For the most stubborn challenge to
the Roman Church came from those who were sickened by the spectacle
of its open alliance with capitalism . . . from those who wished to do away
with the venal elements that were making a mockery of its sacred pro-

If the Church, therefore, is to redeem society, the Christian will have to make many decisions for which he will not be able to find the answer by any direct appeal to the New Testament. Principles, as we have noted, are not decisions; and the Gospel, as we have so often emphasised, does not in itself contain the whole of morality. These decisions can sometimes be agonising – the worst that I can recall in my own experience, apart from the two world wars, was the Suez incident. But we are not likely to reach the right decisions by importing highly-charged religious emotion or by using the language of piety. They will have to be reached by cool, rational argument, based on the great inherited moral axioms, reaffirmed and deepened by Christianity, which belong to the legacy of Western humanism, an informed understanding of the facts and a realistic calculation of the probable consequences of any action, lest the last state should prove to be worse than the first.[1] (It is easy enough to call for the prohibition of addictive drugs or abortion or anything else; but what if prohibition creates a black market?) Christians will rightly expect divine guidance. But those who think that decisions can be reached by a privately intuited 'divine guidance' unchecked by reason and factual common sense might reflect on the story of Charles I and Cromwell. Here were two Christians, involved in a situation which neither of them completely understood, both believing themselves divinely guided, impelled to destroy one another and plunge their countrymen into civil war. Which of them had received 'the Christian answer'?[2]

---

fessions. The Waldensians, the Fraticelli, the Lollards, the original Protestants, were all in opposition to the overheated desire for worldly gain. At its source, Protestantism was an attempt to check the commercial spirit and prevent it from getting hold of the Church; that is why the early Protestants had many allies within the institution itself and had no desire for separation.' Mumford, p. 182.

[1] 'It is most important, in a verbal exposition of an argument about what to do, not to allow value-words in the minor premise. In setting out the facts of the case we should be as factual as we can.' R. M. Hare, *The Language of Morals*, p. 57.

[2] 'Other men with other creeds and other interests would adapt the story to their political arguments, their moral or religious needs, would venerate King Charles or condemn him, would admire the Regicides or execrate them. In other revolutions, other civil wars, the King's name and Cromwell's would become catchwords for parties and doctrines that neither the King nor Cromwell would have understood. The most real thing in their situation – the guidance of God – was to become the least real to ensuing generations'. C. V. Wedgwood, *The Trial of King Charles I*, Collins, 1964, pp. 223, 224.

II GOD AND CAESAR

When our Lord said 'Render unto Caesar . . .' he gave the impetus to the long debate which runs through the whole of mediaeval history and is still, though in a different form, the central question of twentieth-century politics. What belongs to God and what to Caesar? 'Modern philosophy, even when it is far from orthodox, is largely concerned with problems, especially in ethics and political theory, which are derived from Christian views of the moral law and the catholic doctrine of the relation of Church to State.'[1] But he was not thinking in those terms at all. He was not thinking about Church and State. To a Jew, with the Old Testament behind him, such a distinction could have had no meaning; and indeed such words as Church and State are anachronisms before the end of the mediaeval period. At the time Jesus was meeting a catch-question. It was put to him by a coalition of people who held diametrically opposed views on the most inflammable issue of the moment. In Judaea under Roman occupation ought a patriotic Jew to pay the poll-tax? (The 'tribute' would not be levied in Galilee, then under the 'indirect rule' of Antipas.) Was he for the Resistance, like the nationalists and many, at least, of the Pharisean party which had been born in the Maccabean revolt? Or was he, like the Sadducean priesthood, holding on to its vested interests, a collaborator? Whichever answer he gave, he would be caught, either Rome would arrest him as a rebel or the Pharisees could denounce him as no patriot. The answer he gave has become proverbial. Christians are still asking what he meant by it. Like other Biblical texts it can be quoted to support opinions which he could never have countenanced. It can, for example, be quoted as the authority for 'keeping religion out of politics', that is, in effect, for religious and ethical dualism, as though there are two separate departments – public affairs which 'belong' to Caesar and in which religion ought not to 'interfere', and 'spiritual' matters which belong to God. And, as we have seen, some Christians at some periods have come disastrously near to saying that (see p. 218). But let there be no doubt what that means. It means making the State a 'mortal god', its own self-sufficient justification, its own final court of moral appeal, owing no allegiance to any higher law, and completely exempt from the divine sovereignty. Then rea-

[1] Bertrand Russell, *History of Western Philosophy*, p. 326.

sons of State become the *ultima ratio* and Caesar claims that conscience 'belongs' to him. That is the theology of totalitarianism; Hitler and Stalin would readily have agreed with it. But it is inconceivable that Jesus, whose whole thought and teaching were centred in the reign or sovereignty of God, should have said or intended anything of the kind. He would not support the political intransigence which led to the tragedy of A.D. 70. That denarius with Caesar's head on it, he seems to have said, is legal tender: pay him what is his due, what belongs to him. But do not, for the sake of political advantage, withhold from God what belongs to him. That, surely, was where he laid the emphasis. And had he been asked: What belongs to God? nobody who reflects on his teaching and its Jewish background and context is likely to doubt how he would have answered. His answer would have been, in effect, Everything. What is really implied in this famous epigram, and most Christian traditions have so understood it, is that Caesar himself belongs to God. The State is answerable to the moral law.

The issue, then, is not, as the Middle Ages tended to make it, a frontier-dispute between two rival jurisdictions. To say that Caesar is under the law of God is not at all the same thing as to say that the Emperor ought to obey the Pope. To render to God the things that are of God does not mean that the spiritual power can claim to be the superior of the temporal. It means that no human authority, civil or ecclesiastical, is ultimate. Both are under the sovereignty of God from whom all earthly authority derives. In wild, anarchic times the strong Popes like Hildebrand and Boniface VIII interpreted that to mean that kings and emperors 'held' from the vicar of Christ on earth. In its attempt to substantiate that claim the Papacy was tempted to play politics and succumbed to that idolatry of power which the Lord himself had called the worship of Satan (Matthew iv: 8–10). The fatal seduction of the temporal power corrupted the whole life of the Western Church. Yet we must not judge those times by our own. We cannot tell now by what other means, if any, the Church could have managed to avoid being totally engulfed in the feudal system. (The struggle about investitures really turned on that.) If modern Christians are now able to say: We must obey God rather than men, or if non-Christian Humanists are free to express their disapproval of Christianity – if liberty of conscience is respected – that is due to the Popes who in a savage era vindicated, by methods which all now condemn, the independence of the spiritual principle.

Christians now freely accept the idea of the lay State, independent of clerical control. All recognise that a relative autonomy is committed by God to the sphere of secular politics – that the Church must not dictate to the civil government nor try to impose Christian legislation – the marriage-laws are an obvious case in point – on a non-Christian majority. But no Christian can allow that this autonomy means that the State is independent of God or can claim to be exempt from the moral law. (The cliché-words in the theological jargon are autonomy, heteronomy, theonomy.) Thus the question about God and Caesar is now, in twentieth-century language, that of the moral justification of the State.

The first believers, converts from Judaism, would hardly have found any meaning in such a question. They had in their blood the mystique of the Hebrew monarchy as the Lord's anointed and the 'son' of God (Psalm ii: 2 and 7). The monarch derived his authority from God and its moral justification was therefore inherent in it. The main stream of Christian tradition has taken the saying Render unto Caesar as giving divine sanction to the State. St. Paul goes to lengths which some Christians would now find shocking in affirming that the Powers are ordained by God and that therefore disobedience is morally wrong. 'Whosoever resisteth the Power resisteth the ordinance of God' (Romans xii: i–7). It is not merely a matter of 'the wrath' – the restraint of anarchy and violence; the Power is a minister of God for good and is therefore to be obeyed for conscience' sake. (Our Lord's own attitude seems to have been more critical [Mark x: 42 ff., John xix: ii].) At its best it is a magnificent conception – earthly authority consecrated to God, exercised 'by the grace of God' and under the sovereignty of a righteous will – and it is still symbolised in England by the glorious ritual of the Coronation. A semi-mystical attitude to the Monarchy seems to run like a thread of continuity through all the confusions of our national history; partly because of the need for a central government to protect the people against the feudal nobility with its private armies and predatory instincts, but also for fundamentally religious reasons. The English people have never thought of the State – never, anyhow, before the eighteenth century – as a merely utilitarian contrivance. There has, of course, been another side to the picture. Europe has been stiff with Sacred Majesties, some of them doing unconscionably bad deeds, and the great idea of kings by the grace of God has sunk to a theory of passive obedience based on a 'divine right to govern wrong'.

But to invest the State with divine authority is to set a drastic limit to its pretensions. For it means that no earthly authority is absolute. Because it is under the sovereignty of God its right to be obeyed is conditional on its own obedience to the law of God. The Hebrew prophets said that in tremendous tones. 'The Lord hath rejected thee from being king.' 'I will utterly sweep thee away and will cut off from Ahab every man child . . . for the provocation wherewith thou hast provoked me to anger and hast made Israel to sin.' (I Kings xxi: 22. An ambivalent attitude to the monarchy appears in I Samuel viii and xix.)

No such notion appears in the New Testament, although it is really implicit in its premises. It could not have occurred to Byzantine Christianity.[1] But the moral theology of the Western Church has always embraced what has been called a 'Whig' strain.[2] It has always taught that rulers who rule unjustly – or, in other words, violate the purpose for which under God the State exists – forfeit the allegiance of their subjects, for whom it may even become a moral duty to resist or depose a tyrannical régime.

There is therefore for Christians an ethic of rebellion as well as an ethic of civil obedience. That ethic is not to be invoked lightly or without the most careful calculation of consequences. Christians are normally under obligation to obey the government in being because all social stability depends on that – a lawless habit of mind is incompatible with the maintenance of justice or freedom. (What is right under an occupying government, that is, in a non-natural situation, perhaps comes under the doctrine of necessity. Yet it must be remembered that Render unto Caesar was spoken in fact in just that situation.) In principle, the value of standing out may be less than the negative dis-value of undermining the common respect for law.

But all power tends to corrupt and Christians will always do well to be jealously vigilant of all persons who wield political power;[3]

[1] See footnote 1 on p. 120.
[2] Lord Acton called St. Thomas the first Whig. (Dr. Johnson had gone further back!)
[3] See Max Warren, *Perspective in Mission*, Hodder and Stoughton, 1964, Ch. IV.

P

and the civil service through which the power is exercised. Christians should be watching on every Crichel Down. Nor must we forget the Marxian critique. There is always a danger that legislation may reflect the interests of a dominant group or the demands of an organised lobby, and love will require watchfulness against that. But beyond all that, if Christians are confronted by laws which seem to them to be so immoral as to be an outrage against love and justice – not merely injurious or inexpedient – then they must defy them and take the consequences. And that is the Magna Charta of liberty. For 'Freedom depends on there being enough people to say We must obey God rather than men'.[1]

Reason, not force, is the basis of the State. The State is the legal organ of society for the implementation of its social purpose, and therefore exists in a moral frame of reference. Any society needs to be protected against those who will take advantage of its protection, so that there must always be sanctions in the background. The State embodies the force of the society. The employment of force is in itself evil. But it can in fact be employed effectively only because the majority are willing to obey the regulation which it enforces as the expression, however rudimentary, of a recognised moral purpose. It is not the force which creates the society. The 'sovereign' in whom legal force is concentrated is the instrument of the social will. The British and the American constitutions have never been imposed by a 'sovereign': the sovereign accepts obligation to them. (It was the complaint of the American colonists that they were being deprived of their common law rights.[2])

Intertwined with devotion to the monarchy, the recurrent theme throughout English history is the emphatic insistence that the monarch is under and answerable to the law. The phrase was,

---

[1] In this country, one cannot get anything done in politics except through the party political machinery; electoral splinter groups count for nothing. In order, therefore, to secure measures which seem to him to be Christianly important the citizen may have to support a party of which on other grounds he may not approve, and there may be painful problems of conscience. But party loyalty can be taken too far. The appeal to the team-spirit can be moral bromide. Ought one to be 'loyal' to institutions which really need radical change? One blow struck for the Independent is probably a gain for the Christian cause. The trouble throughout public life at present is too much conformism, not too little.

[2] Goodhart, *English Law and the Moral Law*, Stevens and Sons, 1953, pp. 12, 13, 56.

sub rege et sub lege. 'The king,' said Bracton in the thirteenth century, 'ought not to be subject to any man, but he ought to be subject to God and the law, since the law makes the king.' It has been
taken for granted in this country that there is some fundamental
law which is, as it were, part of the Constitution and is indeed part
of the nature of things, which provides a defence against the
sovereign law-maker. '*Nolumus leges Angliae mutari.*' The Norman
conqueror legalised his position by swearing to 'keep the laws of
good King Edward' – though what they were nobody could have
told him. This axiom, partly embodied in the common law, is still
expressed in the Coronation oath. Here is contained the 'Christian' theory of government and the characteristically English
principle that freedom is freedom under law.

The opposite view was violently expressed in Hobbes's view of
the origin of the State. 'Hobbes found official political thought
dominated by the idea that government was to be obeyed because
ordained of God; and he substituted the thought that the State
was instituted by man for his own convenience and that it should
be obeyed because the consequences of disobedience can be demonstrated to be more disagreeable than obedience in almost all
cases. That is to say, experience not morality is for Hobbes the
motive of political obedience ... Hobbes found opposition thinking
dominated by the idea that government should not be obeyed
when it conflicted with divine law, natural law, natural rights;
and he showed that natural law, morality and rights in society are
derived from the State and that it is nonsense to speak of natural
rights antecedent to the State ... That is to say, he made power
not right the key question in politics.'[1] Hobbes had, of course,
had continental predecessors. But this theory, which was called in
aid of, and meant to support, the Stuart absolutism, was a revolution not only in the political but in the moral philosophy of the
West. It was rendering to Caesar the things that are God's and
gave naked power-politics a theology. *Leviathan* is the father of the
police-state.

Mediaeval theory conceived of Law – the divine law, the
Platonic Idea of Law – as being in some absolute sense prior to any
actual positive legislation. The ruler's business was not so much to
make law as to expound, elucidate and express the eternal and

[1] C. H. Hill, *Puritanism and Revolution*, Secker and Warburg, 1958,
pp. 277, 278.

perfect law which was 'there' already. Any human law which conflicted with it was not law at all and ought not to be obeyed. (See p. 225.) One result of that way of putting it was, as we have seen (p. 133), that Christian political thinking was more inclined to uphold the *status quo* than to press for dynamic social legislation. But it was in itself a splendid affirmation which is fundamental to Christian political thinking. It affirms the moral implications of politics. It was the scholastic and mediaeval way of saying Render unto God. It is, however, undeniably difficult to invest law with a hypostatic existence prior to and independent of any actual laws; and this is the real problem about 'natural law' if conceived as something substantially existing. What we *mean* as Christians is that all government, and therefore all law, has a moral frame of reference – Caesar is not his own, he belongs to God. For us today Caesar is the House of Commons, and it is the House of Commons that makes law. The modern form of the God-and-Caesar question is therefore the question, now being widely debated, how is Law related to Morality? Or, in different words, in a secular society who is the arbiter of morals?

III MORALS AND THE LAW

'It was a crime in Iceland in the Viking age for a person to write verses about another, even if the sentiment was complimentary, if the verses exceeded four strophes in length. The English villein in the fourteenth century was not allowed to send his child to school and no one lower than a freeholder was allowed by law to keep a dog. The following have at different times been crimes: printing a book professing the medical doctrine of the circulation of the blood, driving with reins, the sale of coins to foreigners, having gold in the house, buying goods on the way to market, or in the market with a view to selling them at a higher price, writing a cheque for less than one dollar.'[1] Such a list might well discourage any attempt to discuss the relation between law and morals, or even between law and sanity. But it may serve incidentally to remind us how often laws have in fact been promulgated for the

[1] United Nations Congress on the Prevention of Crime (Stockholm 1965). Working paper on social change and the prevention of crime, p. 4, quoting Sutherland and Cressey, *Principles of Criminology*, Philadelphia, 1960, p. 15.

wrong reason or in a fit of temper ('They ought to make a law against it'), on the basis of inadequate information or for the protection of vested interests, and therefore how much all laws need criticism in the light of some recognised and objective principle. The question is, where or what is that principle? If the laws on that list – and thousands of others, such as hanging small boys for stealing apples – seem to us now idiotic or outrageous, it is partly because we have better information, partly because we regard them as just wicked. We criticise them by reason and conscience.

The Hebrew belief in the law as God's will implies, as the Prophets so urgently insisted, that the laws of bad kings were not morally binding, and were, indeed, not 'the law' at all. 'It is', says Professor Lloyd, 'impossible to overestimate the Hebrew contribution to the human spirit in thus rejecting human law as the necessary embodiment of morality.'[1] We have observed how this theme recurs in various forms throughout Western history, whether as the Biblical law of God, the Stoic or Thomist natural law, or in Bracton's law that makes the king. In all these forms it is making the same claim – that law ought to embody moral principles and that this is the real ground of our obligation. Just how morals and law should be related may be, and is now, matter for debate. There may be disagreement about moral principles. But Western civilisation has been built on the conviction, endorsed by Christianity, that 'the ultimate justification of law is that it serves moral ends',[2] that it embodies the conscience of the community. To be legally binding is not to be morally binding. A law may be perfectly valid law, with watertight legislative authority, it can be applied with complete impartiality (and to that extent have some element of justice in it) and can nevertheless be a thoroughly bad law. 'And it makes no practical difference in the end whether I say: This is a bad law and therefore I refuse to obey it, or This violates natural law and is therefore in no real sense a law and I have no obligation to obey it.' Both imply the same moral judgement. 'A rule may be perfectly justly administered according to its tenor and yet may itself embody the most profound injustice. And when we speak of injustice in this sense we refer to that scale of values which, on whatever basis, we

[1] Dennis Lloyd, *The Idea of Law*, Pelican, 1964, p. 51.
[2] Ginsberg, *On Justice in Society*, p. 23.

choose to accept as providing the criterion by which we judge all human rules of conduct whether legal or non-legal as being good or bad, just or unjust.'[1]

To the unsophisticated moral judgement the majesty of the law does mean something – more than the robes and the ritual of the court-room. As Lord Radcliffe puts it, ' "the ordinary citizen" feels in his bones that the law which the learned judge interprets to him from the bench is the voice of something more stable and more fundamental than the aspirations and convictions either of himself or the judge'.[2] Most citizens in this country regard it as a moral obligation to obey the law because they feel that it does reflect, if not a transcendent morality yet at least the general moral consensus of the community with which they identify themselves and whose life and outlook they share. (This makes it, of course, all the more important that the law should not forfeit that support by offending the moral consensus of the community, either by moving too far ahead of it or – what is much worse – lagging too far behind it.) The complexity of modern society involves an immense volume of laws and administrative regulations if the social traffic is not to come to a standstill – or so it can be plausibly made out; brief authority loves elaborating them. Few of them have any real moral content and many can often appear to be merely silly. Yet most of the people obey them most of the time, on the understanding that, by and large, they tend to the general welfare of the community, so that it is a duty to obey them. It need not be denied that good citizens are at least helped to conform to these regulations by the consequences of infringing them; but they presuppose a general will to obey, and this is seen as a moral obligation. Otherwise the whole system would break down.

The theory commonly known as legal positivism tends in effect to deny that there exists any fundamental connexion between what is legal and what is moral, and evacuates law of any moral content. According to this theory, a law is that which is imposed by the sovereign and is constituted and enforced by sanctions. It originates in will, not in reason, and its justification is simply that it is willed. (*Hoc volo, sic iubeo, stet pro ratione voluntas.*) This is in effect the Austinian theory of sovereignty – the sovereign is the

[1] Lloyd, op. cit., p. 133; see also p. 103.
[2] *The Law and its Compass*, p. 11.

de facto 'commander'. The essence of law is the sanctions attach-
ing to it and the will of the commander to impose it. What is legal
is what can be enforced. If this is so, then the State *creates* justice
rather than being its instrument and servant. Justice is therefore
essentially capricious rather than an attempt to embody a moral
principle. This means in the end, as we have seen already in discussing Hobbes's view of the state of nature (see pp. 37, 227),
that the ultimate basis of the State is force. This cuts across the
whole Western tradition and indeed, as it would appear, across any
hope of the vindication of human rights. But the fundamental concept of law, as Goodhart says, is not sanction but obligation[1] and
the total separation of law and morality endangers the very idea of a
rule of law or a *Rechtstaat*, as opposed to a police State.[2] This, it
need hardly be added, is not to say that legal and moral mean the
same thing. It is to maintain that there is some relation, and the
question is just how they are related.

Few people now, outside theological circles, think in terms
of a prior or 'natural' law antecedent to positive legislation. The
need is to find an agreed moral standard by which law can be both
justified and criticised. In a pluralist, secular society, Christianised but no longer Christian, how are moral standards to be defined? Is the Christian standard still to be taken for granted?
If not, is there anything to take its place? Or is it the case that the
West, which cannot live with Christianity, cannot live without it?
Here is the moral and spiritual vacuum with which we were concerned in Chapter One.[3] Beyond that is the question[1] whether and
how far the function of law is to enforce morality.

This latter question has been very fully explored in the public
debate between Professor Hart in his book, *Law, Liberty and
Morality*, and Lord Devlin in his book, *The Enforcement of Morals*,
which arose out of the Wolfenden report. The general terms of that
debate and the points at issue are now so widely known and have
been so much discussed that there is no need to go into them in
detail. But these two books, and Lord Devlin's particularly which
ranges over considerably wider ground, ought certainly to be on

[1] Op. cit., p. 93.
[2] Ginsberg, p. 215.
[3] See the quotation from Lord Devlin on p. 21 above.
[4] As Professor Lloyd pertinently points out, if a lawyer in South Africa
appeals to natural law as against *apartheid*, others will say that *apartheid*
is what natural law requires. Op. cit., p. 103.

the reading-list of any student of Christian social ethics. They discuss the question from which this book started, In a mixed, secular society are a man's morals his own private affair?

Lord Devlin's position is now well known. 'The suppression of vice is as much the law's business as the suppression of subversive activities; it is no more possible to define a sphere of private morality than it is to define one of private subversive activity. Societies disintegrate from within more frequently than they are broken up by external pressures. There is disintegration when no common morality is observed . . . so that society is justified in taking the same steps to preserve its moral code as it does to preserve its government and other essential institutions.'[1] It must, of course, be recognised that 'a state which refuses to enforce Christian beliefs has lost the right to enforce Christian morals',[2] and the question will have to be asked what morals has the State the right to enforce? But the fact remains that the criminal law of England has from the first concerned itself with moral principles. There are, for example, offences against the person for which the consent of the victim is no defence. They are prohibited, says Lord Devlin, not only to protect the individual but for the protection of society and 'of one of the great moral principles on which society is based, that is, the sanctity of human life'.[3]

John Stuart Mill had urged in a 'famous sentence' that the sole end for which mankind are warranted, individually or collectively, in interfering with the liberty of action of any of their number is self-protection. The only purpose for which power can be rightly exercised over a member of a civilised community against his own will is to prevent harm to others.[1] On that ground it is urged by Hart and others, and appears to be urged by the Wolfenden Committee, 'that there is a sphere of private morality and immorality which is, in brief and crude terms, not the state's business'. The Committee goes on to add that 'to say this is not to condone or encourage private immorality'.[2]

Mill's protest still remains invaluable against needless invasions of liberty, but the fact remains that the law as we know it is concerned with protecting society and protecting the moral conven-

---

[1] Devlin, *The Enforcement of Morals*, pp. 13, 14.
[2] Op. cit., p. 5.
[3] Op. cit., p. 6.
[4] *On Liberty*, p. 72; Devlin, p. 103.
[5] The Wolfenden Report, para. 62.

tions of society, not simply with preventing individuals from inflicting injury on one another. In the judgement of the House of Lords in the case of the *Ladies Directory* Lord Simonds said: 'There remains in the courts of law a residual power to enforce the supreme and fundamental purpose of the law, to conserve not only the safety and order but also the moral welfare of the State.'

Professor Hart is entirely right in saying that morality enforced is not morality – everyone on both sides would agree with that. 'The attribution of value to mere conforming behaviour in abstraction both from motive and consequences belongs not to morality but to taboo.'[1] Christians may also well take heed to his protest against overmuch ethico-legal paternalism. It has indeed lately been made by a group of churchmen. 'If the law', they write, 'is extended unthinkingly in a moral direction there is always a danger that a fantastic sense of disproportion can arise. While serious crime is increasing the energies of the police may, for example, be absorbed by investigation of night-club activities . . . If the law and morality are related too closely, there is a temptation to concentrate too much on problems of sexual immorality and to leave larger and more serious crimes alone . . . diverting police to indecency enquiries has a very doubtful usefulness.'[2] But Professor Hart was not in fact arguing that the law has nothing to do with morality. Neither was Mill or the other utilitarians. And the whole debate, at least as it has presented itself in the popular mind, has become a bit unreal. It has become so misrepresented as to make it an issue between enlightened 'moderns' who maintain that their private morals (by which is meant little more than their sexual habits) are nobody's business but their own and a hidebound reactionary Establishment – supported by narrow-minded ecclesiastics – who want to impose antiquated laws on them. If that were so, it would certainly be odd that the bishops in the House of Lords voted for the Wolfenden proposals!

But that is not at all what it is about. Both sides of the House have much in common – if they had not there could have been no debate. Both agree that the law has a duty to defend, if not the 'morals', at least the established moral conventions of the com-

[1] Op. cit., p. 37.
[2] From *Punishment*, a report by the Anglican Board of Social Responsibility, Church Information Office, 1963, pp. 18, 19.

munity. Both would agree that sodomy is immoral: certainly the Wolfenden committee would, and I doubt whether any normal man thinks otherwise. Both would agree in wishing to avoid any *needless* intrusion on people's private lives. The question is not whether homosexual practices between adults in private are 'right' – one has heard even educated people complain that the bishops want to 'condone sodomy'! – but whether they ought to be punishable by law – whether every sin ought to be made a crime or whether that would defeat its own object, whether, in fact, some forms of conduct which many, at least, believe to be morally wrong are not best left outside the legal process to be dealt with by different kinds of remedy.

As to that our law has made up its mind long ago. 'Only a minority of American States do not have statutes making fornication punishable under certain conditions and some States make even a single act punishable.' In Boston in 1948 there were 248 arrests for adultery.[1] English law has refused to take that line. Bigamy is obviously criminal in a country which believes in monogamous marriage. But even incest was not a crime in common law; it was made so by statute fifty years ago.[2] Fornication and adultery are not crimes – partly, no doubt, because they are thought of tolerantly, partly because a law which tried to prohibit them would be so widely and commonly disregarded that it would be totally ineffective and the law itself would be brought into contempt, but partly also because such a law would lead to intolerable snooping and blackmail. Not all sins can possibly be made crimes[3] – what about envy, hatred and uncharitableness, which are in themselves more sinful than fornication? But there are many things that are morally wrong which though they are not punishable as crimes are yet unlawful and, as it were, outlawed. The law protects legally recognised marriage, but it does not extend its protection to concubinage. Prostitution is not a crime; but it is unlawful – the law does not recognise it as a legitimate 'trade, profession or calling'. A contract made between prostitute and client will not be enforceable in the courts, nor the rent of disorderly houses recoverable. Adultery is not a crime, but because it violates lawful

[1] Hart, pp. 26, 27.
[2] Devlin, p. 1.
[3] Politics of the Genevan type – e.g. in New England – have done their best, or worst; but even they could not include more than overt acts. 'Sin' is in fact a religious concept, not another name for wrongdoing.

marriage it is a valid ground for a divorce. We are not, therefore, shut up in the alternative between retaining the present savage law against homosexual offences and appearing to say that they do not matter at all. The really important and weighty argument against accepting the Wolfenden recommendations – and this is what Lord Devlin feels so strongly – is that it would be popularly interpreted as a green light for sexual perversion. It has been proposed that the right procedure would be by an Act stating in the preamble that all forms of homosexual intercourse, including Lesbianism, are *unlawful*, which would then proceed to define as criminal the corruption of minors (everyone is agreed on that), the violation of public decency and (possibly) Buggery and Bestiality – though that would run counter to Wolfenden recommendations – and lay down a maximum, not a minimum, penalty.[1]

I myself agree with the Wolfenden proposals as (I believe) do nearly all the bishops. But the recent debates in both houses of Parliament revealed how acutely divided opinion is, and it was on that ground that the former Home Secretary refused, and probably rightly, to accept them. The same is also true about capital punishment. This will now almost certainly be abolished,[2] but there is nothing like universal, perhaps not even majority support for that. It is broadly true that if a minority lobby manages to drive through a law which has not the support of average opinion, the law will quickly become a dead letter. The classic case is American Prohibition. (I remember being invited to lunch with a highly-placed and well-known ecclesiastic who produced some home-made hooch, with the remark that he now regarded it as a moral duty.) But what about the abolition of slavery, or the laws which brought duelling to an end? The law can educate public opinion. The Volstead act broke down in defiance, but 'it may well turn out that the desegregation laws if persistently enforced may help to bring about a change in attitude, in behaviour and eventually in moral convictions'.[3] Nearly all constructive reform of criminal law has been in advance of public opinion. It is doubtful, as Professor Lloyd says, 'whether the numerous cases to which capital punishment applied would ever have been reduced or that this

---

[1] Quentin Edwards, *What is Unlawful? Does Innocence Begin Where Crime Ends?*, Church Information Office, 1959.
[2] This was written in the summer of 1965.
[3] Ginsberg, p. 235.

penalty would ever be ultimately abolished, if a popular majority had first to be ensured. Higher ethical attitudes may not be sufficiently embodied in popular sentiment to be productive of legal action in conformity with it. Here law may reflect popular morality though the latter is slowly being made to yield to a more refined and humanitarian approach. Much of the activity of early criminal law with its savage penalties for trivial offences . . . and the gradual move towards a more humane penal system reflects this kind of relation of law to popular feeling and the gradual improvement of both moral and legal standards, each reflecting and interacting upon the other'.[1] And it is this kind of moral education, rather than pontifical pronouncements, which should be the concern of Christian social ethics.

But when public opinion is divided where is the moral standard or criterion to which proposed legislation can be referred? 'This is the fundamental problem of social ethics.' 'How are moral standards to be ascertained in the absence of a spiritual authority?'[2] Does it rest with the jury – the men on the Clapham omnibus? Can it be discovered by any kind of opinion poll? That would be, in effect, to equate moral principles with the attitude of the average sensual man. Can we, as Lord Devlin so powerfully argues, continue to try to enforce Christian standards? That could easily prove to be incompatible with the moral and spiritual freedom which is a vital concern of Christianity (see p. 137). There is no clear way out of the dilemma in which Western society is involved, short of such a return to Christian faith as it is unrealistic to expect. Christians, it seems, must simply accept the dilemma and make the best contribution they can within it.

The Wolfenden committee disclaimed the duty of assessing the teaching of theology, sociology or psychology. But surely that is precisely what is needed. In fact 'a double enquiry is needed, a critique of the moral principles and assumptions and an enquiry into the relevant facts and tendencies. We cannot assume that public or positive morality is unchangeable or beyond criticism or that we know enough of the forms of social adjustment that are possible. If law and morals are to be linked we need to reach agreement on the procedure to be followed in bridging the gap between them. This I take to be the task of a critical jurisprudence,

---

[1] Lloyd, op. cit., pp. 63, 59.
[2] Devlin, p. 92.

and a study of recent work on controversial issues – as, for example, capital and corporal punishment, birth-control, euthanasia, divorce – will show that such a jurisprudence must make increasing use of the social sciences, combined with philosophical analysis of the extent and nature of any disagreements there may be on matters of moral principles'.[1] This is just where Christians come in, with their theological valuation of man and their merciful doctrine of original sin.[2]

IV CRIME AND PUNISHMENT

If it is agreed that the primacy of persons is one of the most characteristic notes of any society that can be called Christian (see p. 154), then the attitude of society towards crime is a central concern for Christian social ethics. 'How a society treats its offenders is an index of its basic attitude towards human personality: if, for instance, we ill-treat our thieves, we show only too clearly what we put first, property or people.'[3] The reform of penology is a growing point in contemporary social thinking, and Christian thinking ought to be in the van of it. What constructive critique have Christians to contribute? How can the two basic Christian principles – the command to love and the duty of forgiveness – be brought to bear on the present situation?

The question is clearly one of the utmost urgency in view of the vast increase of crime – proportionately, and not merely absolutely with the natural increase of population – which is reported everywhere in the West and indeed, or so it appears, the whole world over. According to documents published by U.N. there are one or two areas that can report a decrease; but the total picture is one of a mounting problem. In America the F.B.I. stated (1962)

[1] Ginsberg, p. 233.
[2] 'Moral education must not aim at providing a statement of absolutes, but at being a guide to responsible personal and social conduct in situations which are empirically complex and where man's frailty and proneness to sin are realistically acknowledged. There is certainly an urgent need to examine the principles of moral education and to see what is involved in the maintenance of social morality; and serious attention needs to be given to the frontier of ethics and theology, where the traditional mapping has been subjected to severe criticism in recent years by moralists and theologians, believers and unbelievers alike.' From *Punishment*. A report of the Board of Social Responsibility, Church Information Office.
[3] Howard Jones, *Crime in a Changing Society*, Pelican, 1965, p. ii.

that crime in the previous five years had increased four times faster than the population. In this country, the latest report by the Chief Commissioner of Police gave the highest-ever in criminal statistics, and – what was most ominous about it – not just in crime but in the more serious forms of crime among adolescents and even children. Everywhere it is much the same picture, and no one can contemplate it without alarm and very deep searchings of heart. All statistics, of course, need to be broken down before their real meaning can be interpreted. For example, a greater number of prosecutions under the Street Offences Act need not mean an increase in prostitution, as to which no figures can be available. Conversely, if, because of the Betting and Gaming Act, there have been no prosecutions for street-bookmaking, that does not mean that there has been less betting, but only that off-course betting has now been legalised.[1] It must, moreover, always be remembered that the numbers of criminals, in the strict sense of people who have been actually convicted, not vaguely people who do 'criminal' things, is very much less than the number of crimes committed. There are far more crimes known to the police than they are able to bring to a prosecution.[2] And behind these is the wide margin of crimes which are never reported to the police at all or successfully avoid detection.

All this must not be emotionally exaggerated. It must be examined as factually as possible. An emotional approach can result too easily in leaving the problem worse than it is now. It can, for example, lead to a demand for more and more penal legislation which will only increase the number of criminals – for the greater the number of legally defined crimes, the more criminals there are bound to be – or for retrograde forms of punishment which inflict moral injury on society by ministering to a crude desire for vengeance, but do not substantially reduce crime (see pp. 224 ff.). Wherever there are too many laws there will probably be an increase in lawlessness and a weakened sense of social responsibility. The perpetual creation of new 'offences' tends to the blurring of real moral distinctions, and that tends to blunt the social con-

---

[1] Howard Jones, op. cit., Ch. I. This short book offers a perceptive and well-documented statement of the whole question.

[2] Modern transport and communications make organised rackets and white-collar crime easier, and the chances of getting away with it higher. (U.N. Working Paper on Social Change and Criminality. Too much crime does now seem to pay off.)

science. The infringement of byelaws and regulations – producing too many eggs or too much milk (when millions of people are starving for lack of such things!) or selling tobacco after 8.30 p.m. – must swell the total volume of 'crimes', but it would be grotesque to call them criminal; they are more or less on the level of school discipline. But even when we are thinking about real crimes, really serious offences against society, or the moral law, it must not be assumed that more penal legislation is self-evidently the right attack. Some may be better dealt with by other methods. In principle, we shall probably be on the right line if we resist demands for the extension of the area of criminal jurisdiction. Occam's razor may well be employed here: *leges non sunt multiplicandae praeter necessitatem.*

Moral indignation may only blind our judgement. If we love righteousness we must hate iniquity, and it may indeed be true that, as Devlin says, 'No society can do without intolerance, indignation and disgust; they are the forces behind the moral law, and indeed it can be argued that if they or something like them are not present the feelings of society cannot be weighty enough to deprive the individual of freedom of choice'.[1] But they are blind guides to the treatment of crime and may betray society into worse evil. All of us, moreover, need to remind ourselves that the moral indignation that we profess may be in fact a subconscious protest against criminous tendencies in our own souls. What is needed is a dispassionate enquiry into the probable causes of crime, both psychological and sociological, in the offenders and in the social environment. For while the criminal preys upon society, it was society that produced the criminal. For good and for ill, we are members of one another, and any radical study of the problem will be likely to lead to some radical social criticism. Is there anything in the structures of society, or the dominant values by which it lives, that makes for the growth of criminal behaviour? Christianity has always known that no man can be 'saved' in isolation: he can only be saved in a redeemed society.

Love for the neighbour clearly implies protecting him, if need arise, against injury and violence. It would be a very odd kind of love which stood aside and allowed a man to be murdered, taking no steps at all to defend him, not even dialling the police. The Good

[1] Op. cit., p. 17.

Samaritan only found his neighbour after the cosh-bandits had finished with him, but what if he had caught them redhanded? What would be the indications for love then? For our purpose, the neighbour means the whole society, for which love must feel itself responsible and therefore responsible for its protection; and that means that love must support the forces of order and may therefore have to do, or to will, things which seem to be incompatible with itself (see pp. 217, 218 above). But responsibility for the whole society includes responsibility for the criminal. To love the offender means, amongst other things, to respect his human dignity as a person and not to weaken his own self-respect – rather, to try to awaken and to foster it. That may involve a very critical look at some of the present methods of dealing with him.

Goodhart has said that 'a community which is too ready to forgive the wrongdoer may end by condoning the crime'.[1] If forgiveness meant letting off the criminal it would be a violation of the love-commandment. We have no right to be turning other people's cheeks, leaving other people's children to be raped or lonely old ladies to be beaten up, allowing thieves and murderers to run loose. But in Christian theology, forgiveness does not mean being let off the consequences. Forgiveness means reconciliation, the restoration of personal relationships or – in Tillich's idiom – *acceptance*, which is not deserved or earned but freely given. In the present context, the meaning of forgiveness is the rehabilitation of the offender and restoring him to the life of the community.

There may always in practice remain a tension between our obligation to society and our obligation to the offender. But in principle the two go together. For we are not really protecting society unless we are reforming the criminal, unless we are doing our best to guarantee that he will not continue to commit crime. Otherwise the net balance remains unchanged. One way to the prevention of crime is the more effective prevention of recidivism. To say that is to say that the central emphasis must be rather on helping people to go right than on punishing them for going wrong. That, in turn, will involve asking how far punishment is, or can be, a means to regeneration.

Can society, therefore, best be protected by the reinforcement of the police and the strengthening of the criminal procedure, or by constructive reform of that procedure, moral education and

[1] Op. cit., p. 93.

long-term social planning? These are not, of course, sheer alternatives. Quite obviously we cannot sit back and wait till long-term
social planning has done its work. The arm of the law may require
strengthening; if it is too weak anarchy might follow. 'A disquiet-
ing feature of recent wage-robberies is that they have led to the
employment of private security guards, which is the thin end of
the wedge of private armies.'[1] Again, a higher likelihood of detection would probably do a good deal to reduce crime – although, as
Howard Jones well points out, the price of that might be an in-
quisition which a free society would not and should not tolerate.[2]
But this does not impair the general principle, on which almost
everybody would agree, that the true way ahead is positive rather
than negative and concerned rather with causes than with symptoms.[3]

Christian prophets may say that the mounting crime statistics
are but a sign of the mystery of iniquity (Lawlessness), the kind of
thing that happens and is bound to happen when men and nations
forsake belief in God and lose their sense of moral responsibility –
the writing on the wall for Western civilisation. And this may indeed be the sombre truth of it, though even so, there may yet be
place for repentance. But there are two questions at least that have
to be asked. Is there certainly more crime today, proportionately to
the population, than there was in the thirteenth or fourteenth century or in the golden age of Queen Victoria? No adequate information is available, but it is, I should say, at the least extremely
doubtful. And can we too lightly assume that the increase of what
we roughly-and-readily call crime is really an increase in immorality? Not all crime can be ascribed to sin. The heart of man is
desperately wicked and the fundamental health of any society depends on the regeneration of character. But it also depends on the
soundness of its structures, and there are certainly environmental

---

[1] *Punishment*, p. 9.
[2] p. 14.
[3] 'At best punishment is a mechanical and dangerous means of protection. It can rarely be made equitable and if used as a means of reform it
requires a degree of wisdom and humanity rarely attainable. There will
be, it is to be hoped, a shift from purely punitive to protective and remedial measures. Meanwhile punishment may be unavoidable. But we must
look forward to a time when dangerous criminals will be segregated and,
for the rest, society will concentrate on removing the conditions favouring
crime and on the best means of securing a widely diffused sense of responsibility independent of punishment'. Ginsberg, p. 191.

Q

factors which tend to evoke out of human nature either what is best in it or what is worst – need we look further than family life to see that? Nor can any ultimate judgements of that kind absolve the Christian citizen from the duty to investigate secondary causes or to help to provide relative social remedies.

Our grandfathers talked about the vicious poor, and there must clearly have been a correlation between crime and humanly degrading poverty, penned in slums and animal housing conditions. But the slums have gone, or are rapidly on the way out, and crime no longer lurks in Fagin's kitchen, in thieves' alleys and other 'haunts of vice' into which the police were not too willing to penetrate. (It was the Salvation Lasses who went!) It stalks abroad in respectable outer suburbs – white collar crime is said to be on the increase. There are still known and mapped 'delinquency areas' but these are no longer confined to the downtown districts; some are in the new Council housing estates. Moreover it is the affluent society which is throwing up the new wave of crime. 'Juvenile delinquency has tended to increase most in those countries of Europe in which the standard of living is highest – in the poorer countries of southern Europe it has hardly increased at all.'[1] Can there possibly be any correlation between the new affluence and crime, as there was, in the past, between crime and poverty? The improvement of material conditions has not produced a diminution of crime.

The probability is that the crime problem is one aspect of the total problem of any rapidly changing society – the general confusion of moral standards and the weakening of social cohesion through the breakdown of traditional social patterns (see Ch. I). (How much change and at how fast a tempo can any society stand without disintegration?) Much that has been said in previous chapters about the constantly shifting population, due to the need for mobility of labour, and about the changing patterns of family life from the extended family to the nuclear, may be directly relevant to the present question. In delinquency areas, we should remember, what we describe as deviant behaviour does not seem to be deviant at all but as perfectly normal and natural behaviour; it is only 'they' who regard it as objectionable, and 'they' belong to a different culture and an alien way of life altogether. What obligations can anyone have to *them*? A man takes his tune from his

[1] Howard Jones, p. 25, quoting a U.N. report.

social milieu. Perhaps one can hardly exaggerate the part that is played in human behaviour by expectation. Millions of people are now being rooted up from the traditional neighbourhoods and communities – this is happening almost everywhere in the world – and decanted into new housing schemes which are aggregates of insulated families but in no real sense neighbourhoods or communities. People live in them but do not belong to them. There is no standard of social expectation, very little sharing in a common life. For young people, at least, the gang has to supply both, and the gang, being alienated in spirit from the other elements in the population, tends to develop a deviant youth-culture determined to prove its worth and get its own back.

A good deal is known and far more needs to be known about the operation of subconscious motives in producing overt criminal behaviour. Attention is being increasingly directed to emotional frustration and deprivation compensating, through the familiar mechanisms, in self-assertive social defiance. How far, we must ask, is there a correlation between such emotional frustration and the changed social and domestic patterns? It has long been known that violence and sadism and vandalistic destruction of property can provide a substitute sexual gratification. It is clear that much more research is wanted into all these personality-disorders and their relation to sociological facts. It can be said that these are 'abnormal' cases. But what exactly is normal personality? In the present context the question would seem to be whether any practicable social changes would assist a more satisfying identification of the ego with the social super-ego.[1]

Psychiatric treatment will often be required. But what society needs is to take steps to remove adverse conditioning social pressures – more steps to strengthen and stabilise the family, more constructive approaches to town planning (with a critical look at low-density housing), better provision for real community life on the estates and in the rural areas, to arrest the stampede from the countryside and to counteract the lure of the bright lights. It needs also to ask itself searchingly whether existing definitions

[1] In Freud's idiom the super-ego is regarded negatively, as the censor, 'the hostile limiter of the ego's freedom'. More recent work regards the super-ego in a positive aspect as a force 'which does not merely check the ego but strengthens and enhances it as a creator of positive standards (which) nurtures the capacity for expression and life-fulfilment through art, ethics, religion, science'. Mumford, *The Condition of Man*, p. 424.

of crime are all framed in terms of society as a whole, and never in terms of any privileged interest. (It might remind itself of the game-preservation laws.)[1]

But all this leads on to the actual treatment of criminals. Here we encounter the fundamental tension between the reformative treatment of offenders and the vindication of social morality. If two men are found guilty of the same offence by the same court should they both receive the same sentence? There may be degrees of diminished responsibility, indications for very different forms of treatment. Is the primary duty of the court to punish or to set the offender's feet on the way back? How far can sentences be individualised without putting false weights in the scales of justice? Does justice require here treating unequals unequally no less than treating equals equally? But in any case, who are equal and who are unequal? Not the most ideal judge can know all the psychological history of the man in the dock – perhaps indeed he ought not to know, lest his judgement should be swayed by pity. Some American States have made the experiment of removing sentencing from the trial judge and entrusting it to expert committees,[2] the whole emphasis being laid on treatment. This means, in effect, shifting the whole emphasis, as Lady Wootton and others are now urging, from culpability to curability.

Yet this would appear to outrage the demand for the vindication of the law through punishment, that is for punishment as retribution. Is retribution inherent in the moral law? Is there some kind of ultimate moral necessity that wrongdoing should be visited by a penalty, so that thus good asserts itself against evil? Must the offender always be made to pay? This theory, which is deeply entrenched in some of the classical doctrines of Atonement, was stated in its most rigorist form by Kant. It was frequently emphasised by William Temple. It is strongly endorsed by Professor Goodhart. 'Retribution in punishment is an expression of the community's disapproval of crime and if this retribution is not given recognition, then the disapproval may also disappear.'[3] Even those who feel this most keenly would, however, agree that punishment ought, at the same time, to be aimed at the moral

[1] The *Daily Telegraph* carried two good articles by Bryan Wilson on Social planning with special reference to teenage delinquency, August 24th and 25th, 1964.
[2] Howard Jones, pp. 99 ff.
[3] Op. cit., p. 92.

reform of the offender. To what extent are the two things really compatible? For certainly punishment can make a man worse, leaving him embittered and vengeful towards society. Punishment can only be reformative if it is accepted by the offender as being, in some sense, due to him or deserved, or if, as we say, it brings his offence home to him. It cannot be taken for granted that this is always so, and indeed the more far-gone the offender, the less probable is it that it will be so.

Are we, then, to take the utilitarian line and assume the merely deterrent role of punishment? If so we run into further difficulties. Are we justified in inflicting pain on one man in order to discourage other people? How severe a deterrent is justifiable? Is the fear of punishment always a deterrent? For there are well-known pathological cases in which people go out of their way to court punishment under the compulsion of guilt-complexes or by way of asserting their self-importance. (It is arguable indeed that in some cases the death penalty and the morbid publicity were an actual incentive to murder.) All these various questions really reveal the same problem and there is no glib one-word answer to it. There is no one mandarin Christian solution.

The most hopeful line will be the exploration of more constructive treatment and better aftercare. Imprisonment may itself be criminogenic – all concerned are only too well aware of that – and at present the curve of the success-rate for prisons, and for borstals, is falling. It seems clear that social and moral reformation requires a much closer association with normal society and with family life than custodial treatment at present is able to contemplate. Every 'open' experiment ought to be encouraged and the whole idea developed very much further. The licence system could be more widely extended. Prison labour could be so reorganised as to be a retraining for industry. It may be possible to devise means by which offenders could serve a sentence through a system of adult attendance centres while continuing to live with their families. There is very much to be learnt from Scandinavian methods.[1] The safety of society may demand that dangerous psychopathic types must be segregated in maximum security. But, as Alec

[1] And Dutch. The U.N. paper on Measures to Combat Recidivism has an account of the Van der Hoeven Klinic in Utrecht for the treatment of psychopathic recidivists. At every stage the patient is *consulted* about his treatment, and taught to have responsibility for it.

Patteson said in his famous dictum, you cannot hope to train people for freedom behind locked doors. There is also needed far more adequate aftercare and more ungrudging acceptance by society. For if men are cold-shouldered by society when they are released, is it their fault or ours if they revert to anti-social conduct?

Perhaps we shall have to say that in the long run a society gets the criminals it deserves. Are the dominant values of Western society such as to make for social cohesion, mutual trust and personal fulfilment? Is there, as Howard Jones has suggested,[1] a 'reservoir of free-floating hate' which may yet tear society in pieces? And if there is, has this anything to do with that concentration on money and external things which tends to ignore the spiritual needs and emotional satisfactions of persons? May not that be for Christians the fundamental question?

V THE SANCTITY OF HUMAN LIFE

In the Christian tradition the sanctity of life refers specifically to human life. 'Kill not any living thing', says Buddhism; but for Christians the sanctity of life does not mean the preservation of sacred cows or poisonous snakes or plague-infested rats. Indeed that principle, carried to its conclusion, contradicts the preservation of human life. Schweitzer, with all his 'reverence for life', presumably killed the anopheles mosquito. Neither the classical nor the scriptural ethic questions man's right to kill animals for food. (There were vegetarian sects in the ancient culture, but their qualms were bound up with a theory of metempsychosis.) Indeed the modern reader is often shocked, especially if he pictures the scene, with the coldblooded way in which the Old Testament describes the ghastly hecatombs of the sacrifices – even though he hopes that the numbers – a thousand bullocks and a thousand rams – are imaginary or conventional. But a fundamental conviction of the Bible is the sanctity of the life of man – 'For in the image of God created he him' (Genesis viii: 6). One mark of any developed civilisation is the value which it assigns to human life. Christianity reinforces that by its faith that life was ennobled and sanctified through the Lord's 'taking our nature upon him'. The cardinal principle of the Christian ethic is the value and sanctity of human life. 'Ye are of more value than many sparrows.'

[1] p. 160.

Yet the phrase, the absolute value of human life, which is commonly used to describe the Christian attitude, stands in need of a certain qualification. Does Christian teaching really say 'absolute'? That a Man laid down his life for his friends is the supreme example of Christian charity. It is surely inherent in the Christian world-view that what makes life ultimately worth living is that there are values higher than life itself which invest life with its dignity and significance and to which life must, on occasion, be offered. What shall a man give in exchange for his soul? The answer must be, sometimes, his life. Christianity, in other words – this is a point which will be found important when we come to examine 'mercy-killing' – regards life qualitatively rather than quantitatively.

Moreover, as Christian ethics became systematised, it has always been recognised that there are circumstances in which it may be morally right to take life, for example, in legitimate self-defence or by a woman defending her honour. The elaborate casuistry of all such cases may be left to the books on moral theology. Again, perhaps because it had little option, the Church has always conceded the right of the State to require the lives of its citizens in war (or of Christians to kill in 'just' wars) or by way of inflicting judicial punishment. Many Christians, of course, have strongly challenged both. Many have protested that capital punishment is a violation of that which it seeks to defend; but as this is now a dead-letter in this country it need not be discussed further here. (For pacificism, see pp. 267, 271.) Are these the only possible exceptions which can be admitted in Christian social ethics? The commandment is, Thou shalt do no murder, that is, thou shalt not take life unlawfully; and the real question is, what is murder? What taking of life can have moral justification? Are there, for example, any circumstances in which a man may rightfully take his own life? Or is it so true that the Almighty has fixed his canon against self-slaughter that suicide must be morally wicked, as in Law it has been, and is still, a crime and a felony?

SUICIDE

In this country, in 1962, the number of suicides recorded was 5,583, and of course the number of unsuccessful attempts, few of which are ever reported to the police, was indefinitely larger than that. The suicide-rate is an index of social health. There must be something wrong with a society in which so many of its citizens find life so empty and unsatisfying, or are reduced to such ultimate despair, as to throw away their own existence. Moreover, so far as statistics are available, it appears to be true that the suicide rate is highest in countries which have the highest standards of life – standards of life, that is, not standards of living. It would seem that the first concern of the Christian ethic should be with the social implications of suicide and with preventive and remedial strategies. One of the most creative contributions is undoubtedly that of the Telephone Samaritans, which was begun by Christian initiative. But there is need for much more research into both the psychological motivations and the social aetiology of suicide. Vast numbers of people are assailed, from time to time, by suicidal impulses. What are the psychological causes of that, and what are the social conditions which may heal them or which tend to provoke them to their fatal consequences? One of the stock arguments of the moralists, whether Christian or secular, has been that suicide is morally wrong because it deprives the State of a citizen. But the suicide is the product of a society which has made him feel that life is no longer desirable. What is going wrong with the society?

The Christian moral case against suicide, and not least in St. Thomas, is largely formal and seems more like a rationalisation of a deeply felt, instinctive horror of it. To call suicide self-murder begs the question. It must be seen in its wider social reference, and this includes what is sometimes forgotten – the traumatic effect on a man's own family, who will never, so long as they live, get over it. But the fundamental Christian objection can perhaps be sustained only on religious grounds – that we are, as Aquinas puts it, God's property. Life is God's gift and we have no right to reject it. (*Summa* II, ii, Q 59, 64.)

The deeply-rooted horror may be a hangover from primitive magic and fear of the dead man's ghost – and this may explain the burial at the cross-roads. Yet the Old Testament nowhere condemns suicide – it merely records the proverbial act of Ahitophel (II Samuel xvii: 23). The Stoic opposition under the Caesars made a cult of high-minded suicide as the free man's way out – 'the door is open'. Christians had their own grounds for condemning it. The traditional judgement has not been unquestioned. It has, for example, been challenged head-on from two impeccably orthodox quarters. In spite of Aquinas, St Thomas More supported self-inflicted euthanasia, and John Donne wrote a tract in favour of suicide. Hume who, though sceptic as he was always professed to be writing as a Christian, made the same attack with characteristic cynicism.[1] Other Christian writers have taken a similar line. But the main stream of tradition in the Church has been uncompromising in condemnation. Suicide has been mortal, almost unforgivable sin. In English law, suicide has been a felony, and the Crown's greed for the forfeited estates may have encouraged the mediaeval lawyers to lay heavy weight on its felonious character. The horrible consequences of all this ruled out any approach to constructive treatment. People lied or tried to conceal the facts from their doctors and others for fear of the savage penalties.

Parliament has so far been unwilling to remove suicide from the list of crimes. There has, however, been a general liberalising both in public opinion and in legal practice. Comparatively few prosecutions are now instigated for attempted suicide, and when they are there is high probability that the sentence will be no more than probation or direction to undergo medical treatment. (Actually only a small percentage of attempts are ever reported to the police; doctors and clergy and relatives keep them quiet.) The Homicide Act (1957) reduced the charge in a suicide pact to manslaughter – previous to the act it was murder – thus allowing the judge full discretion. He can, if he wills, give an absolute discharge. One of the most difficult legal problems is how to deal with aiding and abetting. So long as suicide remains criminal this can still, it would seem, be technically murder. It may be that it ought always to be punishable. And indeed if no penalty were attached to it, then the door would be thrown wide open to unrestricted legalised euthanasia, and that is a step on a very dangerous slope. If anyone may kill anyone else at his own request – and it might be almost impossible to prove that no request had been made – it might be giving immunity to murderers. In the general interest of society any taking of life by consent or on request must clearly be kept under stringent legal safeguards. But the charge for aiding and abetting suicide might perhaps justifiably be reduced to manslaughter. And it is very much to be hoped that suicide will

[1] Glanville Williams, *The Sanctity of Life and the Criminal Law*, Faber 1958, pp. 277, 238.

soon cease to be a crime at all. Christian opinion would certainly welcome that and has indeed been foremost in pressing for it. It would certainly make for general social welfare if the problem can be handled on its own ground, unconfused by criminal implications.[1]

In any formulation of a Christian judgement, it has to be remembered that suicide is a term that covers many different acts which differ very widely in moral quality. Some, indeed, performed under duress or interior psychological compulsion, are hardly the subjects of moral judgement at all. There are actions which may be technically suicide that call for positive moral approbation. There are some which may seem to be cowardly or selfish and some which remain totally inexplicable. There can be no standardised text-book moral formula.

No one can have anything but praise for a Captain Oates – the inevitable example – or the man who throws himself across his wife's body to shield her from an explosion or a rifle shot. (Moral theologians bring such cases under the principle of 'double effect', but it seems to be rather rarefied casuistry.) It is no doubt true that the end must be great enough to justify even the sacrifice of one's own life. A man would be held morally irresponsible who allowed himself to be run down by the traffic to recover his hat or to shake hands with a friend. There are many men of my generation who have had to face the question in personal terms. Under battle conditions, Red Cross personnel and chaplains are clearly under obligation to take even the most extreme risk to carry in or minister to the wounded. Are they justified in taking the same risk to say the burial office over the dead? My own answer, in principle, was no, but it may have been the answer of cowardice. But if they do take that risk and are killed will any one say that they were committing sin? The very suggestion is morally outrageous. They will be rightly regarded as moral heroes.

About such cases the question does not arise, nor about the martyrs for freedom and faith and righteousness. Indeed there is something unrealistic in including these in the category of 'suicide'.

There might seem to be a distinct moral difference between laying life down for others, or for a great cause, and deliberately taking one's own life, but there is no very clearly-defined frontier.

[1] See *Ought Suicide to be a Crime?*, Church Information Office, 1959.

For example, a man with inoperable cancer may contrive to kill himself by an overdose. But he may have one of two very different motives, either to relieve his relatives from the burden, or to save himself from the pain and weakness; or there may have been a mixture of both. But no human judgement can know which motive it was. Since he was, in any case, going to die, he can hardly be said to have laid down his life for others. Yet in so far as that was his main motive does he really fall under moral condemnation? In so far as his motive was to avoid pain, the Christian is certainly called to accept suffering in the Spirit of Christ and by the grace of God. But how far is he, as a Christian called upon to accept suffering that can be avoided? And as to the purifying effects of suffering, we must be on guard against parsonical clichés. Pain beyond a certain degree of intensity can reduce a man to a whimpering animal. We rightly reverence the heroic virtue of a man who endures to the end and is not defeated, but we surely ought not to demand heroic virtue as a standardised norm for Christian conduct. It *was* morally wrong, no doubt, to take the overdose. But the Christian judgement will surely be very merciful. Can it honestly be regarded as mortal sin? At worst, it was an example of human frailty.

A woman may kill herself to avoid rape. This presumably falls under the same heading as the right to kill the man with the same intent. Women have indeed been canonised on this – including some who perhaps never existed! The act has been judged to be good rather than sinful. A Negro may be pursued by a crowd of lynchers. If he has a gun he may shoot in self-defence; but that will make things worse for him in the end and many other Negroes will suffer for it. What if he turns the gun on himself instead? Officials who had incurred Hitler's wrath were often told of the fate which awaited them and then handed a loaded revolver. In 1940 when invasion was believed to be imminent, many Englishmen known to be on the Nazi blacklist carried a cyanide tablet in their pockets. If it had happened, and if they had been arrested and swallowed the tablet, could that have been called sinful? All such cases are acts done under duress. They are in effect involuntary actions and accordingly do not fall under moral judgement.

The same applies to the large group of cases which are due to psychological disorders in varying degrees of intensity, which range from those of the adolescent suicides (often under examination stress) to that of the self-enclosed, despairing psychopath who has ceased to be able to believe in anything. Moral considerations do not arise. It is recognised that disturbed adolescents sometimes stage elaborate 'attempts', which may accidentally be successful, out of a pathological exhibitionism. They were never intended to end in death but only in forcing somebody to take notice.

There is also a less defined group of cases in which people kill themselves under no compulsion, and indeed with apparent irresponsibility, because life has ceased to bring any satisfaction. The causes may be loneliness, unemployment, the sense of being unwanted after retirement, the breakdown of a marriage or a love affair, or a feeling of being generally 'browned off', which has probably deep psychological roots. Here there is certainly some degree of sin. But often society is far more culpable. Why were they left to feel lonely or unwanted? Christianity knows that 'salvation' begins with the recognition of acceptance, the discovery that someone believes in us.

Suicide, then, ought not to be a crime in law, and it now seems, on closer examination, that although in some cases some moral guilt is incurred, yet it cannot now normally be regarded as a specially grievous or mortal sin. The primary concern of Christian thinking should be with the underlying social causes and with pastoral and psychiatric approaches to it. All this amounts, no doubt, to a revision, even a reversal, of the traditional attitudes. It is however one of the many cases in which new facts and fuller knowledge and a deeper understanding of human nature modify the traditional content of Christian ethics (see p. 32). Christian moral insights are not tied by precedent. Full account ought to be taken of the tradition; but in the end no Christian generation is bound by the moral judgements of its predecessors.[1]

EUTHANASIA

The religious condemnation of suicide seems to rest fundamentally on the argument that our lives belong to God, not to ourselves. We violate the sanctity of life if we cast it away by our own act. That is not for us to decide; we must abide our going

---

[1] For full discussion of the legal position see Glanville Williams, Ch. VII, and for moral and religious appraisal see *Ought Suicide to be a Crime?*, Ch. III.

hence even as our coming hither. I have tried to appraise the Christian attitude and have inclined to a more lenient judgement than every reader may be prepared to endorse. But what if, instead of taking his own life when he is in the grip of a painful illness, the patient asks the doctor to do it for him? (In practice there will normally be an abettor. Someone must put the means within his reach.) Or if the doctor quietly lets him die when he knows that he is beyond human aid? It would seem that the problem of euthanasia is really an extension of the same problem which has been discussed in the previous pages. It involves much the same moral principles and many of the same legal questions. The problem arises not from human wickedness but from two things that are essentially good – first from the advance of medical techniques and then from one of our best moral assets, the magnificient ethical code of the Profession. And here too informed public opinion, and within it Christian opinion, is on the move. Does the Hippocratic oath, reinforced by Christian tradition, necessitate, and does the sanctity of human life imply, that it is in all cases a moral duty to keep men alive to the last possible moment? And in view of the latest medical techniques we must ask what exactly is meant by 'alive'?

The doctor is the servant of life. He labours with dedicated devotion, often against nearly impossible odds, to fight off death and preserve his patient's life. And the trust of the patient and the relatives is based on the knowledge that he will never desist from that. (It is true, we are told, that any skilful doctor could kill a patient without trace if he wished and that there could be no legal protection. But such is the great professional tradition that no one would ever imagine the possibility. The patient knows that the doctor is on his side.) But is there a point when that obligation ceases? In an intolerably painful illness for which there is no possibility of cure, so that it is certainly going to end in death, is he morally bound to prevent the man from dying for one more day or for one more hour up to the very last extreme moment? If pneumonia meanwhile supervenes, is he morally bound to administer antibiotics? If the patient himself asks to be released from what has become little more than a living death, may he justifiably give him his quietus? Does the sanctity of life mean that the prolongation of physical existence, under any conditions and at any price, is an absolute, incommensurable value, or can there be a standard of valuation which is qualitative rather than merely quantitative? If physical death is the worst thing that can happen to us then presumably it is a moral duty to subordinate everything else to its postponement. But that is not a Christian valuation. There is a Christian attitude to death as well as a Christian attitude to life.

Morally, it may seem unrealistic to describe it as murder if a patient is released from life by his own expressed wish. But the law as it now stands is quite uncompromising. If anyone gives the patient a tablet which he knowingly takes and then dies, that is murder. (It is the same crime as abetting suicide.) In such charges consent is no defence. And still more obviously if the other party has given and is proved to have given a fatal dose or injection, that is murder. The doctor has no immunity from that law. On general grounds Christians will support all measures that tend to the safeguarding of life, and they would, I think, rightly resist any proposed changes in the present law which would confer immunity in such cases on anyone other than the patient's doctor. But this is the doctor's position at the moment. It is true, no doubt, that the charge is very seldom brought, though the police may at any time be forced to bring it, and that in practice the judge's direction may allow the substitution of a lower charge or may involve the doctrine of necessity (cp. the judgement in the Bourne case, p. 260 below) or that the jury may refuse to convict. But the full legal consequences *may* fall on him. And the logical implications of the present law, if strictly applied, may even be found to militate against the anaesthetisation of pain.

When a patient is in great agony the minimum dose required to kill the pain may in fact be one that is likely to prove fatal. Is a doctor to be prevented from giving it by the threat of having to face a charge of murder? Again, as a patient becomes habituated to narcotic drugs they may have to be administered in progressively increasing doses, and the time will come when the choice will have to be made between leaving the patient's agony unrelieved and relieving it but by shortening his life or at least by accelerating his death. Few will doubt what the decision ought to be. Yet the doctor *has*, in effect, 'killed' the patient.

Moral theologians justify the decision under the doctrine of double effect and the law may rely on the doctrine of necessity. But how far is there any real moral difference between the deliberate giving of a dose knowing that it will in fact prove fatal and deliberately giving a fatal dose?

The withholding of medical means to prolong life – not striving officiously to keep alive – seems to raise no moral problems, and is said by authorities to be 'probably lawful'. The phrase commonly used in this context is the distinction between the prolongation of life and the prolongation of the act of dying. But the phrase does not really cover the facts. Death and life are no longer so clearly distinguishable. *When* does a man die? When his heart stops beating? The use of electronics in cardiac surgery brings the whole problem into a new phase. It is possible to keep a man 'alive', that is to say to keep his heart beating, long after consciousness has been destroyed, with no possible hope of recovery, by brain injury. I have known of a case that lasted two years, and one of even twelve years has been reported. How far can this be called life? If the doctor switches off the machine can he really be said to have 'killed' that poor body in which the spirit's self had ceased to burn? Can there possibly be any moral obligation to prolong that physical existence and indeed can it even be morally right to do it? Can the sanctity of life require that?

Here it may be repeated that for the Christian there is a value in death as well as in life. For those who share the Christian hope death is a gate into life: *mors ianua vitae*. But for all men, Christians and others, death is a relevant fact of human life and indeed the inescapable condition of it. There is a time to live and a time to die. When that time comes the enemy comes as a friend and the patient should not be held back from joining him.[1]

Christian opinion, in its official expressions, is at present very strongly opposed to any legalising of euthanasia. It is probable, too, that majority opinion in this country and in most other countries would oppose it. No country has in fact yet taken that step.[2] It might result in making life cheap. It might result in all manner of abuses. If suicide ceases to be a crime then it would not be an offence for *anybody* to put the poison into the patient's hand, and that gap would have to be stopped accordingly. There is probably no responsible opinion that would contemplate unre-

[1] *Decisions about Life and Death*, Church Information Office, 1965, p. 7. The whole pamphlet is of great value. For legal facts and assessments, Glanville Williams, Ch. VIII.
[2] Glanville Williams, p. 297.

stricted euthanasia. It would have to be rigorously confined to the doctor and perhaps also to cases of terminal illness. I do not think that with those limitations and those safeguards Christian opinion need resist a liberalisation of the law. Everyone knows that doctors do in fact give drugs that have the effect of shortening life and everyone approves of their doing it – would indeed censure them if they failed to do it. Every day they have to make decisions which involve terrible responsibility in the secret places of their conscience in the light of their own best medical judgement. Public opinion trusts them implicitly. We all put our lives in the doctor's hands. Why should we think that he will become less trustworthy if he is given legal protection?

In a House of Lords debate the Archbishop of Canterbury (Lang) argued, and Lord Horder had given the lead, that the right way of dealing with the question was to suggest no new legislation and not to propose any legalising, but to leave everything where it is in practice, that is, within the discretion of the doctor. Most opinion, Christian or other, would probably at the moment agree with that. But it is most unfair to the doctor, and in the long run also to the patient, to deprive him of protection under the law. He cannot make an objective professional judgement if the threat, however remote, of prosecution or blackmail is sitting on his shoulder. The case could be met by a measure which would not give a patient a right to euthanasia nor be dependent on the consent of relatives (who may have an interest in the death) but would provide protection to the doctor in the exercise of his professional judgement. (He might decide to refuse the patient's request.) It might simply provide that it is not an offence for a qualified medical practitioner to accelerate the death of a patient who is suffering from severe pain in an incurable and fatal illness unless it is proved that the act was not done in good faith and with the patient's consent. The doctor would have to prove the medical facts. It would be for the Crown to prove bad faith. This is suggested by Glanville Williams, p. 303, and, on balance, with some misgiving, I should support that.

ABORTION[1]

We have had to ask, when does human life end? We have now to

[1] This section was written before the House of Lords debate in the autumn of 1965, and the subsequent publication of *Abortion – an Ethical*

ask, when does human live begin? Does the sanctity of human life
extend back into its pre-natal existence? As to that, Christian tradition has been quite solid. Everyone knows that exposure and infanticide were practised freely in Graeco-Roman society. A social
conscience which did not disapprove or try to prohibit the killing
of live babies would certainly feel no scruple about abortion. The
Church took an equally strong line against both. Abortion was
simply another form of infanticide. The two were but different
forms of the same sin, which violated the sanctity of life. All
Christian States have enacted stringent laws attempting to eradicate abortion which was regarded and punishable as murder.
St. Augustine and others were no doubt obsessed with the fate
of infants dying unbaptised. We must also remember the concern
of governments to maintain a sufficient level of population against
high mortality-rates, war and plague; another visitation of the
Black Death would have left Europe cripplingly depopulated.
(The argument here is the same as in suicide; it is depriving the
State of a citizen.) But the same concern is evident all the way
through. Abortion was something morally wrong and criminal
because it was killing a yet unborn child. It was on that ground
that abortion was prohibited, not because it involved danger to the
mother.

English law leaves no room for doubt about that. In its present
form (Offences against the Person Act 1861) any act done with
intent to procure abortion, whether by the woman herself or by
another – even, apparently, if it does not succeed, even if the
woman is not in fact pregnant – is a crime and the maximum
penalty attached is no less than imprisonment for life. (The
maximum penalty for rape is seven years.) The moral implications are perfectly clear. As with murder, consent is no defence.
The action and even the attempted action is prohibited as something wrong in itself. And the reason is ultimately theological –
the Christian valuation of the embryo as a human being with an
immortal soul. It is to protect the sanctity of life.

So far as concerns the mother herself the law is now scarcely
ever enforced. Prosecutions are very rarely instigated. This is
partly, no doubt, because the woman may be needed by the Crown

---

Enquiry by the Board of Social Responsibility, Church Information
Office.

R

as a witness, but is also for more significant reasons – that the jury may refuse to convict and that the sentence in any case will be nominal. In other words, the law is no longer enforced because it is no longer enforceable. Public opinion is no longer behind it. Abortion is one of the texts for Lord Devlin's thesis that 'without the teaching of Christian morality the law will fail'.

Meanwhile judicial opinion is moving towards a quite different reading of the existing law. Lord Goddard said in the case of *R. v. Tate* (1949) that 'it is because the unskilled attentions of ignorant people in cases of this kind often result in death that attempts to produce abortion are regarded by the law as very serious offences'. Here the central emphasis has moved from the life of the unborn child to the life of the mother. This, comments Devlin, 'gives the law a twist which dissociates it from morality and, I think, to some extent from sound sense. The act is being punished because it is dangerous and it is dangerous largely because it is illegal.'[1]

The law has in fact hopelessly broken down. It does not succeed in preventing abortion. But it has vastly increased back-street surgery. Abortion, being illegal, has gone underground. There is no need to enlarge on the results or on the total volume of suffering, illness, insanity and death which is due to the trade of the unskilled abortionist. 'It is hard to visualise the total misery and wreckage of life that must result from this hidden social canker . . .[2] A figure of this order, even if wrong by a factor of ten, demonstrates beyond all argument that the law is ineffective. In the overwhelming majority of cases the illegal operations are performed not by qualified medical practitioners (for these are successfully intimidated by the law) but by unqualified persons under septic conditions.'[3] The last state indeed is worse than the first.

Whether from the strictly Christian standpoint or from that of general social welfare the first step must be to eliminate the black market. (By the Christian standpoint I do not mean concern about 'immorality' in the narrow sense. There is little to suggest that abortion is mainly sought for illegitimate pregnancies.) But it is unrealistic to imagine that more stringent laws and heavier penal-

[1] Devlin, *The Enforcement of Morals*, p. 24. See also Glanville Williams, pp. 140–147.
[2] Glanville Williams, who estimates there is not more than one prosecution in England for every thousand criminal abortions.
[3] pp. 195, 196.

ties are going to stop desperate, frantic women from seeking relief wherever it can be got. They would only drive the black market deeper underground. Half the trouble now is that the qualified gynaecologist and the woman who obliges in the back-alley are put by the law on precisely the same footing. It is obvious that there will always be *some* cases, in which it is right, from the Christian standpoint or any other, to terminate a pregnancy. It is vital on all grounds – physical, social and moral – to keep this in the hands of the qualified practitioner. It seems clear that the only effective means to that is some measure of limited legalisation. There might be a measure making it unlawful for any person other than a qualified practitioner to perform any act intended to terminate a pregnancy in another. Self-induced miscarriage by the woman herself would perhaps be best kept outside the law. Too much snooping is socially corrupting. In any case nothing will stop a desperate woman – the threat of life-imprisonment does not now – and no paper-penalties will in fact be exacted. Dead-letter laws are morally bad for society.

It might possibly be best to leave it at that. It would help to solve one side of the problem – the creation of a new social evil through the attempt to prevent another. Yet no society with a Christian background can contemplate giving unlimited legal sanction for an act which all Christians, and many if not most responsible citizens, regard as immoral, except when there are compelling justifications for it. Any legalisation will have to be strictly defined.

But when, we must ask, does a human life begin? In the ancient language, at what point in the process does the soul come into the unborn child? We cannot use quite that language now. The question will have to be asked in the different form, how soon is there within the womb anything that can rightly be regarded as a *human* life, a rational soul, a personal existence? Is it from the first moment of conception? That is the view presupposed in the present law, but St. Thomas and the canonists distinguished between embryo *formatus* and embryo *informatus*. The foetus was 'ensouled' or 'informed' with life when it became capable of 'movement', i.e. at the first sign of 'quickening'. In common law, according to Glanville Williams,[1] abortion before quickening was not a crime, and only became so in 1803. There is respectable Christian tradition for saying that there is then a human life when

[1] pp. 142–144.

there is a viable child with an independent life of its own, i.e. not before the fourth month. After that abortion really becomes infanticide and revolts all natural human feelings. This limitation, then, might be imposed, that no operation shall be lawful after the twenty-eighth week of pregnancy.

There can, one would think, be little room for doubt that pregnancy may rightly be terminated if the mother's life will otherwise be endangered. Both lives ought to be preserved, but if sheer medical facts make that impossible, then which of the two lives ought to have priority? The same decision may have to be made at a birth, and no different principle seems to be involved. To maintain that in all and any circumstances it is absolutely wrong to remove an embryo seems to me to be morally indistinguishable from maintaining that there are certain circumstances in which it is right to kill the mother. There are, of course, casuistical subtleties; but 'there is such a thing as Christian common sense'. Is this to honour the sanctity of life? There is really no moral difficulty in this case. It comes under the doctrine of necessity, as laid down by the judge in the trial of Mr. Bourne, who bravely insisted on challenging a test case.

The question is whether saving the mother's life may legitimately be extended to include saving the mother from prolonged suffering or severe physical or mental illness which are likely to follow if she gives birth to the child? Christian judgement will probably agree that 'therapeutic' abortion of this kind, under due medical safeguards, is permissible. It may fairly be judged to be governed by necessity, though it may be a delicate matter to decide how far the principle ought to be extended. A woman may suffer acute mental distress and may even be brought near to the point of insanity, by having a baby which she does not want to have. Many Christians, probably, would exclude that instance. Yet it may perhaps be urged that the Christian conscience ought to be more alert than it always is to the moral problem of the unwanted child, with all the disastrous psychological consequences and its well-established bearing on delinquency.

Outside therapeutic abortion, as to which, in general terms, there would now be agreement, are there other grounds for moral justification?

When a child has been raped, moral judgement and human compassion will probably be at one. The conception was forced upon her under duress, so that she was not a responsible moral agent. So far as the law is concerned the decision here seems to have been laid down in the Bourne case. Morally, it may fairly be called necessity.

A very much more difficult group of questions arise if proposals are made to extend the principle from the mother's life to the unborn child itself. If there are compelling reasons to expect that the child will be born so grievously deformed or with such a degree of mental deficiency that it will never have the opportunity of living a normal or real human life, may the pregnancy be legitimately terminated? This requires very much fuller examination. In general terms it seems to involve the question whether the sanctity of life requires the preservation of physical life at all costs. But the answer cannot be given by a formula. It involves, like any moral decision, a scrupulous balancing of conflicting values and a choice between the greater and lesser evil. But at least this, like other similar cases, must be approached with the utmost compunction, and vigilance lest public opinion should come to regard the practice of abortion, as pre-Christian society regarded it, as just a simple and obvious way out.

STERILISATION

If Christians accept family limitation as not only permissible but as a Christian duty (see pp. 197 ff.) how far does that moral judgement carry them? If contraceptive methods are sanctioned, is sterilisation to be ruled out? Is there any real distinction in moral principle? As is well known, some Indian governments, faced with an overwhelming population problem, are conducting State propaganda in favour of sterilisation on a wide scale. (Western contraceptives cost money; and, perhaps because they are Western, are unfavourably regarded in Asia.) Christians in India are asking for moral guidance. There is a small but vocal and persistent demand for sterilisation in this country, both as a means to family limitation and on eugenic and other wider grounds. What is or should be the Christian attitude?

As a means to the limitation of the family there would seem to be no essential moral distinction between this and the use of contraceptives, if it is employed with the same moral safeguards – with deliberate moral responsiblity and the free mutual consent of both partners. (It need not be an irrevocable step: in theory the male operation is reversible.) Though it may be and is in itself an evil – as, for that matter, is *any* operation – in some cases it may be the lesser evil and therefore morally the right choice. In this limited context of family limitation it would seem that, in relevant situations, there is 'no absolute moral bar from the Christian side'. But it must be emphasised that this Christian judgement can apply only to voluntary recourse to it. Any attempt at compulsory sterilisation involves an infringement of human rights and a violation of personal freedom and dignity which a Christian ethic is bound to condemn and resist. This would also apply to any proposal for compulsory sterilisation as a penal measure.

Therapeutic sterilisation, by consent, seems to be covered by the same principles as those which apply to therapeutic abortion. 'There is a growing tendency on both sides of the Atlantic for surgeons to combine sterilisation with therapeutic abortion in suitable cases, because the same condition that indicates the abortion may indicate that the woman should not become pregnant again.'[1]

This would seem also to cover sterilisation, voluntarily accepted, on eugenic grounds. 'Three generations of imbeciles are enough.' (Admittedly, the voluntary consent of mental defectives may come to nothing at all, and this makes it much harder to resist the argument for compulsory sterilisation by the State.) It may be that new biological knowledge may be tending to weaken the force in some of this argument. But it is an exceedingly complicated question which ought not to be closed by over-dogmatic statements.

Contrary to popular opinion, the sterilisation of a 'sex-maniac' offers no protection to society, since, unlike mutilation, it does not affect sexual potency. It need hardly be added that, although St. Thomas was prepared to recognise it as a penal measure and that, however incredible it sounds, the papal choir used to employ *castrati*, mutilation can never be morally justified.

I say nothing here about Insemination. It has recently been discussed by Wassams[2] and there is a new Anglican report[3] which

---

[1] Glanville Williams, p. 79. For full discussion see his Ch. III. See also the Church of England report, *Sterilisation, an Ethical Enquiry*, Church Information Office, 1962.

[2] *A New Introduction to Moral Theology*, S.C.M., 1964, p. 150.

[2] *Artificial Insemination by Donor; two Contributions towards a Christian Judgement*, Church Information Office, 1959.

contains the Archbishop of Canterbury's evidence given before the Departmental Committee.[1] There may be a rather stronger case to be made from the Christian side than has been made yet.

In approaching the group of problems raised in this section we must keep before us two governing principles. First, that the new discoveries of the sciences, in so far as they tend to liberate human life from the sheer determinisms of nature, may serve to enhance the sanctity of life in the will of God, and so call for Christian welcome. But secondly, that obedience to the will of God means bringing science under moral control. Because science knows how to do things, it does not follow that it is right to do them.

VI THE AFFLUENT SOCIETY

'As MR. GEORGE HERBERT saith in his "Church Militant"

> Gold and the Gospel never did agree:
> Religion always sides with Poverty.

Usually the Rich are Proud and Obstinate, and will not endure the due conduct of the Ministry.'[2] Like Baxter himself, who could still assume that 'economics are a branch of ethics', the classical Christian tradition has certainly always been suspicious of wealth. Even today many Christians tend to make out that they are rather worse off than they really are; there is still some sense of guilt about being prosperous. There is no evading the fact that on the whole the New Testament comes down on the side of poverty. This was not from any false 'spirituality' or identification of 'matter' with evil, but because of the moral implications of wealth – that riches tend to harden men's hearts, to make them self-protective and content, and disguise from them their interior destitution. The message of Jesus was to the poor, that is, to people conscious of their need. 'Blessed are the poor in spirit.'[3] The Old Testament, which is as earthy as it could be, quite frankly and

---

[1] See also Glanville Williams, Ch. IV, which is strongly critical of the Church's attitude.

[2] From Baxter's *Reliquiae*, prefaced to *Chapters from Richard Baxter's Directory*, by Jeanette Tawney, G. Bell & Sons, 1925.

[3] Matthew's version is probably the right one. For Luke's version of the Beatitudes, and his general attitude to riches, see the commentaries. James appears to be quoting stock 'labour' rhetoric. What he says, e.g. in ii: 6 and v: 1-6, can hardly have been true within the *Koinonia*.

naïvely accepts material good things – corn and wine and oil and flocks and herds – as gifts from God and signs of divine favour, and therefore as signs of being right with God. (Hence the astonishment of the disciples: If a rich man cannot be saved, how can anybody?)

Scripture and the Fathers and the whole tradition assume that there will always be rich and poor, and that this is part of the providential order, and they assume a background of scarcity. Whenever there have been signs of a new wealth there have been misgivings and moral protests. The eighth-century prophets reacted violently to the first contacts with urban civilisation, as St. Francis did in his own special way to the new trade in the Italian hill-towns, or the Lollards to the beginnings of English capitalism. For nineteen centuries the relief of poverty, the care of the poor and needy for Christ's sake, has been one of the primary and most obvious claims and manifestations of *Agape* – so that 'charity' came to be almost equated with it. In our own day, for the first time in history, it is within man's power to abolish poverty. The whole situation is radically changed. In the post-war affluent society many of the traditional Christian judgements about wealth and poverty are no longer relevant. The new fact – the new economy of abundance – must require a great deal of ethical rethinking; and this will need not only the technical knowledge which the experts alone can contribute, but also a very high degree of perceptiveness – what St. Paul called power to 'approve things that differ' (Philippians i: 10, R.V. margin) or, in other words, discrimination of values.

I shall make no attempt to discuss technical questions of finance or economic theory, for if I did I should only be talking nonsense. (I am on Mr. Munby's episcopal blacklist – p. 62 – I did not read Economics at Oxford!) And this may mean that anything I try to say will be confined to such vague generalities as to be superficial and unrealistic. But I offer a few elementary suggestions as guideposts for further Christian thinking. What, then, has Christianity to say to or about the Affluent Society, and what is the right Christian reaction to it? Where, if anywhere, can we see God's work in it? What is 'for us' here and what is 'against us'? If the devil shows signs of getting hold of it and turning what is good in it to evil ends, how can his plans be foiled and counteracted? For at first sight the devil seems to be very active. 'The love of money is a

root of all kinds of evil' (I Timothy vi: 10). Looking at the contemporary scene, it is easy to feel that here is a society wholeheartedly given over to Mammon-worship, in which material
values alone count, overriding all personal and cultural values,
in which money is the criterion of excellence and getting rich
quick the chief end of man. Nor would such a judgement be altogether jaundiced. Indeed, the prevailing idolatry of money and the
irresponsible exercise of money-power may be doing more to
corrupt the community life than all the less reputable 'immoralities' which incur far more Christian denunciation. But the worship
of money is not the same as money. We are warned that we cannot
serve God and Mammon. But the question is, how can Mammon
serve God? 'Make to yourselves friends,' said Jesus, 'by means of
the mammon of unrighteousness, so that when it fails they may
receive you into everlasting habitations' (Luke xvi: 9) – use it,
in other words, to secure permanent and spiritual values. If we are
not faithful in the unrighteous Mammon, who will commit to our
trust the true riches?

Man in our time enjoys such abundance as no men hitherto had
even so much as imagined. The great masses of the population take
as a matter of course a standard of living – of nutrition, cleanliness,
health, warmth and light – as can never have visited Croesus in his
dreams. And it is not simply a matter of more goods – cars and
refrigerators – but of services – education, social insurance, welfare services, leisure, travel, sports and entertainments – which
not even the most highly-developed civilisation in times past has
been able to provide. And that, not merely for lack of the techniques, but because it was not rich enough to afford them. It is only
the new wealth that makes them possible. We must first of all,
therefore, give thanks to God the Giver for this largesse of a
bountiful Creator, who 'has given us freely all these things to
enjoy', and accept them reverently as a trust from God. For these
wonderful God-given opportunities can raise man to new dignity
and freedom, fuller realisation of human possibility, richer fulfilment of himself as personal. By immensely widening his range
of choice – far beyond the sheer coercion of getting his bread – and
providing stronger defences against fortune, they open to him
wider opportunities of cultural and spiritual enrichment. 'In the
second half of the twentieth century in the highly industrialised
and rich countries, the problem has largely ceased to be one of

abolishing poverty and become one of raising the quality of living.[1]

Clearly the first step that love requires is to see that poverty really is abolished. And behind the glittering façade there are still far too many people – more than politicians like to admit – living on or below the poverty line. The first claim on national resources ought to be to give them their due share in God's bounty.

But how far are the opportunities being used to achieve a new quality of living? It was only a very crude expectation which believed that an economy of abundance would in itself create a moral millennium. It does not in itself improve human character, though it may be used as an instrument to that end. It is obvious that wider freedom of choice brings with it wider freedom to choose wrongly. And it is disconcerting to discover that crime is increasing in the richest countries – though American experience should have warned us that increase of wealth does not bring a reduction of gangsterism. But the real indictment of the rich society is not so much the amount of positive evil in it as the appallingly low cultural level and the sterile triviality of its interests. The picture presented by the West today is one of spiritual destitution in the midst of material abundance. But there is no *necessary* connexion. The two things are not causally related. It is easy for preachers to denounce materialism and ascribe the vulgarity and shallowness and general moral inertia of our age to the fact that people have far too much money which they cannot be trusted not to misuse – though God gives it to man and God respects man's freedom. 'It is so easy to argue that because the modern world has seen a vulgarisation of taste, the wasteful destruction of social tissue in the emergence of a proletariat, the decline in Christian morals and the emergence of shallow this-worldly interpretations of human destiny – that *therefore* all these things are inevitably linked with economic progress. There are complex interrelationships between all these things, and it is the height of folly for Christian apologists to pretend that they are all tied together.'[2]

The question is really one of comparative values and of the true ends of economic progress. Is it an end in itself, as is suggested by far too much political propaganda? (*Panem et circenses* is a haunting parallel.) If not an end in itself, what is it *for*? What

[1] Munby, *God and The Rich Society*, O.U.P., 1961, p. 59. Readers of this book will recognise my debt to it throughout this section.
[2] Munby, p. 185.

kind of society do we want to make with it? How can it be used for
the greater glory of God? Surely the primary Christian contribution will be made in asking and answering those questions.

It may be that a true valuation of material wealth and all that
goes with it – how much it matters and, ultimately, how little – still
requires a dedicated vow on the part of some Christians to total
renunciation. That was how St. Francis understood it. Here one
has to remember the distinction between Christian witness and
Christian policy. St. Francis had no idea of a Christian policy and
indeed even stood in the way of a Christian policy. It has been said
that he 'widened the breach between the Christian ideal of holiness and the new capitalism' in Northern Italy.[1] Yet Francis lit a
candle in the hearts of men and, as St. Paul said of the Lord himself, 'by his poverty many have been made rich'. Holy poverty is
no Christian policy, though some Christians are and always will be
called to it, any more than pacificism is a policy. Both are needed
in every generation as indispensable acts of Christian witness.
But for the great majority of Christians the call is now to the sanctification of wealth. To sanctify it, to use it for God's glory, must
mean to use it for those ends and purposes which God approves
and for which it has been entrusted to us – that is, for spiritual
ends, for the true enrichment of human personality. What we have
to ask is, what measures, what modifications of the social structure,
what replanning or redistribution, what reorganisation of industrial processes, are most likely to conduce to that end? Policies
cannot change human character, but they can control some of the
forces that prey upon it. They can help to fashion a society in
which there are higher levels of expectation and in which the innate
goodness of human nature is given a better chance of coming to the
top.

Ought 'Economics to be a branch of Ethics'? What exactly is
meant by saying that it ought to be? The whole notion of Economic Man and the *laissez-faire* dogmas that supported it were a
repudiation of the belief that there was any relation between the
two. Economic laws were a universe of their own, self-explanatory
and self-justifying, to which moral considerations were irrelevant.
The cynical phrase 'Business is Business' is a trespassing notice:
Morality keep out. Ethics cannot accept that exclusion. Business,
after all, is a human activity and must therefore always have moral

[1] Mumford, op. cit., p. 126.

relevance and, like every other human activity, is answerable to the
sovereignty of God. And in fact the economic activities can be,
at any rate within certain limits, and to a quite considerable extent
already are, brought under social control and therefore 'moralised',
to whatever extent social morality reflects the social purpose and
values. The control could of course be carried a great deal further;
the social purpose could come to set its sights higher; the acknowledged values might be more demanding; but none of this affects
the main point, that there is already implicit recognition that
money was made for man, not man for money, and is meant to
serve human and therefore moral ends. The whole point of what
I am saying is to emphasise that. But this is not the same thing as
saying that there are immediate moral considerations in the detailed working of the mechanisms or that ethics can, or has any
right to try to, prescribe the law for its technical operations. These,
like those of the sciences, have their own laws and are, *in that
sense*, 'independent'.

There is no 'moral' or 'Christian' way of conducting a scientific
experiment. Each must proceed according to its own laws –
autonomous, yet ultimately 'theonomous'.

But how far does that independence go? It is often said, as it is
said about science, that the whole economic system has escaped
from moral control, like a dangerous wild beast which has now
to be got back behind bars again. And of course it is true that
wealth no less than science can be and is being turned to evil ends
such as making weapons of destruction. But a 'system' is in itself
morally neutral, like a material object or a cheque. Its moral
quality comes from the end it serves – how far it serves genuinely
human purposes. That is the subject of ultimate moral judgement.
The system seems to have run away with man, subjecting him to a
vast impersonality which carries him along against his own will
and with no understanding of what is happening to him. But the
system, as Munby reminds us, is a total of an infinite number
of detailed operations, all of which, if investigated piecemeal,
can be morally criticised and so reorganised as better to minister to
men and women.[1] 'The questions that Christians have to face here
have nothing to do with the behaviour of people or with morals in

---

[1] See on this Munby, Ch. VII. Mr. Munby is rightly concerned to turn
off the heat, but I venture to think that he does rather underrate the
'demonic' element in the mass-society.

the ordinary sense. They concern the proper ends of institutions and the framework within which they can be expected to fulfil them.' If so, the central point of the Christian critique will be to ask: What are the institutions *for*? Are they geared to serve human and social purposes or are those purposes sacrificed to them?

Galbraith's title has now become a stock phrase, but not all who use it have read the book and the radical criticism which it develops. It has now become an unquestionable dogma that production is an end in itself. More and yet more must be produced, irrespective of the value of the product, in order to stop the machinery from stopping. This process cannot go on without the creation of artificial needs and a vast organisation to create them. Millions of people are being exposed to a very subtly-directed suggestion that their primary aim is to keep up with the Joneses, that they will be social failures or sub-status or even doing something morally wrong if they do not require the latest gadget, even though they may have no real desire for it or at the cost of something far more necessary. This accentuates the total confusion of values which characterises the affluent society, and leads to many social and domestic evils (H.P., etc.) and tends to spread a climate of envy which poisons social and class relationships. The ethics of advertising and its methods seems therefore, as I have said (see p. 175), to be one of the questions which call urgently for Christian criticism. Beyond that is the much wider question how far in the new economy of abundance more wealth and more effort should now be diverted to cultural and aesthetic ends. Is not too much human potential now being sacrificed to industrial wealth? Production was made for man, not man for production.

All power tends to corrupt and money-power perhaps most of all. How much of the triviality and vulgarity which debases contemporary Western life and is now being exported the world over, is a result of the 'enormous power given by the market to a few more or less irresponsible money-makers to set the pattern of public taste', in the entertainment business, for example, or in the mass-circulation newspapers, which in order to maintain the immense demand without which they cannot survive at all, tend to appeal to their customers at their lowest point of taste, morals or independence of mind? What would seem to be the right approach to this matter is not a closer imposition of censorship but a critical look at the structures of these industries and their professional organs of control; and that may require governmental intervention.

But when all is said, the essential contribution which the Church has to make to the rich society ought to be through the witness of those valuations – with the social and moral criticism inherent in them – which are seen to be embodied in its own life and the general Christian standards of living. If we are quite uncritically 'conformed to the world' of abundance, how can we redeem it? If we try to withdraw from it we remain a ghetto. 'If Christians are to lead men to a greater sensitivity to the ways in which we may learn how to use our riches to the glory of God, it will have to be seen in the style of our lives. We have failed dismally.'[1]

The Scriptural warnings about the corruptions of wealth are coming home to the rich world today. Not only in its hardness of heart and selfishness and its concentration on material values, but also in its spiritual blindness to the claims of the hungry and undeveloped peoples. While the West misuses its superfluity, far the greater part of the human race is living at or far below the subsistence level. The most elementary needs of Justice and Charity require some equalisation of resources, so to enable the newly emergent countries to make their distinctive cultural contribution and take their due place in the brotherhood of mankind. This is far more than a matter of mere 'relief'. The World Council of Churches, Christian Aid, Oxfam and similar agencies have worked miracles of constructive help through the voluntary funds at their disposal – it is one of the epics of Christian history. So, too, of course, has American generosity. But all this touches no more than the fringes. It is not really a matter of 'aid', however generous. It is a matter of seeing it as a right, as a clear demand of the divine Justice. What is needed is large-scale capital investment, without ulterior ideological motive – a lesson which the West will find hard to learn – through the official action of governments on an assessment fixed by a world-authority and a willingness, for the sake of Man as Man, to lower, if need be, our own standard of life. Will the call be accepted while there is yet time? It is one of the acid tests of our sincerity in wishing to use our riches to God's glory.

All this, of course, ties up with the racial question, and with our own immigration policy. The probability is that these two ques-

[1] Munby, p. 57.

tions weigh far more in the balance between peace and war than all
the attempts at controlling the new weapons.

VII PEACE AND WAR

The whole ethical field is overshadowed by the demographic
facts and the fear of war. Unless these two forces can be controlled, there will be no more ethics and few more men. 'Humanity
will prey upon itself like monsters of the deep.' The two threats
are obviously interrelated.

In the present world as it actually is, with its fears and hates and
conflicting interests, not in the world as we should like it to be,
what has Christian ethics to say about war? Apart from sentimental
utopianism, is there a realistic Christian policy? For most of the
traditional Christian ethic – the attempt to define the conditions of
a 'just' war and prescribe the moral rules for the waging of it –
seems now to have been made irrelevant both by the global scale
of modern warfare and by the new weapons of destruction. The
paradox of the whole situation is that quite immoral and cynical
dynastic and trade wars with professional armies were apparently
far less morally destructive than the new-style wars which are
waged for righteousness and become wars of unlimited objective
in which total populations are involved and the righteous cause
is tainted and poisoned. Indeed, the worst thing about modern
warfare, worse even than the appalling wastage of life, is the moral
corruption that it brings with it.

Pacificism, again, is no longer a live issue. If nuclear war on a
world-scale broke loose, Christians would not be called upon to
decide whether they could conscientiously 'take part' in it. They
would not be asked. They would not be there to ask. Within the
first few hours they would all be dead. Millions on both sides
would be annihilated. And in such a war there could be no victor
nor could any cause, however righteous, win. To talk about 'win-
ning' a war today is meaningless.

Perhaps it is well to start by facing the fact that war, as it now
would be, just cannot be 'moralised' – it would be more like an
eruption or a tidal wave. Yet it would be the result of human
actions and of causes which are within man's control. The supreme
moral challenge of our time is to eliminate war and create peace.
But peace is not merely the absence of war.

Christians must face the realities of power, and power cannot be tamed by pious speeches. ('How many divisions has the Pope?') One lesson past experience may have taught us – if we are afraid of taking the risk of war we may well end in bringing it about. In the twenties and early thirties, in this country, Christian and Liberal opinion concentrated attention on disarmament and brought successful pressure to bear on governments. But the results of that were disastrous. At the time when Hitler occupied the Rhineland, I remember myself telling a minister that if the Cabinet ran risks of war for that, it could not be justified to God or Man. Yet had France and Britain made some show of force, the Second World War would probably not have happened. Force is not in itself morally evil – must 'Christian' action *always* be non-violent? It can surely be morally right to use force – which need not necessarily mean fighting – to hold the dykes of a peaceful civilisation or to prevent the outbreak of major war. (Current sentiment tends to underrate how much the growth of free institutions, including those in the United States, owes to the shield of British naval hegemony.) It is hard to believe that it would be a Christian policy which allowed a higher type of civilisation to be overrun and destroyed by a lower – 'better red than dead' is not a Christian sentiment.

So long, then, as the deterrent does deter – and it did deter both sides in the Cuba incident – it may have relative moral justification, even if we hold that it was morally wrong to make use of the atomic bomb in the first instance. At the moment, the fact that these ghastly weapons exist has created an equilibrium of fear in which the threat of an East–West armageddon seems to be rather less imminent than it was. But fear is a dangerous ally of peace; and these weapons can only too easily provoke the very thing that they are meant to hold. Indeed it is at least arguable that Christians ought to support a policy which entails much stronger conventional forces in Europe – even though it would probably mean conscription – so as to guarantee that frontier incidents and small local wars can be contained, without 'escalating' to all-out nuclear warfare. It is urgently necessary that governments should continue to do whatever is humanly possible to secure even the most elementary steps for inspection and control of nuclear projects with a view to reaching agreement on limitation and ultimately – the only long term aim which is tolerable to the conscience of humanity – their total destruction by all Powers concerned. Even the smallest agreement would make for confidence and might thus prepare the way for a further step. It is no less important, by way of guarantees and mutual organisation of defence, to prevent the dissemination of nuclear bombs, which would then simply run away with humanity beyond all hope of legal or moral control, and mankind would be brought to the edge of self-destruction. But, as past experience should warn us, unilateral disarmament is no answer. Nevertheless, it is better to march to Aldermaston than to sit around and do nothing or assume that there is nothing that can be done. (One of the strange things about human nature is the amount of virulence and hatred that consist with anti-war demonstrations. C.N.D. seems to have gathered round it an infection of that 'free-floating hate' – see p. 246 – which is epidemic throughout the world today and could lead to disruption and anarchy.)

But behind all this there is a wider question. The scientific research of the West today is being monopolised for its own purposes, captured by Pentagons and War Offices and locked up behind the ban of official secrets, so that to communicate new knowledge to the world at large is punishable as treason. Is it not committing a crime against humanity and the international commonwealth of science? For all this is in order to defend itself against a danger which it is creating by a myth sustained by out-of-date thinking – that is, the myth of the Free World *versus* Communism. (How much freedom is there in the 'free' world?) The obsessional American fear of Communism is keeping the West anchored to a policy which is becoming increasingly unrealistic. With the emergence of Asia and Africa the whole alignment of world-power is changing. A show-down between Washington and Moscow becomes every day more improbable. Indeed what seems far more likely to happen is that these two giant concentrations of power will become increasingly assimilated. The war that might happen is not that. It is one the very mention of which is abominable – a war of the rest of the world against the white races. That unspeakable horror can yet be averted. A minute fraction of the brains and manpower and the well-nigh incalculable expenditure now being diverted to military ends, if it were invested in international services to raise the standards of life the world over, could give substance to the peace we hope for.

S

Too many of the prayers for peace which are offered in Christian churches are bromide. What Christians ought to pray for is justice. Armaments are symptoms rather than causes. Peace is not the mere absence of war but the bloom on the fruit that grows on the tree of justice. 'The fruit of righteousness is peace.' Disarmament propaganda starts at the wrong end. The constructive policy is to remove the causes – the fear, the envy, the desperate hunger and the humiliating inequalities by which the demonic drives to war are generated. The main pressure of Christian opinion should be along the line of its own love-commandment, for an equalisation of the world's resources.

Like so much else that we have been considering, much of the problem comes back in the end to the need for revising an antiquated structure. 'The great challenge of our time is presented by the fact that the constitutional machinery of the world has proved inadequate alike to its material needs and its spiritual aspirations . . . There is no contemporary human society whose needs – economic, social, political or even military – do not transcend their national boundaries.' It may well be indeed that national sovereignty which has brought strength and enrichment to mankind during the last few centuries of its history is something which God's ongoing purpose requires now to be outgrown and transcended. Be that as it may, the urgent need of the time is for a workable international law administered by a world-authority which will not be defeated at every crisis by the national claims to be judges in their own cause – the contradictory of natural justice – which are now asserted through the veto. 'We have been attempting to outlaw war without really substituting law or anything like it at all . . . the crying need is for a whole new range of legal conceptions in the international field starting from the fundamental issue of what are (or rather should be) the juridical persons recognised by international law and proceeding to a full code of behaviour for civilised States; covering the whole range of conduct at sensitive spots, capable of being judicially ascertained and capable in principle of enforcement.'[1]

That would be a kind of secular Christendom. Such a world court is still on the far horizon. It could only be given effect by a world-conscience. And to that Christians can contribute richly by pressing on with the ecumenical movement. One of the most im-

[1] Hailsham, *Science and Politics*, pp. 76, 77, 85.

portant facts of the time is that there is already in existence a world-wide spiritual community, transcending race, colour, nationality and all the divisive political ideologies. The most potent force making for peace and justice and the brotherhood of mankind in the will of God – stronger than any that can be exercised by political or economic agencies – would be the unification of all Christians in one holy universal Church.

EPILOGUE

'My kingdom', said Jesus, 'is not of this world.' Yet he taught us to pray 'Thy Kingdom come on earth'. That tension, that bi-polarity of outlook, is inherent in any distinctively Christian ethics, and in Christianity itself as an incarnational religion which claims to stand on historical events. If it is not something from 'beyond' – the spatial language can hardly be avoided – or if it is not committed to history – the actual life of societies in the world – in neither case is there a real incarnation. The contemporary concern with the 'secular' – which seems to some Christians the betrayal of an essentially 'supernatural' faith – is indeed a belated re-discovery of what Christianity is about, or at least of an ineradicable strain in it. Yet taken alone it can be so one-sided as to empty the Gospel of its redemptive power.

Throughout this book we have been discussing the Christian life in secular society. We have rejected the false other-worldliness which leads to contempt of this present world or neglect of social and civil responsibilities. A Church that is only concerned with saving 'souls' out of the world has no message for the world, or 'for man in the wholeness of his human nature and for the history of the world as a whole' (Hodgson, *The Doctrine of the Atonement*, Nisbet, 1951, p. 122). The Church must be involved in the secular, as Jesus himself was, without reserve, because the secular world is God's world; and there it must serve him – there is nowhere else. Yet a Christianity perfectly content with the secular and completely at home in it would have nothing important to contribute. Jesus identified himself with men in their given historical situations; and in its condemnation of Docetism the Church made a Christian ethic possible. But there is throughout the Synoptic record, as well as more obviously in the fourth Gospel, a mysterious note of distance and detachment. He was in the world, but he was not of the world (John xvii: 14, 16); and the Church,

277

in its insistence on the 'two natures', protected itself against 'secularisation'. It was in the Lord himself, and in him alone, that the tension has been completely resolved.[1]

Jesus was not concerned with 'religion' in the narrow sense now imposed upon it as a departmentalised activity – the word 'religion' is not found in the Gospels – but with man's total response to life as a whole. But that response was centred in faith in God. ('Religionless', as Bonhoeffer used the word, really means non-pietistic; he did not mean that the coming Christianity will cease to be rooted in faith and worship.) And God is not part of the world, he transcends it – that is implied in speaking of 'God' at all – and apart from him the world could have no existence. God is not the prisoner of the space-time process. His purpose cannot be exhausted within history. Neither can man's relationship to God, with all its implications, be fully realised within spatio-temporal experience.

I have just re-read words which are worth repeating. 'If there is a meaning in history, it lies not in the systems and organisations that are built, but in something more essentially human, something in each personality considered for mundane purposes as an end in itself . . . History is not like a train, the sole purpose of which is to get to its destination . . . each moment of it is its own self-justification . . . We envisage our history in the proper light if we say that each generation – indeed each individual – exists for the glory of God; but one of the most dangerous things in life is to subordinate human personality to production, to the state, to civilisation itself, to anything but the glory of God.'[2]

But that gives life in this world an eternal reference. Here we have no continuing city. History and its achievements are transient. Civilisations are subject to mortality. If men indeed exist

---

[1] 'Sacred and secular, otherworldly and this-worldly, my conclusion is that Christianity is uncompromisingly both, but not in any facile Anglican or archiepiscopal compromise, but in a costly interrelation. We follow Christ who, in the form of a Servant, made himself utterly one with humanity, but was no less so, but rather drew the power to be so, because he was found a great while before day alone in a desert place praying to the Father. As Christ was in the world and not of the world, so is the Church called to be.' (A. M. Ramsey, Archbishop of Canterbury, *Sacred and Secular*, Longmans, 1966, p. 70. The whole subject is admirably discussed in Chapter V of this book, 'The Christian and the Secular World.)

[2] Butterfield, *Christianity and History*, G. Bell, 1949, p. 67.

for the glory of God then their final end and their destiny as persons are not to be found in this passing world – a world which Christians see as a vale of soul-making – but in a communion with God which time cannot terminate nor death destroy. God is not the God of the dead but of the living.

Whatever the symbols and metaphors employed – a city in heaven, Jerusalem the Golden, 'a country far beyond the stars' – it lies at the heart of the Christian world-view that we are inheritors of a 'living hope, incorruptible and that fadeth not away'. The Church was created by the Resurrection – there were no Christians before Easter Day – and, though it exists as the servant of God's world, its centre of gravity is not in this world. It knows that here men are strangers and pilgrims, spirits 'seeking a country of their own' (Hebrews xi: 14). The Christian valuation of the secular, both positively and negatively, depends on its faith in God and eternal life. Its power to serve, to redeem and transform the secular will be beyond measure weakened and impoverished if, in identification with the world, it loses hold on its faith in the world to come and the 'blessed hope of everlasting life which God has given us in our Saviour Jesus Christ'. (Prayer Book Collect for Advent II.)

INDEX